Black Superheroes,
Milestone Comics,
and Their Fans

Studies in Popular Culture
Nancy Walker, General Editor

University Press of Mississippi / Jackson

BLACK
Superheroes,
MILESTONE
Comics,
and THEIR FANS

JEFFREY A. BROWN

www.upress.state.ms.us

Illustration on page iii courtesy of DC Comics and Milestone Media, Inc. Used with permission.

09   08   07   06   05   04   03   02   01   4   3   2   1
∞
Library of Congress Cataloging-in-Publication Data

Brown, Jeffrey A.
Black superheroes, Milestone comics, and their fans / Jeffrey A. Brown.
p.   cm. — (Studies in popular culture)
Includes bibliographical references and index.
ISBN 1-57806-281-0 (alk. paper) — ISBN 1-57806-282-9 (pbk. : alk. paper)
1. Comic books, strips, etc.—United States—History and criticism.   2.
Afro-Americans—Comic books, strips, etc.   3. Milestone Media Inc.—History.   I. Title.   II.
Studies in popular culture (Jackson, Miss.)

PN 6725.B76   2000
741.5'089'96073—dc21
00-021978
British Cataloging-in-Publication Data available

For Mary Plouffe

Contents

Illustrations

Acknowledgments

I am extremely grateful to a number of people who have helped make this study possible. First and foremost, thanks to Ivan Kalmar, who offered exceptional advice and guidance throughout every stage of this research project. My thanks also go to Craig Werner, Hy Luong, Bonnie MacElhinny, Richard Lee, Marcel Danesi, Grant McCracken, Trudy Nicks, and Caryl Flinn for their supportive and constructive comments on earlier drafts and for general encouragement. I would also like to thank Seetha Srinivasan and Anne Stascavage of the University Press of Mississippi and Karen Johnson for their excellent work on this book.

Of course, this entire project would not have been possible without the participation of countless informants. Dwayne McDuffie, Derek Dingle, Denys Cowan, and Christine Gilliam from Milestone Media all deserve a special thank you for opening their doors and contributing valuable insights about their company, their goals, and their world of comic books. The comic book fans who participated in the study are too numerous to thank individually, but each and every one of them was an incredible wealth of information without which this project would not have existed. Thank you.

Prologue

It was a Saturday afternoon when I first came across Galaxy Comics and Collectibles, a comic book and gaming specialty store located in a middle-class neighborhood on the fringe of downtown Toronto. I had been in dozens of comic book stores before and was confident about what I'd find inside, past the larger than life superheroes painted on the glass window. What I wasn't prepared for was the sheer volume of activity I found. On this day, Galaxy Comics and Collectibles was abuzz with more energy than I had ever seen in a comic book store before. Though every independently run comic book store has its own unique personality, they all have a certain ambience in common. In many ways Galaxy was no different from the thousands of other comic book specialty stores spread across North America.

Like almost every other comic book store, Galaxy was a cramped shop with a slight odor of old newsprint and its walls were covered with promotional posters featuring muscular men and busty women in colorful, skintight costumes. Some of these stylish advertisements were adorned with such immediately recognizable cultural icons as Superman or Batman, while the others depicted a collage of heavily muscled characters with dramatic names like Savage Dragon, Deathblow, and Ripclaw, all of whom seemed to be bursting right through their two-dimensional confines. Higher up on the walls, out of the reach of grasping hands, was an array of older, rarer, and thus more valuable comic books, each safely enshrined in a plastic Mylar bag with acid-free cardboard backing.

Waist-high tables loaded with countless boxes of less prestigious back issues were lined up end to end down the center of the store. Several of the store's young patrons were bent over the narrow boxes, flipping through the various leftover comics seeking that elusive issue that would fill the gap in their own collections or hoping against hope to discover a rare and expensive comic that had some how been mispriced and lumped in with the remainders. All of Galaxy's new comic books were displayed at the back of the narrow shop on a wooden, and obviously homemade, magazine stand. An alphabetical list of the thirty or so books that had come in the previous Wednesday was scribbled on the chalkboard beside the display. A full third of the titles listed already had a line scratched through them to indicate they were sold out.

At the front of the store, near the entrance doorway and the pile of backpacks scattered underneath the "Please Leave All Bags Here" sign (cheerfully subtitled "Shoplifters Will Gladly be Beaten to a Pulp!"), was a glass display case that doubled as a checkout counter. Behind the counter were two teenage clerks, both of whom were busy tallying up customers' purchases while simultaneously trying to explain to an older gentleman why his ragged old copy of *The Phantom* wasn't worth thousands of dollars. It seems the man had heard a story on the radio about someone who had found comic books from the 1940s in the attic and had sold them for over a hundred thousand dollars, and now he wanted the same windfall. A couple more typical patrons, prepubescent boys in baggy jeans and oversized T-shirts, were impatiently attempting to squeeze past the unsatisfied attic cleaner so that they could get a better look at the completed sets of trading cards housed on the three shelves inside the makeshift display cabinet/checkout counter.

What did, at first, seem different about Galaxy Comics and Collectibles that Saturday afternoon was the noise. Often comic book stores are quiet places, each customer silently perusing the multitude of titles vying for his attention. But on this occasion the store was overrun with boisterous grade-school kids who had just started their summer vacation the week before. All around me were boys from seven to twelve years old excitedly talking not only about what they were going to be doing over the summer holidays, but also about what comic books they were most looking forward to reading. During the summer months the comic book publishers pull out all the stops. They use every gimmick possible to make their books stand out from the hundreds of others that crowd the display rack. As I moved through the store I could hear snatches of conversation peppered with a fannish lingo: "chromium cover die-cast design," "multi-universe crossover," "free holographic card," and "mini graphic novel movie adaptation." The adrenaline was high among Galaxy's young customers. You could almost feel the anticipation of the coming heroic battles that would be played out on glossy four-color pages for two to six dollars an adventure.

To the left of the cash register, in front of a display of various superhero action figures, there was a relatively subdued black child of about nine disappointedly telling his mother that they didn't have the hero he wanted. "There's no Icon or Hardware here," the boy, Mike, complained.

I interrupted, informing the exasperated looking mother that I had been doing some research on Milestone Media, the African American comic book company that published the exploits of the black superheroes Icon and Hardware, among others, and that there were no available toy versions of these characters yet.

"But I saw an Icon figure in that magazine," Mike said as he pointed to a recent copy of *Wizard: The Guide to Comics* that was sitting on the display counter.

"Oh, I know what picture you're talking about," one of the employees manning the cash register offered. "But that wasn't a real action figure. It was one of those homemade ones that people send in so they can get their name in the magazine."

"That figures," the boy's mother said, as Mike and his younger sister quietly moved to the back of the store to look over the new comics, "I was hoping to find a couple of black hero dolls for him to play with this summer. I guess we'll just have to stick with the Batman stuff for now."

Mike's mother, Sondra, explained to me that her son had been interested in comic books for the past couple of years and had become a voracious reader, devouring as many stories as he could get his hands on, sometimes twenty in a day. "I thought it was great that he was reading so much and having a lot of fun," Sondra said. "I suppose all young boys enjoy comic books at some point in their lives. For a while Mike was reading anything he could get his hands on. I was really happy, though, when he found a few of these books that starred black superheroes. I think it's important for a child to read about people of his own color as heroes sometimes. Now Mike buys these comics almost exclusively," Sondra nodded at a Milestone poster promoting an upcoming meeting of Icon and Superman, the original Man of Steel himself, "except for Batman, he still *really* likes Batman, too." She laughed. "But now he plays Icon and Rocket [Icon's female sidekick, think of Robin with an attitude] with his little sister all over the house. That's good. I like that. Now he doesn't *have* to pretend to be Superman or Batman, or any other white guy superhero. That's good. It's about time we got some new heroes around here."

New heroes indeed.

Black Superheroes,
Milestone Comics,
and Their Fans

1

Introduction: "New Heroes"

I like the phrase "new heroes." I have heard it a lot over the past couple of years while exploring the world of comic books and their readers. It is a phrase that is almost deceivingly concise. It is a simple enough combination of words, but it alludes to a culturally important change in the way we see our world. "As anyone involved in fiction and its crafting over the past fifteen or so years would be delighted to tell you," wrote acclaimed comic book auteur Alan Moore, "heroes are starting to become rather a problem. They aren't what they used to be . . . or rather they *are*, and therein lies the heart of the difficulty. We demand new themes, new insights, new dramatic situations. We demand new heroes" (1986, 3). In a world that is continually growing, continually changing, the old paradigms just don't cut it anymore.

One of the ways the world has been changing, at least in the West, is reflected in the manner in which the traditional monolith of popular culture has sought to (re)address divergent audiences. This study offers an account of one comic book company's attempt to address divergent audiences through new heroes and how the readers of these texts come to understand them through interpretive strategies and subcultural practices specific to the comic book industry and comic book fandom. Specifically, this study focuses on the African American comic books published by Milestone Media and how fans relate to the stories and the new black heroes according to six fundamentally interconnected principles and points of comparison. The interpretive strategies used by comic book fans revolve around (1) their recognition of Milestone's corporate and creative identity as *the* mainstream publisher of African American superhero comics; (2) their awareness of the debate between Milestone and other African American comic book creators regarding the authenticity of creating black characters in cooperation with one of the dominant (i.e., white) publishing companies; (3) their reliance on subcultural principles specific to comics fandom, such as the collecting principle, whereby the readers' recognition of specific artists and/or the potential market value of the comic book allows the fans to accumulate cultural capital within the subculture; (4) their knowledge of the superhero genre's history and of earlier attempts to create black heroes; (5) their familiarity with formalized genre conventions and Milestone's place as an innovative publisher which retains most of the "classic" elements of the superhero formula; and (6) their comparison of the Milestone books to the market-dominating comics published by other young companies which promote a popular trend of gender extremism.

For many fans the reading of a comic book is far from a passive activity. That does not necessarily mean that comic book fans are active resisters of hegemonic meaning, as several audience ethnographies have argued (most notably, Radway 1984; Jenkins 1992). Rather, for the devoted comic book fan interpretation is a complex process shaped by inter- and intratextual information shared with, and about, other fans and the creators themselves. As popular texts, the reading of comic books is interpreted according to the ideological encodings of the producers *and* the socially positioned, fandom-based, decodings of the audience. For readers familiar with the history and/or the conventions of comic books, the Milestone superheroes function as a focal point for interpreting revisionist notions of African American characters in comparison to more mainstream comic book ideals; and, further, they facilitate a progressive interpretation of black masculinity which incorporates intelligence with physicality. In other words, there is a sort of "contract" of meaning that exists between the two sides and positions any interpretation of textual ideology as both a personal and mutual concept. In this case, the contract is such that the producers have created black characters who fulfill a need for new heroes and operate according to certain principles of non-extremist racial politics, thus allowing the readers to interpret the texts in cooperation with the producers' intended meanings as revisionist black hero texts and personally as alternative models of masculinity, models which stress holism rather than the one-dimensional hypermasculinity found in other contemporary comic books.

Because the comic book industry is a medium very clearly dominated by some of modern popular culture's most quintessential images of heroism, it is also one of the most obvious examples of unequal representation. Since its inception more than sixty years ago the world of comic books has been populated with the same type of characters in magazine after magazine. Chief among these ever popular characters is the seemingly endless variety of Superman-like costumed crusaders. Almost without exception these archetypal do-gooders, these modern mythological heroes—Captain Marvel, Captain America, Batman, Spider-Man, Thor, etc.—have been white-bread defenders of "truth, justice and the American way." Like most other forms of North American mass media in the twentieth century, comic books have more or less managed to erase all evidence of cultural diversity. For decades young readers have encountered a defining and idealized image of heroism that was explicitly honest, law abiding, chaste, excessively masculine, and above all, white. For the majority of readers these caped avengers who could fly, bend steel bars with their bare hands, and deflect bullets with their broad chests were the ultimate power fantasy played out in flashy monthly installments. Yet for comic book readers from different ethnic backgrounds there were no heroic models that they could directly identify with, no heroes they could call their own. Instead, they were required to imaginatively identify across boundaries of race since the only depiction of visible minorities in most comic books were the nameless criminals and barbarous savages that the real heroes defeated month after month. But just as the "truth" and the "justice" of the American way have begun to be questioned by voices that have previously been suppressed or marginalized, the heretofore unchallenged privilege of the white-bread comic book hero is on the decline.

The potentially harmful racial bias of comic books was so obvious by the early 1970s that the Black-Owned Communications Alliance (BOCA) sought to capitalize on this image of unequal identification in their public service advertisement promoting the need for responsible racial representation in the media (fig. 1.1). "What's wrong with this picture?" asks the advertisement's copy in bold letters under the photograph of a young black boy striking a heroic pose in front of the bathroom mirror—a towel tied around his neck for a cape, chest puffed out, fists defiantly resting on his hips. But instead of his own idealized image staring back at him, he sees the reflection of a generic, white costumed hero. "A child dreams of being the latest superhero. What could be wrong with that?" the promotional copy continues. "Plenty," is the answer, "if the child is Black and can't even *imagine* a hero the same color he or she is." The concern of the BOCA advertisement is clear. Children are impressionable and learn from what they see. And, the copy text goes on to argue, with the traditional white images of heroism that dominate popular culture, black children rarely get to see "Black men and women doing positive things besides playing basketball and singing songs." The BOCA advertisement is a call not only for more frequent and more diverse positive black images in the media, but also for the development and support of black-owned media production companies that would best be able to provide these much needed new heroes. On numerous occasions during the course of this study I was

1.1   *Black-Owned Communication Alliance advertisement*

reminded of this advertisement, whether it was while rummaging through academic texts, talking to superhero fans, or self-indulgently reading huge piles of comic books. This advertisement, although dated, seemed to crystallize the all too common discrepancy between young comic book readers and the one-dimensional heroic types usually portrayed within those books.

   In the 1970s the two major comic book publishing companies, DC Comics and Marvel Comics, both tried to create legitimate black superhero characters. Both companies failed to achieve any long-lasting success because their black characters were too closely identified with the limited stereotype commonly found in the blaxploitation films of the era. More recently, in the spring of 1993, Milestone Media, an African American–owned and controlled comic book publishing company, began to provide the world with some new heroes. Included in their monthly roster of heroes are such popular characters as Icon, a super strong and straight-laced hero in the Superman mold, and Icon's partner, Rocket, the first unwed teenage mother to don the costume of a superhero; Hardware, a genius inventor who has constructed his own high-tech armor; and Static, a wise-cracking high school nerd by day and an electricity-wielding superhero by night. Where once visible minorities were almost exclusively depicted on the comic book page as villains, indistinguishable petty criminals, screaming savages, and occasionally as comic relief sidekicks, today's characters of color are finally starting to emerge as real heroes, as new heroes, demanded by new audiences.

This study offers an examination of contemporary comic book fandom as it relates specifically to the texts published by Milestone Media and the particularly loaded and problematic representation of the black superhero. As the field of audience studies has developed in the 1980s and 1990s, in both the class-oriented British and the populist American traditions, numerous critics have increasingly emphasized the role of the audience as active interpreters in their everyday use of mass media, interpreters who can, and do, construct unique readings contingent upon their own cultural position and personal experiences. However, most of these audience studies, which I will return to in more detail later, are critically informed by where they consider the "true" meaning of the cultural texts to reside—with the producers or with the consumers. Since the primary concern of this study is how the adolescent members of the comic book reading audience use mass-produced genre texts in their personal and social lives to construct an understanding of race and gender, I feel it is important to focus not solely on either the creators, the text, or the audience members, but on all three. Yes, the media can exert power and influence over the audience but only in so far as that audience might allow them to, and it is the readers who negotiate the degree of that power and the direction of that influence.

The research presented here is based primarily on such qualitative methods as participant-observation, textual analysis, and most importantly, interviews with several comic book creators, retailers and over a hundred fans. For more than four years now I have been deeply involved in the somewhat transient and loosely structured world of comic book fandom. Comics fandom is a subculture that I have known of since I first began reading comic books as a child, but I had never become unconditionally involved with it because I, like many comic book readers who remain on the periphery of fandom, often thought of it as a little too *fanatical* for my own tastes. As a subculture, comic fandom is an overwhelmingly male enclave (see appendixes for a detailed breakdown of the informants by age, race, and reading habits). There are female fans, but they are much less in number and usually much less demonstrative about their passion for comics. While there is a wide age range among comic book fans, I have focused here on the younger and still the most common enthusiasts: preadolescent and adolescent males. I have been reading the books and the fanzines, frequenting a variety of comic book specialty stores, attending the local and national and international comic book conventions, and cruising various computer chat lines devoted to comic books. I have experienced the anticipation that many fans savor when they rush to their local comics shop on Wednesday afternoons eager to discover what has become of their favorite heroes, who more often than not were left in the clutches of evil arch-nemeses just a month before. At more than one convention I have witnessed firsthand the awe in the eyes of young enthusiasts who have just spoken with their favorite writer or artist after standing in an autograph line for hours. I have haggled over the price of back issues I needed to purchase, and I usually lost the negotiation, except when a particularly knowledgeable twelve year old consented to be my price advisor. And I have commiserated with fans and retailers over the demise of comic book series that were abruptly cancelled due to low sales figures and the highly competitive nature of the market.

In conjunction with participant observation, I have relied heavily on interviews as a source of insight into what these fictional adventures mean to individual readers. Most of this research was conducted in and around the greater Toronto area and was supplemented by stints in New York City and Chicago. The research in Chicago proved especially fruitful because it coincided with one of the world's largest annual comic book conventions. Since my central focus involves the contribution of the producers' intended meaning in collaboration with the consumers' interpretation, I was fortunate to have been able to interview the cofounders of Milestone Media. I was amazed and grateful at the cooperation and encouragement that they and their corporate publishing partner, DC Comics, afforded me. As the creative forces behind a new publishing enterprise, the Milestone founders were quite aware of the complexity of their relationship with fans and about the intentions, political and otherwise, of their comic books. I have tried to supplement any holes in my interviews with the Milestone executives through the numerous pieces that have appeared about them in both the mainstream press and the fan-based magazines and newspapers.

For logical reasons the Milestone audience was much more difficult to pin down than were the Milestone creators. I am now well aware of why Janice Radway (1988) has referred to ethnographic studies of media reception as the problems of dispersed audiences and nomadic subjects. There is no single central event where comic book fans can be observed. The most likely places to find comic book readers is at comics specialty stores and at conventions. But even with these identifiable locations there is no guarantee that you will come across the same subjects more than once. Moreover, conventions are typically loud and energetic environments, and while this can provide a wealth of observational material it also proved very distracting for fans. It is not easy to get a ten-year-old boy to answer a question about why he prefers one character over another when a model dressed in a skimpy Vampirella costume is walking by. Initially I attempted to organize relatively structured interviews with comic book fans through connections I had established at local specialty stores. That strategy turned out to be entirely unsuccessful. It was next to impossible to arrange meetings, I was frequently stood up, or when the meetings did occur there was often an obvious lack of enthusiasm for the subject of comic books, an enthusiasm which I had previously seen the subjects display in abundance in the stores or at conventions. Ultimately, most of my ethnographic research was conducted "on the hoof," as it were, talking with comic book readers anywhere I could get them to talk to me—in the stores, at the conventions, in shopping malls, and even while standing in line at the movies. On occasion this proved to be more than just a little frustrating because it limited my opportunities to revisit some particularly insightful informants. Eventually many of the people I interviewed became very familiar faces, popping up at the same stores at the same time each week, or frequenting every comic book convention in the area. Of these familiar faces, a core group of twenty-five spirited comic book fans from different parts of the city became particularly important informants—always willing to help illuminate my understanding of their readings, to clarify my mistakes of interpretation, to provide background information about characters, story lines, and creators, and even to offer their market expertise on several occasions when I needed to buy hard-to-find comic books.

Rather than a formal interview, which all too often implies an unequal relationship in favor of the interviewer, who controls the subject, the tempo, and the very language used, I consider my interactions with the readers to be more akin to conversations. In this case conversations were much more effective because the age difference between myself and the majority of the subjects, 84 percent of whom were between five and nineteen years old (see appendix A for an exact breakdown of informants by age), proved even more distancing in a formal setting. I wanted to avoid the fans' perception that I was an authority with some sort of judgmental agenda. Instead of trying to "get at" certain perceptions that I was developing through direct questions, I found conversing about a shared interest to be much more conducive in a collaborative sense. Here I have taken a cue from Lindlof and Grodin (1990), who discussed the practical advantages of the collaborative, unstructured style of interviewing as especially effective when faced with the difficulties of studying a dispersed audience and a system of media use (e.g., reading) that can not be observed directly. Moreover, conversation based on affiliation seemed to encourage the readers' enthusiasm because it is the way fans speak with each other, a way that, as previous audience researchers have often pointed out, is very similar to gossip.

Where possible I have tried to include the age of the informant, and where relative I have included mention of their ethnicity (see appendix B for an exact breakdown of informants by race). Although this study is concerned primarily with the development and the reading of black superheroes, I did not want to restrict myself solely to black comic book readers. Instead, I think it is important to consider how readers from a variety of ethnic backgrounds respond to, and make use of, these new heroes as they are incorporated into their understanding of cultural concepts such as race and gender. It would have been too transparent to write about these new black superheroes as a one-dimensional gesture against the status quo, or as a hegemonic means of colonizing images of black anger and/or masculinity. It is much more interesting to look at how these new heroes rework existing paradigms by including African American identities within the conventional narratives and iconography of the superhero formula, and to consider how these new heroes reflect audience members' interpretive practices by keying on their subcultural knowledge of the medium and the genre and how the texts facilitate an alternative reading of black masculinity. I want to emphasize that this study is an exploration of young male readers from a diversity of cultural backgrounds and how they read symbolically loaded texts across, and along, racial lines rather than just a look at how the comics speak directly to black audience members.

As a point of clarification, I should explain my use of the terms "African American" and "black" throughout this study. While I realize that there are very real political contingencies inherent in the use of particular names for visible minorities within the current social climate of contemporary America (see, for example, Baugh 1991), a thorough examination of these contingencies is beyond the scope of this study. I do not, however, use the terms interchangeably. "Black" is used as a general term of reference, and "African American" as a specific term of reference. In other words, because much of this study was conducted in a Canadian context, the phrase "African American" was effectively inaccurate as many of the informants who identified themselves as black were from non-African or non-American slave-descendant cultural and historical backgrounds (e.g., those with a Caribbean heritage resisted the label of African American if I accidentally used the phrase in conversation). Even the phrase "African Canadian" rested uncomfortably with many of the fans whom I spoke with because they felt it portrayed them as merely in the shadow of African *Americans*. Thus I use the term "black" more liberally here than a study solely about race might because it is a term that can transcend certain cultural boundaries which the fans deemed relatively unimportant to their understanding of the texts. When I do use the phrase "African American" it is because I am specifically referring to a person or a character who is clearly identifiable as such.

Although I have already mentioned identification as an important factor in the development of black comic book characters, it is not my prime concern, at least it is not my prime concern in the limited one-to-one sense in which the term is commonly used to imply that men can only identify with men, women with women, whites with whites, and blacks with blacks. In fact, if theoretical and ethnographic considerations of media audiences have proven anything in the last twenty years it is that audiences are more than capable of manipulating the text in order to find a meaning that is applicable to their own social position. Whether it is Australian Aboriginal children cheering on the Indians in American Western movies (see Fiske 1989a), lesbians viewing television's *Cagney and Lacey* (see D'Acci 1994), or housewives writing *Star Trek* slash fiction (see Bacon-Smith 1992), media audiences have repeatedly shown that they can read between the lines to create their own heroes. As I have argued elsewhere in relation to film theory and celebrity identifications (Brown 1996), I think that to assume audience members need fictional characters with the same skin color, the same gender, or the same sexual orientation as themselves is to underestimate the polymorphous nature of identification. But, still, the desire to see heroes who at least look like one's self represented directly on the screen or the printed page is natural. There is no reason (other than the often cited excuse of economics) why some audience members should always be required to project their imaginative identification across boundaries of race, gender, or sexuality. Here, then, identification is not always an explicit concern but it does seem to continually lurk just beneath the surface of many of the issues raised, particularly when it comes to interpreting models of race and gender.

The research presented here is an attempt to fill a void in media and audience studies, a void in both topic and focus. While several areas of adult media fandom have been thoroughly explored in recent years, such as the audiences associated with science fiction, soap operas, and romance novels, the large, widespread, and highly visible world of comic book fandom has until recently been relatively unstudied. This is a curious oversight considering the extreme popularity of comic book characters in our culture and the amount of attention, often negative or condemning, given to the comics by other media and concerned parents, educators, or religious groups who worry about possible harmful effects. The fact that the more frequently studied media fandoms are composed primarily of adults probably accounts for their legitimacy as research subjects either in defense of or in question of the popular perception that these fan groups are cultural deviants behaving in a childish manner. On the other hand, because the principal audience for comic books has always been children there is still an impression that these books are mere chewing gum for young minds and are thus unworthy of serious consideration. Likewise, some critics feel that comic books are so simple that they can be dismissed without really being looked at. The sheer size of the industry alone should be some indication of how important a topic comics are—publishers sell millions of books worldwide every week. Yet, for the most part, comic books and their readers are still looked down upon by both academics and the general public. Comic books, it seems to most people, are not to be taken seriously. Comics are to be casually read by young children and then outgrown, with as little thought as outgrowing an old pair of shoes.

In addition to looking at a relatively unconsidered medium, this study is also an attempt to integrate what often remain as divergent interests in many considerations of popular culture. My focus here is neither the audience nor the text, exclusively. Where others have chosen, for ideological reasons, to concentrate on one or the other of these points of access I hope to bridge the gap, as it were, between the different (but not necessarily opposing) domains by addressing the fans, the texts, and even the producers of the texts. This tripartite division can be seen, for example, within the realm of television studies. While a few researchers, (e.g., Gitlin 1983; Feuer et al 1984) have focused on the economic and institutionalized logic of production, others have concentrated on detailed analyses of particular television programs or genres (Deming 1985; Mayne 1988; Williams 1988), and a growing number of scholars have centered their attention on the actual audiences and the often oppositional meanings that they extract from television spectatorship (Ang 1985; Fiske 1987a, b; Jenkins 1988, 1991; Lewis 1990, 1992). Of course, there are practical as well as political reasons why most media research concentrates on one specific element of the producer-text-audience equation. It would take scores of researchers working around the clock and across the map to even begin a truly comprehensive study, and the financial and physical restrictions inherent in any such project would in all likelihood be insurmountable. It would also be unfair to claim that even the most narrowly focused of past media studies did not pay some attention to the interrelatedness of the different cultural factors. For example, out of necessity, every consideration of producers or audiences also addresses the text to some degree. Still, I think, cultural studies are only beginning to emphasize how the different elements of popular culture production and consumption work together so that the realms of what Stuart Hall referred to as "encodings" and "decodings" are understood as intricately interrelated on a number of levels.

As a medium, the world of comic books is an especially clear example of the interrelatedness that is possible between producers and consumers. Instead of seeing the creators and the consumers of mass-produced cultural products as distinct groups, with the producers manipulating and capitalizing on the needs of the consumers or with the two groups locked in a struggle over the ownership and the meaning of popular texts, we need to start considering the relationship of production as potentially collaborative and mutually satisfying. We all too often demarcate the two sides as agents of contention rather than looking at them as an integratable whole. The linearly perceived relationship of producers to text to consumers does not have to be a rigid top-down or a resistive bottom-up situation.

The blurring of the boundaries in comic book production is a clear example of what might be happening in less overt ways in other media systems. In his insightful essay on the history and nature of the audience for superhero comics, one of the very few essays to address the topic in a discerning manner, Patrick Parsons argues that "more interesting in many ways than the influence of content on the special or at-large audience is the influence of the audience—the specialized comic audience—on the content itself, and more to the point, the manner in which the audience has been responsible for the changing nature of the content" (1991, 84). Parsons goes on to point out that the impact of the audience on the producers and the product can be articulated in at least three main forms: "the changing demographics of interested readers; the direct communication between fans and comic artists and writers; and the rise of writers and artists out of the fan audience" (84–85). As an entertainment medium the world of comics is relatively close-knit. The creators and the consumers are often in fairly direct contact with each other at conventions or through letter columns, and more recently over the internet. This contact between the two sides has the potential to influence the stories themselves. The most literal and sensationalistic example of this negotiation of meaning occurred in 1988 when DC Comics allowed readers to decide the fate of Batman's sidekick, Robin, through a 1-900 telephone poll (they chose to kill the character by a slim difference of 5,343 votes to 5,271). On a more typical level, the constant reader feedback helps the creators to fine-tune the characters and the plots from one adventure to the next.

Texts can and do influence readers, producers can and do socially manipulate consumers both intentionally and unintentionally, and audiences can and do interpret texts in a variety of active ways, including resistance and playful cooption. It would be foolish to unconditionally deny any of these possibilities that exist in the system of reception. But, as I hope the following chapters will demonstrate through the examples of specific comic books, their creators, and their readers, it is also possible that popular media texts are constructed and interpreted through the negotiation of interests shared by the audience and the producers who both work in cooperation to create a narrative that operates as a source of social and a personal meaning.

Though one of my central premises is that the medium of comic books is a closely interrelated world with strong and influential links between the sides of production and consumption, I have, for the sake of clarity, separated some of the constituent parts into distinct chapters. Chapter 2 deals with the emergence of Milestone Media as a mainstream comic book publisher made possible by specific historical conditions such as the blaxploitation comic books of the 1970s and the rise of comics fandom as a consumer community. Most importantly, chapter 2 addresses Milestone's status within the mid-1990s publishing industry as a primarily African American line of comics criticized by several smaller African American comics companies for not being "black enough" and how this debate consciously effects the way that the books are approached by both the creators and the readers. Chapter 3 moves from the creators to the audience to outline the scope and characteristics of modern comic book fandom and the cultural principles that underlie the most common (and often the most criticized) activities of fandom, such as collecting and memorizing canonical comics. I argue that there is a clear subcultural logic, or cultural economy, enacted in these practices, a logic that plays an important part in how readers approach and interpret individual comic books. Progressing from the general to the specific, chapter 4 profiles eight individual comic book readers chosen from a cross section of cultural and economic backgrounds. A central theme discussed in this chapter is the readers' parasocial relationships with the texts and how the comics help them form an understanding of masculinity in contemporary culture.

Chapters 5 and 6 are directly concerned with how the Milestone comic books are understood in relation to specific influential factors. Chapter 5 examines the readers' perception of the Milestone heroes as variations on the well-established genre of superhero comic books in general, and more specifically as a reworking of the earlier blaxploitation model of heroism that has haunted the image of black characters for over twenty years. Moreover, chapter 5 explores the idea that shared expectations based on established genre conventions result in an interpretive contract which is a central source of meaning construction for fans. Building on the importance of genre awareness for fan interpretations, chapter 6 argues that a central appeal of Milestone comic books is how they are read by many fans as an alternative masculine ideal, a masculine ideal that reverses the most prevalent contemporary superhero model of hypermasculinity by emphasizing brains over brawn, a reversal that is especially powerful and progressive because it is written on the bodies of black men, who have historically been aligned with the unthinking, bestial side of Western culture's nature-versus-civilization dichotomy.

Chapter 7, the conclusion, returns to the question of meaning construction and stresses the various ways that the Milestone texts are understood by many fans not in blind compliance nor in active resistance, but in negotiation as the media producers and the audience struggle with changing notions of race, gender, and heroism. The six main interpretive strategies employed by the fans of Milestone comics are recapped and contextualized in relation to each other. Though for purposes of study these points are encountered separately throughout this study, in fandom they are never distinct. The points of comparison are completely interrelated and should be understood as such. For example, the fans' recognition of Milestone's position in relation to the overall history of comic books and the superhero genre is part and parcel of the fans' awareness of Milestone's black heroes as a reworking of earlier stereotypes. The conclusion also suggests what this study can contribute to our overall understanding of media audiences, race relations, and the intersections where the cultural industries meet with real people. It also dwells on what this study *cannot* tell us about popular culture: where are the pitfalls of overgeneralization and what are the limitations of niche-market entertainments as agents of cultural change.

The following chapters also include numerous illustrations of the comic books themselves. I have reproduced these images for a variety of reasons. First, I think it is important that the reader should see as much of the primary text as possible in order to get a sense of the actual comics, their style, their energy, their intricate integration of narrative, dialogue, and illustration. Second, I hope the visual examples help to support some of the claims that I make during analysis, by very literally illustrating points to which pure prose might not do justice. Some comic book analysts who work from within the field they deconstruct have used the illustrated narrative style of the comics to its logical extreme for supporting difficult concepts. In *Understanding Comics* (1993b), for example, Scott McCloud has written, or rather I should say drawn, an entire book about comics as an extended cartoon strip with himself as an illustrated host. Third, by including visual examples I hope to avoid the trap of figuratively erasing the media text from the readers' view. As Martin Barker pointed out in his study of British funnies, "it is nigh on impossible to see the original materials being analyzed in most critical studies. Too many critics expect us to take their descriptions on faith" (1989, 4). Due to the structural difference between the mostly one-page funnies that Barker was concerned with and the lengthy composition of the comic books under consideration here, I have obviously not been able to reprint the stories in full. Instead of complete stories I have used single pages or covers as examples, but I think that even these samples should be enough to put the commentary to the test, as it were. This is one of the main advantages to studying comics as a media text. Comic books are reproducible whereas other media forms such as film, television, music, or live performances can only be described. And I have always found that mere description, no matter how colorful, is a process that necessarily reduces the vibrancy of a subject that so many audience members find exhilarating.

This research project started with a simple question: How do fans make sense of the comic books they read? Along the way the issues of race and gender became inextricably linked with the subcultural modes of evaluation that fans use. As a specific instance of contemporary culture, comic book fandom can reveal much about the way that Western society deals with complex and abstract issues in very concrete and media-influenced ways. There is much we can learn about fans and much they can teach us about culture. More than just contributing to current academic debates about audiences and media studies, I hope this research can help substantiate the importance of media use in the lives of young consumers trying to negotiate their understanding of our society and their place in it.

A Milestone Development

This racist administrative government with its Superman notions and comic book politics. We're hip to the fact that Superman never saved no black people.

—Bobby Seale, Chicago Seven trial, 1969

Once every two weeks the promotional posters are changed by the owner of the Comics Kingdom, a medium-sized comic book and fantasy games specialty store located in downtown Toronto. On the third Wednesday of January 1993, the group of boys who made their lunchtime trek from the junior high school three blocks away were surprised to find a new "teaser" poster on display. The poster depicted seven heroically garbed black characters flying directly out at the viewer from above a burning cityscape. In plain large print across the top of the poster was written, "Milestone: 2/27/93," and at the bottom, centered between the DC Comics and Milestone Media corporate logos, was the simple declaration "If you're not there, you just won't get it."

I watched from the far side of the store, next to the display of new comics that were quickly being picked over and bought up. A small group of fans gathered around to ponder the promotional poster. "What's this Milestone thing all about?" asked Jim, a Comics Kingdom regular, while he waited for one of the part-time staff members to retrieve his reserved books from the back room.

"It's a new independent company," explained Barry, an aspiring comic book artist in his early twenties who also worked the cash register most weekday afternoons. "They're totally black-owned and they'll be publishing a whole line of black superhero books."

A few other customers, eager to hear more about any upcoming series they might be interested in, gathered around Barry. He explained what he knew about Milestone: that it was a black-owned company, that it was to feature an entire universe of ethnically diverse super characters, that all the stories would be set in the fictional city of Dakota, and that it was the brainchild of a couple of popular comic book veterans, Denys Cowan and Dwayne McDuffie. Milestone, Barry predicted, was going to be one of the most interesting independent comic book publishers around.

"I don't get it," said Jeremy, another regular who had just finished paying for his stack of comics and had returned to inspecting the poster. "If they're an independent how come the DC logo is on the poster?"

"Well," Barry hesitated, "they're an independent who is published and distributed through DC's system."

"Doesn't sound too independent to me," Jeremy countered.

"Is it like the Vertigo or the Piranha Press stuff?" somebody in the small group asked.

"No!"

"Is it like *Brotherman*-type books?" someone else asked.

"No!"

"Is it going to be all the black DC heroes in one team book?" asked another.

"No, it's going to be really different," Barry assured them, "and the books are going to be better quality, not like some of the underground black series that hardly anybody reads."

"If you say so Bear," said Jim with more than just a hint of friendly sarcasm in his voice. Some of the other young customers laughed outright, the rest merely smiled to themselves. Knowing how hard his audience was to please, Barry simply responded with a noncommittal shrug, a pantomime gesture which implied they should all hope for the best but be prepared for the worst.

None of these comic book fans, a third of whom were black themselves, expected much from the fledgling company which had grandly named itself Milestone Media Incorporated. They had all seen some of the embarrassing black superheroes that the mainstream industry had created in the past, and more than a few of them had tried reading the uneven and politically motivated black books that were currently on the market. Political rhetoric wasn't what these young fans wanted, nor did they want more rehashed characters who were already out of date when they first appeared in the 1970s. What these readers wanted were great superhero stories and art. They wanted new heroes.

When the Milestone poster promising dramatic things to come began appearing in comic book stores across North America it was, for some, a first glimpse at a new universe of superheroes, while for others it was the beginning of the much anticipated launch of Milestone's line of comic books featuring ethnically diverse heroes. In this chapter I want to introduce Milestone Media, the comics, the characters, and, behind the color pages, the men who feed the fantasies of adolescent boys around the world. Fans read comic books across key points of comparison, and the unique situation of the Milestone line facilitated very specific access points along the seams of race, genre traditions, and independent publishing. Fans construct their interpretations according to the logic of their subcultural values, and, more specifically, they read the Milestone books in comparison to other independent black publishers, in comparison to earlier blaxploitation-influenced characters, and in comparison to the market-dominating superhero types on offer from the popular creators at Image Comics. As subsequent chapters will explore, all of these interpretive points lead Milestone fans to weave an understanding of masculinity that differs from the standard perception held by many other comics fans, a concept of masculinity that privileges intellect as much as it does naked muscular power. As the case of Milestone and its fans demonstrates, we can best understand the process of media reception used by comic book fans as an active strategy. It is not necessarily active in the sense of being oppositional or counter-hegemonic but in the sense of being a negotiation of meaning premised on a wide but limited range of meanings made possible between the producers, the readers, and the comics. All of these points will be explored further in subsequent chapters. Here I want to detail the problematic position held by Milestone Media. I say "problematical" because of Milestone's identity as a black publisher who is corporately aligned with the industry giant DC Comics. This is a position that is compounded by the contentious and disputed nature of African American cultural politics and the lack of consensus that surrounds the debates about the legitimacy of a Black Aesthetic.

Because the Milestone books are produced by black publishers and creators who are sensitive to the way minority characters have been portrayed in the past, they represent not a perpetuation of negative stereotypes but a redressing of many of those detrimental images. Instead of concentrating solely on the comic books themselves, it is essential that we also consider the information which circulates around the primary texts. With comic book fandom the readers are often well aware of the creative forces behind the texts and incorporate as much extratextual information as possible into their interpretation of the stories, information such as previous comics that the creators have worked on or the creators' relationship to the rest of the industry. While some fans may have been caught off guard by the appearance of Milestone's first promotional poster, their lack of awareness did not last long. Comic book fans are voracious consumers of extratextual information related to upcoming projects—so much so that an entire support industry of fanzines and internet chat lines has flourished. Insider reports about the development of Milestone Media soon circulated throughout the fan community, and all of the associated knowledge about the company's editorial agenda and the criticism of Milestone by other black comics creators became an important ingredient in fan readings. The following pages will describe the creation of Milestone, its corporate structure, and its creative agenda and will review its core line of comic book titles. I will also address the dispute over the authenticity of black comics characters, a dispute that plagues Milestone, and suggest how their contentious political position actually facilitates reader acceptance and identification.

Ever since the launch of the archetypal superhero Superman in 1938 the comics industry was dominated by Aryan men (and occasionally, Aryan women) in tights, men who would save the world from supervillains, aliens, and mad scientists on a regular monthly schedule. It wasn't until after the cultural and political turmoil of the late 1960s that superheroes of color began appearing in comic books. A major turning point came in 1971 when the restrictive Comics Code—which had been implemented as a self-censoring board following the great comics scare of 1954—began to expand its definition of acceptable content as the industry fought to present more socially relevant stories (for a detailed history of the Comics Code, see Nyberg 1994). First Marvel Comics ran a story line in their Spider-Man titles where Spidey, or Peter Parker's college roommate, suffers from a drug overdose; then DC Comics paired two of their most popular heroes, Green Lantern and Green Arrow, for an epic series of adventures addressing such controversial issues as drug use, pollution, political corruption, religious cults, and racism. Written by Denny O'Neil and illustrated by Neal Adams, the Green Lantern–Green Arrow story arch[1] was obviously inspired by real-life developments, including the Civil Rights movement, which served as the catalyst for the heroes' soul-searching journey. Early on in Green Lantern #76 (fig. 2.1) an elderly black man confronts the costumed hero: "I been readin' about you. How you work for the blue skins, and how on a planet someplace you helped out the orange skins, and you done considerable for the purple skins! Only there's skins you never bothered with . . . the black skins! I want to know how come?! Answer me that, Mr. Green Lantern!" Green Lantern cannot answer the question but vows to begin exploring the social injustices found on Earth as well as in space. By issue #87 the story line featured the character of John Stewart, a black man

2.1   Green Lantern (costarring Green Arrow) #85 (1972). *Illustration courtesy of DC Comics. Used with permission.*

who temporarily replaces Hal Jordan as Green Lantern and who, by the mid-1980s in issue #182, becomes the new Green Lantern (sometimes referred to by fans as the Black Lantern) when the original hero decides to resign.

The impetus of social relevance in the comic books of the 1970s is apparent in the short-lived explosion of minority heroes. In the early 1970s, with the loosening of the Comics Code and the industry's subsequent search for appropriate socially relevant topics, comics turned, as the industry had so often done before, to other media for inspiration and found it in the era's popular blaxploitation movies. The blaxploitation films seemed to have the blend of action, heroism, and profit that the comics industry could easily incorporate into the world of the superhero. Although not pervasive until the 1970s, the first real black superhero in comics was Marvel's Black Panther, who emerged briefly in 1966 as a guest character in *The Fantastic Four* #52. Under his form-fitting cat suit the Black Panther was really T'Challa, the king of the fictitious African nation of Wakanda. The character was not overtly related to the Black Panther political movement, but Lee and Kirby had obviously been somewhat inspired by the organization, and at the very least the character's name was a hip reference to the struggles of black American culture. The Black Panther appeared sporadically over the next few years as a member of the superhero team the Avengers, and in 1969 Marvel added the second-ever black superhero, the Falcon, a reformed criminal who became a sidekick for Captain America. Although the Falcon would become a popular character in his own right and was given his own miniseries in 1983, he was destined to remain in the shadow of Captain America; their often unequal relationship was seen by some as an unintended metaphor for the black experience in white America.

The term blaxploitation has been used most recognizably to describe the sixty or so black-oriented action films produced between 1970 and 1975. But blaxploitation has also been used to describe a small group of mainstream black superhero comics published during the same era and inspired by the films. The blaxploitation films were generally low-budget productions which centered on the action-adventure exploits of a sexually charged black protagonist, a character type that critic Daniel Leab dubbed "Superspade," as he (and later she) defeated a white villain or a corrupt system, all set against the backdrop of a large urban ghetto. The genre emerged in response to two separate problems faced by the film industry in the late 1960s. The first problem was political, as a large, post–Watts riot black community began to demand that Hollywood rescind its racist hiring practices and its tradition of unequal or degrading cinematic representations. In his study of African American film images, Ed Guerrero notes that blaxploitation films "were made possible by the rising political and social consciousness of black people—taking the form of a broadly expressed black nationalist impulse at the end of the civil rights movement—which translated into a large black audience thirsting to see their full humanity depicted on the commercial cinema screen" (Guerrero 1994, 69). The second influential factor was economic. The film industry was in serious financial trouble due to a wave of failed big-budget epics. In fact many of the major studios teetered on the verge of bankruptcy and were forced by the banks to completely restructure their production and distribution systems. "At a time of financial exigency," Tommy Lott pointed out in his discussion of black film theory, "some Hollywood studios discovered that there was a large Black audience starving for Black images on the screen. This situation provided an immediate inducement for them to exploit the box office formula of the black hero which, subsequently, became the earmark of the blaxploitation flick" (Lott 1991, 43). The cheaply produced blaxploitation films satisfied, for a time, the immense black audience looking for heroic characters; and more importantly, from a production standpoint, the films managed to earn significant profits for the studios.

Although there were dozens of famous blaxploitation feature films, or rather I should say *infamous* because the short-lived genre is typically recalled by critics and fans alike as a somewhat embarrassing moment in film history and racial representation, I want to briefly outline only two of the most famous films here, *Sweet Sweetback's Baadasssss Song* and *Shaft*. These two films represent the earliest instances of the genre. They also represent an important dialectical split in racial politics, a dialectical split which would be echoed over twenty years later in the differences between the comics characters published by Milestone Media and those produced by other, primarily African American, comic book creators. *Sweet Sweetback's Baadasssss Song* (1971), written, produced, and directed by, and starring, Melvin Van Peebles, tells the story of Sweetback, a "bad nigger" sex stud who was raised in a whorehouse. The thin plot has to do with Sweetback's journey through the underbelly of the ghetto while being pursued by the police for nearly killing two officers who were brutalizing a black revolutionary leader. Along the way Sweetback repeatedly proves his manhood by out fighting and out screwing a number of adversaries. *Sweet Sweetback* cost Van Peebles only $500,000 to produce, but it became an immediate success grossing over $10 million nationally in its first year of release. Despite the film's financial success and its undeniable popularity with black audiences, *Sweet Sweetback* also set off a series of debates among black critics regarding the aesthetic value of the film and the dangerous ideals it portrayed. Essentially, the debates inspired by *Sweet Sweetback*, and its subsequent imitations, were divided across the long-standing political rift between black America's aspiration to harmonize with the dominant culture and its impulse to separate from it. For some, the film was a revisionist portrayal of a black hero and compensated for years of desexualized, Sidney Poitier–type black images that promoted stoic perseverance and conformity as the only legitimate means for acceptance by the larger society. For others, blaxploitation was a degrading representation of a black culture populated with nothing but pimps, hookers, dealers, druggies, and macho studs. The only aspect of the film that was uniformly regarded as a positive step was that *Sweet Sweetback* was, at all levels, a completely independent black production.

In contrast, *Shaft* (1971), directed by Gordon Parks and starring Richard Roundtree, was a studio-backed project that openly sought to capitalize on the newfound black audience by formalizing the conventions of the black action hero. *Shaft* was less politically contentious and became a smash hit with both black and white filmgoers. Rather than a "Sex Show" performer, John Shaft was a more traditional hero, a hard-boiled, macho private eye who also happened to be black, hip, and sexually active. The film's plot revolves around Shaft's effort to rescue a mob boss's kidnapped daughter who is being held by members of a downtown white Mafia. Like Sweetback (or a black James Bond),

Shaft also gets to sleep with numerous women, both black and white, over the course of his adventure. *Shaft* was a huge success and spawned the sequels *Shaft's Big Score!* (1972) and *Shaft in Africa* (1973) before the genre quickly exhausted itself. Although *Shaft* reproduced many of the key ingredients of the blaxploitation film as established only months earlier by *Sweet Sweetback*, it garnered a different reception from critics. Most critics applauded it for creating at least a marginally more positive black role model, while more politically extreme critics ridiculed it as a white-produced film which basically presented white heroic fantasies in a black face. Mark Reid, discussing *Shaft* in his review of black action films, argues that, in their "obvious effort to attract a black popular audience through rhetoric and images appealing to that audience, MGM, like other major studios, invested black heroes with mainstream values. In doing so, they did not create mythic black heroes. Instead, like doll makers who painted Barbie's face brown, they merely created black-skinned replicas of the white heroes of action films" (Reid 1988, 30–31). Though the images presented in both films are problematic by today's standards in regard to racial stereotypes, they are also indicative of the demarcation in black cultural politics whereby *Sweet Sweetback* becomes aligned with a segregationist position, and *Shaft* with a integrationist position (see Lott 1991; Guerrero 1994).

The comic book industry was quick to take its cue from such popular blaxploitation films as *Sweet Sweetback's Baadasssss Song*, *Shaft*, and their numerous imitators, including *Superfly*, *Top of the Heap*, *The Man*, *The Mack*, and *Black Caesar*. Publishers were eager to tap into a market segment that they had ignored for far too long. But instead of producing straight blaxploitation heroes, the comics publishers melded the superficial conventions of the film genre with the characters they knew best, the superheroes. The comic book versions may have looked and talked like John Shaft, but they were given fancy costumes and superpowers. The comic book blaxploitation heroes were also watered down for a younger audience so that such prominent film conventions as the hero's sexual prowess were left out of the stories. The ingredients that the comics did retain were usually much more in line with the politics of *Shaft* than they were with *Sweet Sweetback* or any of the other films that took professional criminals as their heroes. Though they were occasionally reformed criminals or wrongly accused criminals, the comic book blaxploitation characters were always very clearly heroes. They were hip black heroes with a streetwise agenda to clear drug dealers out of the ghettos that they defended. Like the films that inspired them, the blaxploitation heroes of the comics did not last for very long. By the late 1970s they had all disappeared except for the intermittent guest appearance in a more popular character's book. Still, because comic book fans are so well aware of the medium's history, it has been hard for publishers to shrug off the ghost of the jive-talking blaxploitation heroes. The characters are still available in back-issue bins in every comic book store and many of them still make the random guest appearance in a variety of contemporary comics. As I will explore in later chapters, even today's young fans interpret modern black comic book heroes in relation to those who emerged for a brief period in the early 1970s.

Undeniably, the most widely recognized blaxploitation character in the comics was Marvel's Luke Cage, who first appeared in 1972 in his self-titled series *Luke Cage: Hero for Hire* (fig. 2.2). Far from Marvel's earlier venture into black heroes with the noble Black Panther, who was obviously constructed as a positive role model for black children, Luke Cage was a trash-talking, streetwise, ex-con forever on the run from the law. Originally scripted by Archie Goodwin with art by Billy Graham and George Tuska, Cage is the epitome of blaxploitation's angry young black man. Sent to prison for a crime he did not commit, Cage volunteers for a medical experiment that gives him extraordinary strength and steel-hard skin. Cage escapes and sets up shop near New York's Times Square as a mercenary "hero for hire." By issue #17 Cage is granted a

2.2   Luke Cage: Hero for Hire #1 (1972). *Courtesy of Marvel Comics. © Marvel Entertainment Group, Inc. Used with permission.*

more conventional superhero name and the title of his book is changed to *Luke Cage: Power Man.* But by 1986, after having the longest run ever for a book featuring a black protagonist, the series was finally cancelled due to declining sales. Many loyal readers were upset by the demise of the character, and in 1991 Marvel briefly resurrected the hero in a comic simply called *Cage.* Faced with the dilemma of a purely 1970s character existing in the 1990s, *Cage* writer Marcus McLaurin undertook the novel task of what the *Village Voice*'s Gary Dauphin describes as "dialogu[ing] with '70s black macho—the historical space of Cage's origin—hoping to critique the type while still relying on it to make the comic fun. It's a neat enough trick when it works, but when it doesn't, today's Cage is a skipping record, hitting the same blustery note over and over" (Dauphin 1994, 35). Apparently Cage's appeal had worn off and *Cage* completed its run after only twenty issues. The character still appears occasionally as a guest hero in other ongoing Marvel comic books.

When Tony Isabella moved in 1976 to DC Comics from Marvel, where he had worked on Luke Cage, he was given the task of developing the company's first black superhero. DC had in mind a character dubbed "the Black Bomber" who was actually a bigoted white Vietnam veteran who had undergone wartime experiments that would cause him to turn into a black hero during times of stress. Fortunately, Isabella persuaded DC to drop the concept and accept his character, Black Lightning, instead. The electricity-wielding Black Lightning was actually Jefferson Pierce, an ex-Olympian turned inner-city schoolteacher with a passion for cleaning up the ghetto in which he lived and worked. Like Cage, Black Lightning was inspired by the blaxploitation heroes of the screen. His self-titled series was launched in 1977 with a cover illustration featuring Black Lightning beating up a warehouse full of baddies while he declared, "You *Pushers* have wrecked the city long enough—Now it's my turn to wreck you!" Like all the other blaxploitation-inspired comic book heroes, Black Lightning was a watered-down nod to the black power movement of the 1970s, and the stories concentrated on his war on drugs. The series only lasted eleven issues, less than a year, but the character was popular enough to garner numerous guest appearances. One such appearance occurred in 1979 when Black Lightning was asked to join the all-white Justice League of America (fig. 2.3). In an issue surprising for its admission of racial politics among superhero characters, the writers had Black Lightning turn down Superman's offer on the grounds that he didn't want to be the league's token black hero. In the 1980s Black Lightning became a team leader in the series *Batman and the Outsiders.* In 1994, following this time in the steps of Milestone's new heroes, Black Lightning was relaunched in a second ongoing series of his own.

Luke Cage and Black Lightning are not the only blaxploitation heroes to

2.3 Justice League of America #173 (1979). *Illustration courtesy of DC Comics. Used with permission.*

appear in the comics, they are just two of the most widely recognized ones, the ones that modern fans and creators cite time and again as influential on the new heroes of today. Following the early success of Luke Cage, Marvel began to feature the Black Panther in lone action in 1973 in the sixth issue of a comic book entitled *Jungle Action*. By 1977 the character was given his own book, *Black Panther*, which lasted only fifteen issues before being cancelled in 1979. But the Black Panther, the landmark hero, has subsequently been re-vived for two miniseries, one in 1988 and the other in 1991. Marvel tried for a third solo black superhero with the size-changing Black Goliath in 1976, but the series never caught on and was finished by *Black Goliath* #5. Aside from individual minority heroes, the 1970s also saw a revamped version of Marvel's X-Men emerge as a racially diverse team that would become one of the most popular comic books of the 1980s and 1990s. Reworked in 1975, the new X-Men helped to expand the presence of ethnically and nationally diverse characters as heroic ideals by including Storm (African), Colossus (Russian), Nightcrawler (German), Thunderbird (Native American), Banshee (Scottish), and Wolverine (Canadian). Over the years the X-Men would constantly revise their roster to include almost every nationality possible and would expand on their metaphorical nature as mutant heroes to encompass an overriding narrative on the evils of bigotry and discrimination.

The Milestone line of comics was officially launched in 1993, yet throughout 1992, a full year before any of their comic books were even printed, Milestone Media was already receiving a great deal of attention within the pages of industry magazines and professional fanzines such as the *Comic Buyer's Guide*, the *Comics Journal*, and *Wizard: The Guide to Comics* as well as in the mainstream press with articles about the developing company appearing in the *New York Times*, the *Washington Post*, and *Newsday*, among others. At a time of incredible growth within the comic book industry, Milestone was immediately distinguishable from the numerous other high-profile independent publishers by virtue of its designation as a black-owned company featuring black characters. From the very beginning many fans understood Milestone as something more than just a new line of books, as more than just another superhero blank slate onto which they could project their own fantasies. Milestone was, and is, seen as a culturally loaded property—"loaded" because it is different from the norm, because it is a conscious attempt to rework industry conventions—whose obvious inclusion of racial identity into the often all too white world of comic book superheroics has alternately been embraced, rejected, ignored, and negotiated by readers from across a wide spectrum of predisposed social positions. Contrary to the assertions made in recent years about the open-ended qualities of media texts by some of the cultural studies scholars, Milestone is a clear example of a popular medium whose political nature, both inherent and ascribed, works to inform and define certain readings.

Milestone Media is an independent publishing company. It was initially owned and controlled by four young black men: Derek T. Dingle, Dwayne McDuffie, Denys Cowan, and Michael Davis. Davis, an experienced comic book artist and Milestone's original director of Talent Development, left the company in its first year when he was appointed the CEO of Motown Animation and Film Works. The three remaining owners are uniquely qualified for their venture into the risky business of distributing comic books featuring black superheroes. President Derek T. Dingle brings to Milestone an acute publisher's business sense from his previous experience as the managing editor of *Black Enterprise* and as a staff writer for *Money Magazine*. Dwayne McDuffie is the company's editor in chief as well as one of its most prolific and popular writers. McDuffie is a former editor and writer for both Marvel and Harvey Comics and at one time or another has worked on almost every character in the Marvel universe, with particular success on the Deathlok and Spider-Man titles. Perhaps the best known of the Milestone founders is Creative Director Denys Cowan, who is regarded as one of the industry's leading illustrators. Cowan has worked professionally since he began as an inker at the age of fifteen and has developed a fan following for his distinct artistic style on such comics as DC's *The Question* and *Batman* and Marvel's *Deathlok*. Milestone is the brainchild of these creators, Dingle, McDuffie, Cowan, and Davis, in both its corporate structure and its narrative message.

Seeking to redress the lack of minority characters in the world of comic books, the Milestone founders were able to take advantage of the industry changes in the early 1990s, changes that were conducive to the formation of high-profile independent publishers. The notion of creating comic books about black characters by black creators was not in itself a new idea. As early as 1947 the privately produced *All Negro Comics* appeared on the newsstands but only lasted for a single issue, and in an early editorial Milestone itself paid tribute to previous efforts at creating African American comics by people such as Arvell Jones, Keith Pollard, Ron Wilson, Aubrey Bradford, and Skip Kirkland in 1976 (see "The Company Line" in all Milestone March 1993 issues). And several independently produced and distributed black comic books were already in limited circulation by 1993: *Malcolm 10, Nog,* and *Sustah-Girl* from the Chicago-based Onli Studios; Jason E. Sims's critically praised *Brotherman* from Big City Comics out of Texas; and the work of Seattle's Stan Shaw and Toronto's Ho Che Anderson. What was different about the creation of Milestone was that Milestone chose to create its comics independently from within the mainstream system. Rather than self-publishing in limited runs Milestone entered into an arrangement with DC Comics, an arrangement guaranteeing that their books would be printed in a quality format and would be fully distributed at an international level along with DC's own books. This business deal has allowed Milestone to flourish and has also been the object of some criticism from other black comic book publishers.

With the launch of Milestone in February 1993 following so soon after the ground-breaking success of the Image line of comics, and given the separatist tone of some African American movements in the United States, one cannot help but wonder if the impetus for Milestone's creation was in some way reactionary. But the three Milestone principals, Dingle, McDuffie, and Cowan, deny the perception that they were inspired by what they saw happening at other companies. "We got together to fill what we saw as a lack of minority representation in comics," argues Cowan. "It wasn't like Image where we got mad at somebody and broke away. That's a very sexy story but it's not what happened to us. We could have done any of our books at Marvel or DC or Dark Horse but we wanted to ensure we maintained all of the creative control over our characters no matter what. Besides we started to develop Milestone long before the Image guys became thoroughly disenchanted with the established system." According to McDuffie, their approach to creating Milestone was much more organized than the approach that some of the other new companies might have used: "We were so meticulous about our business plan and the creative concept the business plan supported that it took us one and a half to two years from the time we began meeting every week to meeting daily to set the company up." Yet McDuffie adds, "It was while we were in the planning stages that Image was announced and we thought 'great, there must be something in the air.' " What was indeed "in the air" was the financial viability of independent comic books driven by creator recognition and supported by the proven basis of the direct market. Rarely had the world of comic books been more ripe for diversification.

In much of the early press coverage the Milestone founders suggest that their earliest dreams of creating black superhero comics came while they were still young fans, long before any of them had actually entered the business professionally. Cowan and Dingle in particular were childhood friends who would read comics and then experiment with making up their own stories starring black heroes. In an interview for the nationally distributed fanzine *Wizard: The Guide to Comics,* Dingle described Milestone Media, "[It is] an outgrowth of what Denys and I started as children. We were classmates, we read comics together—and when we read comics, we found a paucity of Black characters . . . We started creating our own characters, as a lot of fans did, and they reflected ourselves and our experiences. Fast forward 20 years later, Denys became a very accomplished artist in the comic book field. I stayed in publishing management; Denys, along with Michael Davis and Dwayne McDuffie, decided there was a need to establish a line of Black comic book characters and then they expanded from that to multicultural comics.2 In order to preserve this idea and to protect it, they needed a company and someone with experience in publishing. That's when they called me" (O'Neill 1993, 44). Once the idea started to take shape, around June of 1991, the group began to meet every Thursday evening at Cowan's Brooklyn studio to work out their shared vision.

All four of the principals were in agreement on two points that would be fundamental for the Milestone ethos. The first point was that they wanted their comic books to reflect people from a variety of cultural backgrounds. Although three of Milestone's original four comic book series focused solely on black heroes, the creators are always careful to declare that their line emphasizes multicultural characters. According to McDuffie, the editorial goal that they have maintained from the very first stages of planning has been "to increase the diversity of the comics industry by reflecting the complexity and the diversity of the real world that we all live in. We could have done just African American comics because that is obviously the experience that we understand best, but we realize that that is only one of many possible viewpoints that we want to bring forward for our readers." The second crucial point that the Milestone founders agreed upon was the need to reach the largest audience possible through a professional system of distribution. With their combined experience of the comic-publishing business they knew that creating quality books would not be a major problem. Distribution difficulties, on the other hand, have often been the downfall of new companies without the manpower or the established contacts to see that the books get into enough stores on time every month. Consistency of printing and distribution is a key factor in establishing a large and loyal fan following. If a reader picks up an issue and is intrigued by the book the publishers need to build on that interest immediately. If the next issue does not appear on the stands for another four months there is a good chance the reader will have moved on to other titles or not be willing to invest his or her dollars in a series that is difficult to follow on a regular basis. Even the extremely popular line of comics from Image have been harshly criticized by retailers and fans alike for their inability to meet monthly release dates.

In order to fulfill their distribution goals the Milestone group struck a cooperative deal with DC Comics, the industry's second largest publisher. DC's status within the industry and their experimentation throughout the 1980s with such cutting-edge concepts as prestige format books, maxi-series, intercompany crossovers, and their AIDS awareness program made them a likely partner for the Milestone group. On a practical level Denys Cowan's long and notable career at DC helped to open doors and ensured that the Milestone proposal would reach the desk of Paul Levitz, DC's vice president in charge of business operations and legal negotiations. The initial formal proposal put forth by Milestone outlined three major areas: strategic marketing information, a detailed description of the four original books, and a profile of the company's financial and corporate structure. DC was immediately interested in the potential partnership. During the fall and winter of 1991 the two companies entered into a series of meetings to hammer out the legalities and establish a suitable system that would essentially see DC operating as the printer and distributor for Milestone's comics. The arrangement in negotiation had never been tried before in the comic book industry. The nearest model was the work undertaken by the Will Eisner and Jerry Inger studio in the 1930s and 1940s. The Eisner/Inger studio would be contracted by a publisher to create a comic book that the larger company would then print and distribute. The work was freelance in nature and Eisner and Inger always relinquished all legal rights despite some-times inventing the entire concept, character, and book from scratch. Such was the case with almost all of the Eisner/Inger work of the period (except for Eisner's enduringly popular *The Spirit*), including their production of the Super-man inspired *Wonder-Man* for Victor S. Fox in 1939.

Fundamental to Milestone's agreement with DC was that they would not relinquish any of the legal or creative rights to their work. Throughout the negotiations Milestone, and their lawyers, insisted on three basic points: (1) that they would retain total creative control; (2) that they would retain all copyrights for characters created under the Milestone banner; and (3) that they would have the final say on all merchandising and licensing deals pertain-ing to their properties. Rather than the work-for-hire deals of the Eisner and Inger era, the Milestone-DC contract, which was finalized in May of 1992, is comparative to the standard relationship between independent film production companies and major Hollywood studios. Much like large film studios who pay small independent production companies a creative service fee and a share of the royalties in exchange for the distribution rights of a movie, DC Comics has in effect licensed the characters, editorial services, and creative content of the Milestone books for an annual fee of $500,000 to $650,000 and a share of the profits. In addition to printing and distributing the books DC is also respon-sible for promoting the Milestone titles within the pages of their regular comics, in all marketing materials, at conventions, and in any other media, such as the recent venture of the DC family of comics going interactive through a special promotional arrangement with American Online. By entering into a partnership with DC, which is a subsidiary of the multimedia conglomerate Time-Warner, Milestone became an immediate presence in the comic book industry. Their books were guaranteed to be produced and distributed on time, automatically appeared in all the major retail ordering catalogues, were granted better shelf space in comic specialty stores, and were made available in convenience, gro-cery, and regular book stores. DC also serves as Milestone's licensing agent for other media and ancillary products and helps to arrange lucrative deals like the award-winning one-hundred-card set of Milestone trading cards produced by SkyBox International.

This innovative relationship meant that Milestone could avoid the precari-ous dangers faced by most independent publishers. Although the early 1990s was a period of incredible growth for the comic book industry with over twelve hundred individual titles being released every month, it was also a time when many lower-profile books could be lost in the crowd. Don Thompson, coeditor of the weekly trade paper *Comics Buyer's Guide,* has noted, concerning minor-ity-based comics, "There have been some independent publishers, but they aren't reaching a real wide audience. This [Milestone] is the first independent company to get any major financing. Others are run on a shoestring. This deal makes them a major force" (quoted in Silverman 1993, 31). The Milestone founders point out that the deal with DC also freed them up to produce an entire line of comics rather than a single title, and the conventional wisdom is that a publisher needs a minimum of four books that are recognized as a cohesive group. By starting with four books, fans were exposed to a new Milestone issue every week and could begin to recognize character and company consistency even if just from the covers. In addition to the practical business aspects, the prospect of launching multiple series simultaneously was also a crucial element for the presentation of Milestone's political agenda. The central goal of Milestone in their attempt to address the lack of minority representation in comics, and the often stereotypical nature of that representation when it does occur, is to show the quality and diversity of African American life. "To," as Dwayne McDuffie puts it, "break up the idea of a monolith."

In a special edition of the critical fanzine *Comics Journal,* an edition focusing on black comics artists, McDuffie explains their desire to create an entire line:

There's a creative freedom that we gain by doing more than one book. My problem— and I'll speak as a writer now—with writing a black character in either the Marvel or DC universe is that he is not a man. He is a symbol. Like Wonder Woman—if you write Wonder Woman, she is all women. You can't do a character. On the other hand, if I write a white character—as I have in most of my career, because that's what's available—like Dr. Doom or Captain America, neither one of them represents white Americans. Cage is all black people. Deathlok is all black people. It limits the complexity and the roundedness of the characters. If Milestone had done just one book, whoever that character was would have been limited to being like what Sidney Poitier was in the 1950s movies. But we present a range of characters, guys who are all different from each other, as different as all of us are from each other. We all share an interest in comics, but we all are very different politically and socially—what we think is important, who we think should be president, and any other issue—just like any other group of human beings. By putting a line of characters out, suddenly there is enormous creative freedom. I would not presume to speak for black people in this country. It's ridiculous to attempt to do that. An analogy: you watch the news every night and the anchor man will say, "Black opinion on this issue . . . [laughter] is this." No one would even begin to try to do that with whites. It's ludicrous for me to sit here and say, "White opinion on abortion is this." But because we are so used to dealing with blacks or with anyone considered the other as a monolith, we think it's okay to say, "This is their opinion." Well, in my house there are different opinions, much less within my community and within all blacks in America—we all agree on every single thing? We're all the same guy? Of course we're not. And as long as the media keeps presenting us that way, it promotes racism. (Norman 1993, 68–69)

While other independent black comic book titles such as *Ebony Warrior* or *Zwanna: Son of Zulu* contain much more overtly political messages about cultural nationalism, to the point of their being accused of promoting racism against whites and other groups, Milestone has tried to avoid the stigma inherent in "message comics" in favor of emphasizing cultural diversity.

From the very beginning the Milestone creators have made clear that their comics are meant to be entertaining stories that seek to promote racial understanding as a consequence of portraying hitherto underrepresented groups as complex and diverse people. It was a conscious decision by the founders that in approaching their creations as entertainment first and a source of political agency second they would be better able to effect cultural change without alienating the core audience of comic book readers. Months before the books were released, Michael Davis stressed in a *Washington Post* piece, "We are not going to produce preachy comics. What we want kids to do is pick up our books and get a better understanding of the multicultural experience" (Singletary 1992, E-4). In the introductory editorial page of all four of the first issues, Milestone openly declared their general agenda: "Diversity's our story, and we're sticking with it. The variety of cultures and experiences out there make for better comics in here. When people get excited about the diversity in here maybe they'll get just as excited about the diversity out there—Call it a mission." This political message writ large does not mean that the Milestone titles have stayed away from specific controversial topics. Within the first year the various story lines had explored a variety of sensitive issues including gang violence, drug abuse, teenage pregnancy, and the often strained black and Jewish community relations. But despite these progressive topics, Editor in Chief McDuffie maintains that Milestone's "major job is to entertain people, because even if you want to send a message you need to recognize that the best propaganda is the kind people don't notice. Nobody wants to sit through a lecture."

At the end of January 1993, DC Comics' free promotional pamphlet, Direct Currents, boldly announced: "It's a major milestone in comics . . . Milestone Media, that is! Milestone is an all-new line of comics featuring the adventures of a culturally diverse mix of superheroes, battling in the city of Dakota, and driven by internal conflicts that shape them in ways rarely explored in comics" (Kupperberg 1993, 1). *Hardware* was the first series released on February 23, *Blood Syndicate* followed the next week, with *Icon* the week after, and *Static* rounded out the month. A year later the original four books were joined by *Shadow Cabinet, Kobalt,* and *Xombi.* The diversity that Milestone hopes to represent is apparent in the fundamental differences of each of the titles. Yet despite their differences, the metaphorical nature of the first mainstream culturally diverse comics universe is expressed in the titles' shared heroic responsibilities. "Linked in their struggle to defeat the S.Y.S.T.E.M.," a Milestone press release declared, the battle of Dakota is a "clash of two worlds: a low-income urban caldron and the highest level of privileged society."

Hardware (fig. 2.4), written by Dwayne McDuffie and initially drawn by Denys Cowan, is the story of Curtis Metcalf, an exceedingly brilliant inventor employed by Alva Industries, an incredibly high-tech corporation. Metcalf has a father-son relationship with his white boss, Edwin Alva, Dakota's most prominent businessman and leading industrialist. Alva had sponsored Metcalf's education and encouraged his achievements since discovering him at a grade-school science fair. Believing that he is a favored son, Metcalf is shattered when he discovers that Alva has only been exploiting his genius all along and really sees him as no more than a useful servant. Hand in hand with this personal revelation, Metcalf realizes that Alva's industrial empire is a front for his illegal activities as one of Dakota's leading organized-crime bosses. Metcalf feels compelled to seek vengeance on Alva's criminal empire and uses his unparalleled skill as an inventor to create a super state-of-the-art cybernetic battle suit to wear into his personal war. Armed with an array of plasma guns, laser can-

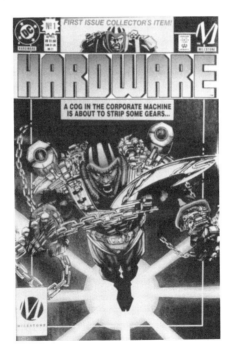

2.4   Hardware #1 (1993). Illustration courtesy of DC Comics and Milestone Media, Inc. Used with permission.

nons, micro-rockets, and jet packs, Metcalf becomes Hardware and sets out to destroy Alva: "A cog in the corporate machine is about to strip some gears." Hardware is Milestone's angry black man who fights against personal injustices and battles the powers that be, which are clearly represented by the corrupt, all-powerful figure of Alva, the white father.

As the series has continued, Hardware's role has developed beyond that of an extremely disgruntled employee to a more mature hero. Unlike more traditional comic book characters who seem to embody noble heroism as an innate personality trait, Hardware is portrayed as a man who must learn to conquer his own rage. Writer Dwayne McDuffie describes the series as "about a very confused man who has to come to terms with his own life, his own morality and his responsibilities before he can truly be a hero. Hardware is a book about a man who must overcome his worst instincts and rise above his personal problems." Thanks to the help and criticism of Hardware's cast of supporting characters—including Metcalf's girlfriend, Dr. Barraki Young, a professor of African American Studies at Medina University, and Deacon "Phreaky Deak" Stuart, a computer hacker extraordinaire and clandestine information gatherer for Hardware—Metcalf is slowly learning to channel his anger into more than just personal vengeance. Throughout the series Hardware has fought to understand his world and to atone for the lives he callously takes in his initial battles with Alva's forces, and he eventually even enters into an uneasy alliance with his former nemesis.

Milestone's second core title to see publication, *Blood Syndicate*, is also perhaps their most controversial. Written by Ivan Velez Jr. and illustrated by Chris Cross, Blood Syndicate (fig. 2.5) is the story of a racially mixed, superpowered street gang. The origins of the characters' superpowers can all be traced back to the night of the Big Bang, one of the fundamental events of the Milestone universe. The Big Bang was supposed to be the final turf war between all the major gangs on Dakota's downtrodden Paris Island. The police intervened by firing a radioactive gas into the melee; they thought that the gas would act as a marker, allowing them to arrest over five hundred gang members by morning. Instead, the experimental gas killed hundreds and left the few survivors with superhuman abilities. A group of the powerful "bang babies" banded together to form the most formidable gang ever: the Blood Syndicate. Among the gang's members are Wise Son, whose molecular structure has been converted into ultradense matter, making him impervious to any physical harm; Fade, a ghostlike transparent character who, we later find out, is also HIV positive; Flashback, Fade's sister, who can rewind time at will but only for a few seconds; Masquerade, who can manipulate her appearance to take the shape of any object or person she desires; DMZ, a mute and masked

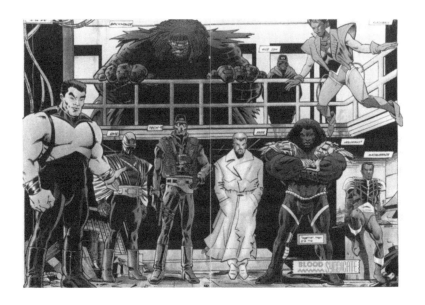

2.5   Blood Syndicate #1 (1993). Illustration courtesy of DC Comics and Milestone
Media, Inc. Used with permission.

mysterious character with powers of flight, invulnerability, and superhuman
strength; Third Rail, who takes on the equivalent power of any energy source
he touches, be it an attacker or an electrified subway rail; and Brick House, a
female bang baby who was fused with a solid brick wall and has become incredibly strong and virtually unstoppable.

The Blood Syndicate is clearly not a team of superheroes. They are a street
gang of urban outcasts more concerned about protecting their turf and garner-
ing respect than about doing good for the greater community. The members
of the gang often fight amongst themselves as much as they fight their ene-
mies. Among the story lines that Blood Syndicate has dealt with are Fade's
sexuality, Flashback's problems with drug addiction, and the ongoing reliance
of the characters on the gang as a surrogate family. A central theme of the
book is the bleak reality of gang violence. Unlike other comic books about
superteams—comics like DC's The Justice League, Marvel's The X-Men, or
Image's Youngblood—Blood Syndicate is a consistently realistic treatment of
violence and its repercussions, or at least as realistic as is possible in a book
populated by superpowered beings. As McDuffie, who also edits Blood Syndicate, tells Comics Scene magazine in a special issue on the rise of new comic
book universes, "The primary rule in our universe is that actions have consequences. If you punch someone through a wall, it hurts. If someone gets shot,

they bleed. You can't deal with this kind of violence and tell people there are no consequences. That goes across our entire line. Hardware killed some people in the first issue—he was absolutely wrong—and he will pay for it." Denys Cowan adds, "A lot of the violence in *Blood Syndicate,* the down-and-dirty violence as well as the mental violence, can be much scarier because you can relate to it. That's why we feel that the violence in Blood Syndicate affects people much more than any other titles, because it's real violence" (Nazzaro 1993, 49). Although the characters of Blood Syndicate are quick to resort to violence, the Milestone editorial stance tries not to glorify the street-gang mentality but to reveal the flaws and effects of that violence.

Contrary to the antiheroics of Hardware and Blood Syndicate, Milestone's third book, *Icon,* is a traditional superhero series. Written by McDuffie and drawn by M. D. Bright, Icon (fig. 2.6) is often referred to as the flagship title of the Milestone line. Icon's story really begins in 1839 when an escape pod from an exploding extraterrestrial starliner lands in a cotton field in America's Deep South. A slave woman named Miriam discovers inside the pod a little black baby who is actually an alien being whose appearance has been altered

2.6　Icon #1 (1993). Illustration courtesy of DC Comics and Milestone Media, Inc. Used with permission.

by the ship's defense mechanisms to resemble the first type of life form encountered. Miriam christens the child Augustus Freeman and raises him as her own. Seemingly immortal, the adult alien now resides in Dakota as the successful corporate lawyer Augustus Freeman IV. Freeman is an extremely conservative Republican who continuously espouses the virtues of a Horatio Alger "pull yourself up by your own bootstraps" philosophy while keeping his Superman-like powers a secret. On one fateful night a group of teenagers from a nearby housing project attempt to rob Freeman's luxurious home. With his extraordinary powers of flight and strength and his bulletproof skin Freeman scares away the intruders and admonishes them for their unlawful ways. Among the teenagers that night is Raquel Ervin, an idealist streetwise girl from the inner city who revisits Freeman the next week and convinces him to use his powers on behalf of those without any. Ervin designs their costumes and Freeman becomes the red, yellow, and green clad Icon while Ervin, with the assistance of an alien power belt that allows her to absorb and refocus energy, becomes his partner, Rocket. An early company preview describes their relationship: "Because Augustus has had so much for so long, he doesn't fully understand the needs of the people whom he protects. The teenage girl who insists on becoming his sidekick, Rocket, is a product of Dakota's worst section, Paris Island. She and Icon have a profound effect on one another. Rocket gets a glimpse of Augustus' affluence, and inspiration from his mighty deeds. Icon, in turn, learns of a world of misery and failed expectations that he didn't believe still existed in this country. Together, Icon and Rocket tackle the world's toughest villains—and some of our biggest problems."

The partnership between Icon and Rocket is an uneasy one. The two characters represent different ideological poles politically and they often act as platforms for the narrative to work out diverse reactions to controversial issues. On the one side Icon is a very conservative persona very much akin to the Booker T. Washington success-through-perseverance philosophy he has adopted, while on the other side Rocket, a Toni Morrison and W. E. B. Du Bois fan, stresses the social injustices at work in the world, injustices that subjugate the downtrodden. The characters have clashed over such things as Rocket's decision to keep her baby when she accidentally becomes pregnant (thus becoming the first superheroine who is also an unwed teenage mother) and Icon's decision to support a new amusement park that caters to the rich but is being built on the ghettoized Paris Island, thus displacing poor people with nowhere else to go. Derek T. Dingle points out that "Despite, or perhaps because of, their different viewpoints Icon provides us with the opportunity to explore opposing ideas about how Black Americans should operate. In effect you get these two people, these two political ideals who challenge each other to better themselves. She challenges Icon to be a real hero for the people who need one, and he in turn challenges her to become more responsible." Rather than taking a solitary political stance according to one racially informed position, Icon carefully illustrates the various personal and political perspectives that are possible within a single cultural community.

The final title to be released in Milestone's initial line was *Static* (fig. 2.7). The most lighthearted of the four original books, Static is the story of Virgil Hawkins, a typically geeky fifteen-year-old student at one of Dakota's troubled public schools, Ernest Hemingway High. Trying to impress some of the guys at school, Virgil sneaks off to witness the gang warfare on the night of the Big Bang. Sprayed by the same radioactive gas as the gang members, Virgil survives to discover that he now has the ability to manipulate electromagnetic currents; he can generate force fields, "taser punches," lightning bolts, and can even fly by surfing on electrically charged discs of metal, such as garbage can lids or manhole covers. A comic book fan himself, Virgil relishes his chance to don his homemade blue and white tights and one of an assortment of baseball caps to become the dashing teen superhero with the ready quip, Static.

2.7   Static #1 (1993). Illustration courtesy of DC Comics and Milestone Media, Inc. Used with permission.

Like the early Spider-Man stories, to which Static bears more than just a passing resemblance, Virgil's adventures always incorporate the realistic dilemmas faced by a kid who is also secretly one of Dakota's greatest heroes. He still has problems with girls, homework, bullies, his older sister, and with trying to keep his part-time job at a fast-food franchise despite consistently being made late for work by supervillains. Among his eclectic group of adolescent friends, the only confidant who is aware of Virgil's secret identity is Frieda Goren, Hemingway High's most popular babe and girlfriend of one of Virgil's buddies. Static is a fun-loving book that explores the troubles and pleasures of modern adolescence at the same time that it offers traditional superhero fare and not so traditional problems, like trying to defuse the bombs and the propaganda of a militant black terrorist, accepting that one of your best friends is gay, and losing your virginity.

Static is definitely the kid in the Milestone lineup. He reacts to things as an average adolescent does. He doesn't have all the answers, he doesn't even know all the questions. Like many of Static's readers, Virgil Hawkins is trying to be the best possible person he can be despite what seem to be overwhelming odds. Virgil/Static sometimes behaves badly but his exploits usually take on the aura of a moral parable about the need to be responsible, kind, understanding, tolerant and to find peaceful solutions to frustrating problems. Since Virgil is the youngest, and clearly not the most powerful, of Dakota's heroes, Static often focuses on his ability to outthink rather than outgun his opponents. Denys Cowan describes Static as "by far our funniest book—a lot of humor and wit that works well with the character development of the stories—but it also deals with the belief that the underdog can win by not succumbing to the I'm-bigger-and-stronger-than-anything-in-the-universe-so-I'll-just-smash-your-head-in mentality that we see in some comic books." As Static, Virgil must learn to mature in order to survive. He is not Billy Batson, who can just shout "Shazam!" and become the full-grown and supremely powerful Captain Marvel. Underneath the costume and the witty repartee Static is still the same geeky kid struggling to defeat the bullies and keep his world in order.

In the spring of 1994, one year after the Milestone universe was launched, the company undertook its first crossover event. A crossover is a marketing strategy to boost sales of interrelated series and is generally considered a momentous occasion in the world of comics. All of the titles in a company's line are engaged in a single epic story line that affects each of the characters in the fictional universe. The "Shadow War" crossover was used to reveal the government treachery behind the Big Bang, the initial riot that created Static and the Blood Syndicate as well as countless villains, and to launch Milestone's second wave of comic books, *Shadow Cabinet, Xombi,* and the short-lived

Kobalt. In *Shadow Cabinet* a covert team of superpowered operatives are assembled by Dharma, an all-seeing Eastern Indian, to undertake Mission Impossible–style assignments in order to secretly protect humankind. The Shadow Cabinet team includes a resourceful array of heroes including Iron Butterfly, a headstrong Iranian woman with the ability to reshape any metal to her will; Sideshow, a black neo-hippie shape-shifter who takes on animal forms; Iota, a playful woman who can shrink herself or any object she touches to the most miniscule proportions; Donner, a superstrong woman created by her father's genetic experiments in Germany; and Blitzen, a superfast woman who is both Donner's usual assignment partner and her lesbian lover. *Xombi* is less a super-hero series than an unusual combination of supernatural science fiction and various religious mythologies. The main character is Dr. David Kim, a Korean American research scientist who is accidentally injected with his own nanotechnology—microscopic robots which can manipulate atoms and rearrange molecules. Kim, in effect, becomes a man who can never die. His body is capable of immediate self-regeneration. The final title to be added was *Kobalt,* which writer John Rozum describes as the sole proprietor of the "post-modern weirdness corner of the Milestone universe." The series is a semi-tongue-in-cheek spoof of the ultra-hard-boiled characters popular at other companies. The rough and grim Kobalt is forced to take on a teen sidekick and the new partnership becomes almost a comedy of errors in the way of superhero crime fighting.

As a distinctly innovative change in the comic book publishing industry, the launch of Milestone was reported in dozens of newspapers, more coverage than any other new comic book publisher had received in the last fifty years. In fact, any coverage by the popular press is considered a remarkable boost for the entire comics industry since even after more than sixty years the medium has never managed to achieve the status or public notice accorded to other entertainment media such as film or television. Clips about the formation of Milestone appeared in the entertainment news broadcasts on CNN, MTV, and *Entertainment Tonight,* and Milestone was mentioned on such fan-based programs as the Canadian cable show *Prisoners of Gravity.* The press surrounding the formation and development of Milestone Media commonly fell into three overlapping categories: (1) general praise for the multicultural agenda of the company, with a particular emphasis on the need for positive role models for black children; (2) business-oriented profiles of the unique publishing arrangement between Milestone and DC Comics; and (3) coverage of the criticisms directed toward Milestone by smaller independent black comic book publishers. Though intense media focus on a new product can usually help ensure public awareness and increased sales, for Milestone it became a double-edged sword. On the one side the media attention was a welcome and positive exposure, but on the other side the tone of the articles portrayed Milestone as a specifically black company to such an extent that the progressive racial element of the books overshadowed any other perceptions. In other words, the Milestone comics were somewhat marginalized as black comics rather than as entertainment that just happens to feature black characters. In an entertainment industry, especially one geared toward a young audience, to be perceived as political is really the kiss of death.

Without fail the newspaper articles praising the development of Milestone dwell on the founders' experiences as black childhood comic book fans. "As a child Derek T. Dingle, president of Milestone Media Inc., loved comic books," reported the New York Times. "But when he and a friend, Denys Cowan, read about the superheroes and their mythical powers, they sensed that something seemed wrong besides just creepy villains and criminals. 'We didn't see any heroes in the comic books that looked like ourselves . . . None of the characters were African Americans' " (Byrd 1992, F-8). Or as quoted in *Newsday:* "As youngsters, when we read comic books, we never found Black characters. There were green and blue characters, but no one of a black hue" (Silverman 1993, 31). These accounts then segue into casual comments by current young readers bemoaning the lack of black superheroes. For example the *Washington Post* reported the somewhat muddled comments of an eleven-year-old comic book fan who claims, "Sometimes I want a Black idol. Sometimes you want an idol to be like you in the comic book. They don't have anybody that involves people like me. If I wanted to be like one of them, my idol would have to be white" (Singletary 1992, E-1). In addition to illustrating the fan origins of the Milestone founders, these early articles emphasize that the Milestone comics are positioned to fill the enduring void of positive role models for black children. There is little or no mention of these young black readers' lives outside the realm of their association with comic books. While there may not be a strong presence of heroic black characters in the comic book pages, that does not mean that these children might not be finding positive role models in other areas of their lives, such as through sports, music, film, friends, and family. The sense presented in the press coverage is that the Milestone comics are not just one of many possible sources these children might have for developing an affirmative sense of self based on skin color but perhaps the only or most fundamental source.

The thrust of much of the newspaper coverage was that Milestone was at the forefront of a new, more enlightened age in the world of comic books. As the title for another piece in the *New York Times* declared, just a few months after the Milestone books began to appear on the stands, "New Superheroes

Free the Comics from the Old-Boys' Network." The article actually is concerned with a variety of changes in the industry including a marked rise in the popularity of female superheroines like Marvel's She-Hulk and Dark Horse's Ghost and Barb Wire; the popularity of serious comics aimed at an adult audience, comics such as those in DC's Vertigo line (e.g., *The Sandman, Hellblazer,* and *Enigma*); and the acceptance of several outed gay and lesbian characters in mainstream comics, for instance, Northstar in Marvel's *Alpha Flight* or the Pied Piper in DC's *The Flash*. But the article focuses on the black characters of the Milestone books as the vanguard to this supposedly new and enlightened age of comic books and includes an illustration of Icon and a photograph of the Milestone creators. Other articles, including one in *Black Enterprise* magazine, refer to Milestone's development of black superheroes as a full-blown "revolution." In fact the "revolution" catchphrase became an essential and defining element in the public perception of Milestone. While coverage of this type is undoubtedly good exposure for a new line of comic books, it also set up Milestone as the black comics publisher. The revolution rhetoric espoused by the press was reinforced by Milestone's own promotional materials, such as their posters and in-comic advertisements that carried the tag line "This Revolution Will not Be Televised" and subscription forms declaring, "A Revolution in Comics, Ongoing Monthly." Despite the founders' constant claims that their comics would be first and foremost good superhero stories regardless of the color of a character's skin, Milestone was placed in the bind of being perceived not just as a producer of another new line of comic books but as a producer of revolutionary, pro-black stories, period. The necessarily narrow focus of the media items so clearly linked Milestone with an agenda of creating black superhero role models that some readers thought, as one fifteen-year-old fan told me, "Oh, I don't pick up Milestone books 'cause "I already know what they're about. It's a black thing." However much Milestone wanted to start from scratch and have their success or failure determined by the quality of their storytelling, they quickly became burdened with their target audience's preconceived ideas of what identifiably minority-based comics must, or at least should, be about.

The second main focus of the press coverage surrounding the creation of Milestone Media concentrated on their unique relationship with DC Comics. All of the media reports at least mentioned the unprecedented publishing agreement, and the industry fanzines often described the deal in great detail due to its potential to reform company alliances and the very nature of independent publishing. The corporate structure of a major publisher taking a small independent group under its wing also garnered attention strictly as an innovative business arrangement and as a potential model for minority-based companies to achieve widespread success and, conversely, for established corporations to diversify their interests. The weekly business newspaper *Crain's New York Business* gave the cooperative deal front-page coverage and argued that if Milestone succeeds in breaking the dominant white mold "they may create opportunities for Latino, Asian and female writers and artists by broadening the established market for comic books" (Breznick 1993, 1, 28). Likewise, a piece in the business section of the *Wall Street Journal* reported thus: "Established companies are joining forces with small and minority businesses that understand niche markets. The partnerships grew out of decisions by the big companies to look outside their corporate cultures to add ethnic diversity to their product lines. Simply hiring Black artists and editors wouldn't achieve the same result, says Paul Levitz, publisher of DC Comics, which will distribute the Milestone produced comic books. 'By reaching to an outside structure, you can tap into a passion that you couldn't put together on demand,' Mr. Levitz adds" (Wynter 1993, B-6).

The most detailed account of the Milestone Media/DC Comics deal was the cover story in the November 1994 issue of *Black Enterprise*. The article stresses that "Partnerships between large corporations and small independent companies are hardly new, but Milestone serves as a model of how a small black firm can benefit from forging a strategic alliance with big business" (Brown 1994, 84). But in addition to the potential benefits of these possible unions, the piece's author, Carolyn M. Brown, is quick to point out that such affiliations often bring with them their share of criticism from other black organizations. Indeed, most of the attention in the popular press was concerned not solely with the groundbreaking development of Milestone Media but with the apparent clash between Milestone and some of the other, smaller independent black comic book publishers. Foremost amongst Milestone's critics was Ania (Swahili for "protect" or "defend"), a small consortium of black independent comic book publishers, based in Oakland, who accused Milestone of Uncle Tomism. Ania argued quite vehemently for any reporter willing to listen that Milestone was callously creating white superhero clones merely painted black. Upon hearing about the publishing and distribution deal arranged by Milestone with DC Comics, Ania's president, Eric Griffin, began to slander Milestone in the industry trade magazines for not being "black enough" and for selling out by working with (or for) a large, predominantly white multinational corporation. Ania's primary allegation that the Milestone line is a whitewashed sellout stems from the fundamental ideological difference between the two organizations. Ania's perspective is a more radically political belief in Afrocentrism as an empowering force, whereas Milestone's approach to presenting black characters in comic books is not an attempt to create overtly political role models but to demonstrate the diversity and complexity of the black experience in contemporary life.

The different approaches adopted by Milestone and Ania reflect the divergent African American political strategies that Ed Guerrero has described as a constant "oscillation between two polarities: the impulse to integrate with the system and the urge to separate from it" (1994, 71). While I, and I suspect Guerrero as well, realize that there is a much wider range of political strategies than these two poles, and a variety of complex cultural aspirations beyond the binary of assimilation and separation, these are particularly cogent positions relating to the images on offer from Milestone and Ania. Indeed, though I run the risk of simplifying these issues of media representation into a two-dimensional dichotomy, it is still an important dichotomy to discuss. Moreover it is a dichotomy set up not by me but by the media coverage of the black comics debate and by the rhetoric of the two publishing concerns. At stake for these two comic book publishers is the problem of representing black characters who retain a certain amount of legitimacy within the black community. Clearly Ania is of the opinion that Milestone's characters are not authentically African American because they are under the supervision of DC Comics. Conversely, Ania believes that their own characters are legitimately African American expressions because they are completely independent publishers. This dispute over black representation in the arts and independent control is not a new one. Ever since the Harlem Renaissance the dilemma of how to properly represent the black experience has been pondered by the likes of Langston Hughes, W. E. B. Du Bois, and Richard Wright. In fact the clearest expression of the debate occurred in the early 1970s (perhaps not so coincidentally at around the same time that blaxploitation films were becoming popular, as were the original black superhero comics inspired by those films) under the rhetoric of the Black Aesthetic. The most representative expression of the black nationalist movement in the arts was the volme of essays reproduced in the book simply entitled *The Black Aesthetic* (Gayle 1971).

Mirroring many of the more militant, post–Civil Rights era, Black Power sentiments of groups like the Black Panthers, the essays collected in *The Black Aesthetic* called for black artists to create works that address the unique lifestyles, beliefs, mythologies, and problems of the black community. Larry Neal, for example, wrote in his contribution, "The Black Arts Movement is radically opposed to any concept of the artist that alienates him from his community. Black Art is the aesthetic and spiritual sister of the Black Power concept. As such it envisions an art that speaks directly to the needs and aspirations of Black America. In order to perform this task, the Black Arts Movement proposes a radical reordering of the western cultural aesthetic. It proposes a separate symbolism, mythology, critique, and iconology. The Black Arts and the Black Power concept both relate broadly to the Afro-American's desire for self-determination and nationhood. Both concepts are nationalistic. One is concerned with the relationship between art and politics; the other with the art of politics (Neal 1971, 272). According to the argument put forth by Neal and other contributors to *The Black Aesthetic* (see, for example, the essays by Gayle, Fuller, Mayfield, Gerald, and Miller), for artists to continue laboring under the yoke of white culture and the white aesthetic is to pursue cultural genocide (Gayle 1971). The black artist, the argument continues, must create new forms that speak only to a black audience and are governed only by black authorities, creators, and critics.

The example of blaxploitation films is useful because it succinctly demonstrates the principles of the Black Aesthetic and because it closely parallels the point of divergence between the strategies used by Milestone and Ania (not to mention the influential historical link that exists between blaxploitation films and black comic book superheroes). *Sweet Sweetback's Baadasss Song* and *Shaft* not only stand apart as the progenitors of blaxploitation film but also represent distinct approaches to the portrayal of black masculinity and heroism. Of the two films, many critics consider Sweetback to be the most legitimately African American production according to the principles of the Black Aesthetic. Sweetback was produced by, written by, directed by, and starred black artists completely independent from any of Hollywood's major studios. Shaft, on the other hand, despite being directed by and starring black artists, has often had its authenticity as a black film questioned because it was produced and distributed under the control of MGM, a major Hollywood studio. In short, where Sweetback was clearly marked as an independently created and politically motivated black film, Shaft was strictly a studio-backed moneymaking project framed by Hollywood's ideology of inclusionary entertainment and thus was safer and less militantly antiwhite.

Although both films were very well received at the box office, the critical responses they provoked were clearly divided according to political factions. Political extremists like Huey Newton and the Black Panther Party praised Sweetback for assembling "the first truly revolutionary Black film ever made . . . [which] presents the need for unity among all the members and institutions within the community of victims" (Newton 1971, A). Other black critics regarded Sweetback as anything but revolutionary or positive. In the more politically conservative *Ebony* magazine, for example, Lerone Bennett chastised the film for romanticizing the poverty and misery of the ghetto and argued that "some men foolishly identify the Black aesthetic with empty bellies and big bottomed prostitutes" (Bennett 1971, 108). Conversely, Shaft was generally applauded by conservative critics, both black and white, for expanding the representation of blacks in mainstream cinema, while radical black nationalists derided the film as a prepackaged production which emphasized middle-class (white) ideals. In his review of black film heroes and the blaxploitation genre, Mark Reid reiterates this extreme position when he writes of *Shaft* that despite the film's "obvious effort to attract a black popular audience through rhetoric and images appealing to that audience, MGM, like other major studios, invested black heroes with mainstream values. In doing so they did not create mythic black heroes. Instead, like doll makers who painted Barbie's face brown, they merely created black-skinned replicas of the white heroes of action films" (Reid 1988, 30–31).

The split within African American political ideology, a split which is indisputably represented in the contrast between *Sweetback* (independent, separatist) and *Shaft* (commercial, integrationist) is reiterated in the juxtaposition of Milestone and Ania. While certainly there other contingent issues of representation involved in this split between *Sweetback* and *Shaft*, and for that matter between Milestone and Ania, it was the separatist-integrationist antagonism that was primarily of concern at the time (see Guerrero 1994; Reid 1988). Likewise, it is the same sense of binary opposition between Milestone and Ania that informs many of the fans' understandings of the two companies' debate over representation. The political differences between Milestone (commercial, integrationist) and Ania (independent, separatist) are strikingly apparent in the contrasting content of their comic books. Ania essentially consists of four companies: Africa Rising, U.P. Comics, Afrocentric Comic Books, and Dark Zulu Lies, each the producer of a single-color title. Africa Rising's *Ebony Warrior* by writer Eric Griffin and artist Steven X. Routhier is the story of Komal Jackson, a high-tech genius who turns down lucrative offers from large corporations in order to return to his southern home of Yorktown. During the day Jackson teaches children but at night he dons a high-tech suit of armor to fight street crime as the Ebony Warrior. In essence Ebony Warrior is much like Hardware except for the emphasis placed on Jackson's turning down the Fortune 500 companies so that he can actively participate "in the struggle to uplift [his] people." U.P. Comics' *Purge* (fig. 2.8), written by Roosevelt Pitt Jr. and illustrated by Bill Hobbs, is an all-out action title where the title character seems to exist solely for beating up criminals, one after another, in a relentless pursuit of the real problem, the evil (white) drug importers. The first issue of *Purge* gives little information about the character, but an insert card does describe Purge's alter ego as Richard James Kincaide, the owner of a multibillion-dollar corporation, who has set out on a "Purification Agenda" to rid his city of crime. The most critical of the Ania titles is writer and artist Roger Barnes's *Heru: Son*

2.8   Purge #0 (1993)

of Ausar from Afrocentric Comic Books. Set in ancient Egypt, Heru is the tale of the miraculous appearance of the magical Heru at a time when hordes of light-skinned Arab and Mediterranean savages from the north invade the king-dom of Pharaoh Akhenaton. Heru arrives just in time to drive away the barbar-ians who were corrupting the richness of the Egyptian culture. Barnes, who holds a graduate degree in African history, bases his work in Heru on texts from ancient Egyptian mythology and reworks the events and the moral para-bles into a comic book format without losing sight of how these sacred legends might still be applicable for people living in contemporary American culture.

Perhaps the most visible, certainly the most controversial, of the Ania books is Dark Zulu Lies' Zwanna: Son of Zulu (fig. 2.9) by artist John Ruiz and the outspoken writer Nabile P. Hage—who dresses up as Zwanna for comic book conventions and once, in full costume, was arrested for climbing the Georgia capitol building and tossing down copies of his comic book. Spouting funky Luke Cage–inspired dialogue like "I got that jungle love for you, baby!" Prince Zwanna is a student from Africa, a descendant of the legendary Chaka Zulu, living in the United States and attending Black American State University. At

2.9   Zwanna: Son of Zulu *(1993)*

the hint of trouble Zwanna "zhaabs out" and becomes a ruthless black avenger clad in nothing more than a loincloth and a tiger-tooth necklace. With the aid of his magical spear, Zwanna fights racism to the extreme, skewering skinheads in the street and impaling and decapitating a group of white transvestites out to destroy world leaders and rape Zwanna himself. An unabashedly radical comic book, Zwanna has itself been accused of racism against whites, not to mention sexism and homophobism. The extreme image of Zwanna was often used as the public face of Ania in mainstream articles chronicling the clash of the black publishers. In contrast to the slicker and much more conventionally heroic portraits of Milestone characters such as Icon, Rocket, and Hardware, Zwanna became his own worst enemy. As Gary Dauphin noted in his *Village Voice* cover piece on the rise of the black superhero, it was the ugliness of Zwanna's image of racial struggle that probably prompted Nabile P. Hage's departure from the Ania group. Others contend that Hage left the fold when Ania eventually softened its stance against Milestone.

In addition to the *Village Voice* review, the Ania versus Milestone debate was mentioned in nearly every newspaper article about the two companies and was prominently featured in such widely read magazines as *Entertainment Weekly* and *Newsweek*. Ania's Eric Griffin claimed that the Milestone books were not true black voices: "Basically what Milestone does is create white characters painted Black. They're not culturally aware" (Spotnitz 1993, 12). And the flamboyant Nabile Hage told *Newsweek*, "Milestone is coming from a corporate American perspective. When your superhero is a Black Republican, that just doesn't work for inner-city kids. Our [Ania's] stories are uncensored and straight from the streets. We're not afraid to offend the establishment" (Waters 1993, 58). On the other side—although in hindsight Milestone now denies ever publicly responding to Ania's remarks—Milestone was reported as responding defensively to the accusations with comments like Michael Davis's "How many black publishers are there in this country? What we need are 78,000 more of them. What we don't need is to be jumping on each other's throats" (Spotnitz 1993, 12) and Dwayne McDuffie's "[T]he idea that the black experience is limited to one kind of person is ridiculous" (quoted in Waters 1993, 58–59). Other independent black comic book publishers, including Alonzo Washington, the creator behind Omega 7 Comics, and Jason Sims, president of Big City Comics and creator of the popular *Brotherman* series, joined in the fray by openly accusing Milestone of selling out. The two main points of criticism were that Milestone's characters are nothing more than "Superman in blackface" or "a chocolate-dip Superman" and that rather than being truly independent Milestone's publication and distribution deal reduces them to the status of DC Comic's token black creators and characters.

The "Superman in blackface" comment was initially heard quite a lot in reference to Milestone's most conventionally superheroic series Icon. The parallels between the two characters are undeniable. Both are alien castaways discovered as infants in small rocket ships which crashed in farmers' fields. Both are raised by their rural foster parents who teach them that with great powers comes great responsibility. Both are incredibly conservative and almost comically straight arrows. They wear similar costumes and possess almost identical powers. At first glance the only difference seems to be the color of their skins. But it is the marked similarities between Superman and Icon, the degree of conformity to the well-established superhero genre, that allows the series to explore how conventional heroism might differ from a minority perspective. Thanks primarily to Rocket, Icon's partner and social conscience, Icon is often forced to confront not only criminal masterminds and supervillains but also the social injustices that dominate the world around him. Ironically, this attention to social injustices is also depicted as one of the reasons why Icon is in fact more conservative than Superman. Given that both Superman and Icon are regarded as establishment heroes and given that, all other things being equal,

Icon is still seen as a minority hero, Icon writer McDuffie describes Icon as "much more straight laced than Superman who is actually way more liberal in his outlook. By virtue of Icon's Blackness, and his presence as a symbol, he has to be a lot more careful about what he says and does than Superman would . . . because nine times out of ten Superman is going to get the benefit of the doubt where Icon wouldn't automatically be granted that privilege." Once the reader digs below the surface similarities to appreciate the narrative differences between the characters and their story lines it becomes difficult to see Icon as merely a chocolate-dip Superman. As the fanzine *Hero* put it in their description of Icon as one of the best ongoing series of 1994, "Anyone who still hasn't picked up a copy of this series because they believed all the Superman-in-blackface hype is missing out on one of the best comics available today. Icon and Rocket are complex characters that deserve a following in their own right."

The parallels that many critics seemed to focus on, between not just Superman and Icon but between all of the Milestone titles and the entire Superman line, were explored in Milestone's second year of publication. *Worlds Collide* was a fourteen-issue intercompany crossover event during the summer of 1994 and ran through all four of Milestone's original series, DC's Superman line including *Superman: The Man of Steel, Superboy,* and *Steel,* and a special collaborative *Worlds Collide* #1. Since Milestone is an independent company with an independent universe of characters, the first problem the creators from both sides faced was finding a way for their heroes to come in contact. The solution was a typically comic-bookish scenario wherein Lois Lane's mild-mannered mail carrier, Fred Bentson, finds that every night when he goes to sleep in Metropolis he instantly wakes up in Dakota, where he leads a second life as another mail carrier. Obviously distraught by sleep deprivation, Bentson alternately seeks help from research scientists in Metropolis and Dakota. Manipulated by Hardware's arch-nemesis, Edwin Alva, Bentson is soon stretched to the point where he metamorphoses into the nearly omnipotent creature called Rift. The warped Rift somehow unites the two realities, and the heroes of Metropolis and Dakota must combine their efforts in order to save at least one of their worlds from Rift's wrath. The similar characters from the two universes are matched up: Icon with Superman (fig. 2.10), Static and Rocket with Superboy, Hardware with Steel (DC's African American, armor-wearing superhero who emerged in the wake of Superman's much publicized death and resurrection story lines in 1993). In addition to the financial success of Worlds Collide (the Milestone titles sold better than ever before and found new fans amongst Superman's regular readers) the crossover gave Milestone the opportunity to highlight the differences between their characters and the similar characters of a more traditionally white superhero universe.

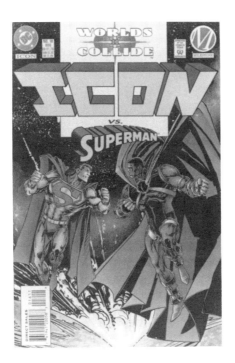

2.10   Icon #16 (1994). Illustration courtesy of DC Comics and Milestone Media, Inc.
Used with permission.

The second main criticism voiced by Ania and a select few other black independent comic book publishers was that Milestone's publishing and distribution deal meant that they were really under the control of DC Comics. Both
Milestone and DC steadfastly deny this perception of their relationship. Milestone's Denys Cowan points out, "We began Milestone as an independent
project long before we even entered into discussions with DC. Dwayne, Derek
and I personally pooled together over $300,000 of our own money to get
things going. We are responsible for all of the creative and editorial content of
our books, and we retain all of the legal rights to our characters and any other
properties related to the Milestone universe." Likewise, Milestone president
Derek T. Dingle adamantly says, "We are an independent producer of comic
books in every sense of the word, DC is just our distributor not our parent
company." But despite Milestone's protestations, the company's critics doubt
their creative freedom. The skeptics feel that Milestone can only grow as much
as DC allows them to and can only publish racially aware stories so long as
they fall within the general guidelines of the DC worldview. "The proof of our
independence," the Milestone founders say, "is in our stories." They point to

the controversial topics that DC would never touch in their own books, topics such as homosexuality, race wars, and teenage pregnancy; to their well-rounded treatment of characters from all sorts of minority backgrounds; and to their indifference in seeking the Comics Magazine Association of America seal of approval for their titles, particularly when the CMAA requires the removal of all racial epithets, which the Milestone books often include as an intricate part of stories dealing with racism (see Newswatch 1993, 12).

But Milestone's claims to true independence and creative freedom were recently challenged by DC's decision to censor the cover of the much anticipated *Static* #25. The special anniversary issue centered on the impending ordeal of Virgil (Static) Hawkins losing his virginity. To accompany the sensitively told story of this very real phase of Virgil's adolescence, Milestone commissioned a fully painted illustration from artist Zina Saunders to grace the cover. The painting depicted Virgil, with the mask of his Static costume pulled back, kissing his girlfriend, Daisy, while reclining on a couch, a sex manual and a strip of condoms scattered on the floor. DC Comics balked at the prospect of publishing the painting as a cover image. Despite Dwayne McDuffie's offer to have the condoms airbrushed out of the picture, DC still refused to print the cover because, according to Paul Levitz, DC's executive vice president and publisher, "DC Comics has a policy of not showing sex on covers." Regardless of the fact that the proposed cover did not show sex but only the likely preface to a responsible sex act, DC deemed the illustration too suggestive and effectively censored Milestone's creative vision. As a token compromise Milestone was forced to accept DC's criterion and the special anniversary issue of Static #25 hit the stands with a mostly blackened cover and a heart-shaped close up of Virgil and Daisy kissing. The full version of the originally planned cover appeared on the second page of the book. It would seem that when push comes to shove Milestone is limited by the corporate decisions made by DC.

Essentially, the short-lived debate between Milestone and Ania—a debate that greatly affected how the Milestone books were initially received—is a single expression of a long-standing cultural dilemma. What is at stake is the very definition of a black identity. In this case the debate is over comic book superheroes, in other instances it has encompassed film, television, religion, music, sports, and politics. The argument about whether or not the Milestone characters are really black is, at least for most comic book fans, ridiculous. "Of course they are" is the audience conception. But within the realm of cultural politics the debate is much more important and much more complex. It is a question of establishing identity based on either visible ethnicity or a cultural criterion, both of which are indecisive and constantly changing variables. The fundamental accusation made by Ania is that the Milestone characters (and by implication the Milestone creators) may be visibly black but they are not so culturally. There are, of course, numerous problems with defining black identity through this essentialist type of criterion. It assumes constants that simply do not exist in the real world. For example, the essentialist view assumes that black culture can be reduced to a particular set of experiences and ideologies, and no matter how many caveats are applied to the definition of this culture it still reduces countless complexities of lived experiences to a few commonalties which are privileged over others. Furthermore, even the concept of biological criteria for defining black identity is well recognized as problematical. Exactly where does one draw the line that distinguishes someone who is biologically black from one who isn't? Skin color? What about light-skinned African Americans? Blood percentages? What about people of mixed parentage? In short, even biological definitions are hard to pin down. As Tommy L. Lott quite correctly points out in his discussion of black identity and black identified films, "[T]he tension between biological and cultural criteria of black identity is resolved in terms of a political definition of black people" (1991, 49). Black identity is defined by politics. In other words, the question of biological and cultural identity becomes inextricably linked to the notion of political identity.

This association of black identity with political identity is clearly the problem that underlies the differences between Milestone and Ania, a problem that goes far beyond whether Icon talks like Superman or not. It is a disagreement that won't be resolved within the pages of a comic book, but it does influence how those pages are read. Moreover, the connection of black-identified comic book characters with a grounding in political agency has been a fundamental preconception associated with the Milestone books. Because the Milestone characters have been so readily identified as black by the mainstream audience for comics, they have also been limited by being identified as "political."

Before going on to examine how actual comic book readers have responded to Milestone's line, it should be pointed out that en masse the Milestone titles have proven neither an incredible success nor a disappointing failure. In the few years that the books have been on the market they have garnered a relatively large amount of media attention, praise from critics, and numerous fan awards from specialized subgroups, particularly those who participate in the on-line comics bulletin boards via Genie, Compuserve, and American Online. And while the books have notched up impressive sales and are almost always in the top two hundred of the over twelve hundred comics published monthly, they rarely break into the realm of the "Top 100" list. They have managed to outlast many of their competitors who came on the comics scene at about the same time, most notably the Ania group, none of whose books made it past the first issue. Despite award-winning stories, first-rate artwork, and favorable endorsements, Milestone has had to struggle with public resistance. In the fall of 1994 Denys Cowan told the leading professional fanzine, *Wizard*, "I have been completely surprised by the resistance our books have received from the direct market. I thought there would be some resistance, but I also thought that our idea would have appeal. I didn't expect the scale of resistance we've seen. Having been in the comics field for 20 years, it's frustrating" (quoted in Shutt 1994, 81).

The most obvious reason for Milestone's disappointing sales figures could possibly be simple racism. After all, according to the limited statistical information available about the audience for comic books (see Parsons 1991), the majority of comic book readers are white males between eight and twenty-five years of age (comics fandom as a subculture will be explored in more detail in chapter 3). But the issue is much more complex than the oversimplified and reductive "white-boys-don't-want-to-read-about-black-superheroes" logic. Indeed, the Milestone principals point to the fact that regardless of the ethnicity of the core audience for comics their books routinely "sell through." In other words, all of the copies put on the stand by retailers are sold and Milestone books rarely hang around long enough to end up in the back-issue discount boxes. The central problem would seem to be that in the direct market retailers are ordering fewer copies of the Milestone books than they do of more easily recognizable series, thus restricting the sales potential of a new company whose titles fall just outside the margins of traditional comics fare. Comics specialty store owners calculate their orders based on how many copies they believe their patrons will buy. The problem is that some of the retailers feel as several told me directly: "I don't have a lot of black customers so I'd never be able to sell a lot of black books." Jake, the owner and until recently the sole staff of All-Star Heroes, claimed that he never ordered more than six issues of each Milestone title, issues that were requested by some of his members, because he did not want to get stuck with a bunch of "activist" books that no one else would be interested in. "My customers are on the younger side," explained Jake. "They want to read about superheroes, not about politics and race problems." These retailers, the gatekeepers between the publishers and the consumers (see chapter 3), have been swayed by the attention given to Milestone's status as the black comic book company and have assumed that because Milestone is a "black thing;" nonblack readers would find little to enjoy in their books. This perception is mirrored by many comic book readers, and I will return to this problem in greater detail when I discuss the readers' understanding of the Milestone books.

Ideologically, the comic books published by Milestone Media are caught in a bind. They are simultaneously criticized by the likes of Ania and other African American activist creators for not being political enough and by the mainstream, mostly white, audience for being too political. In fact Milestone treads that thin line between racial politics and entertainment, a difficult position to occupy. Like other forms of mass media, it is important for Milestone to avoid being perceived as political. In our culture for a media text to be perceived as political is for that text to be marginalized. Herman and Chomsky, in their analysis of how modern news coverage is made to conform with the beliefs of a dominant elite, argue that any mass media will be disregarded if it is characterized as biased, as too politically oriented. "In the media, as in other major institutions," write Herman and Chomsky, "those who do not display the requisite values and perspectives will be regarded as 'irresponsible,' 'ideological,' or otherwise aberrant, and will tend to fall by the wayside" (1988, 304). If mass-produced texts appear to be too politically informed they are often ignored as merely ideological preaching, complaining, or propaganda.

Milestone's editorial claims for being a multicultural line of comic books rather than strictly an African American line is part of their attempt to be perceived as less extremist than the tag of being a black company implies. Yet, while many fans do embrace the Milestone books as entertaining comics first and as black comics second, others are still wary of the potential politics that might overwhelm the entertainment value—something a young consumer with a limited budget is very wary of when single comic books can cost up to seven dollars. This tricky bit of market positioning is one that Milestone has yet to master. The overriding image of Milestone as a black company interferes with the audience's ability to move beyond simple preconceptions, preconceptions that assume the fans already know what the books are about, in this case, political rhetoric. While the novelty of Milestone as a mainstream, black-owned publishing company gained them a lot of attention it also limited their ability to move beyond that one-dimensional status. Case in point: by the fall of 1995 weak sales forced Milestone to cancel four of their seven series, *Blood Syndicate*, *Xombi*, *Shadow Cabinet*, and *Kobalt*. Interestingly, the titles that were cancelled all featured non–African American characters or racially mixed teams, while the ones that remain, *Icon*, *Hardware*, and *Static*, are all headlined by black superheroes. Some of the cancelled series, such as *Xombi* and *Blood Syndicate*, were highly praised by critics, so difference in quality does not seem to be the only reason that some of the Milestone titles failed while others have lived on. Rather, it appears that comic book readers, influenced by all of the publicity about Milestone as the black publisher, are willing to except black superheroes by black creators (though not all of the Milestone creators are black, a point that many fans are unaware of) but do not look to Milestone for superheroes that fall outside of their perceived specialty. In other words, Milestone is restricted by the market perception that has pigeon-holed them as only a black, and hence inherently political, publisher of superhero comics.

In addition to the racially informed perception of the Milestone books, a perception that restricts open-ended interpretations, the fans' reception of the comics is likewise contingent upon how they are perceived in relation to the rest of the industry. The Milestone books are interpreted in comparison to other black comics and in comparison to other currently popular series, particularly the highly influential titles produced by Image Comics. The acceptance or rejection of the Milestone stories at a general level has also been shaped by their conformity, or lack of it, to popular comic book trends. For example, in the three years since Milestone began publishing they have avoided participation in two trends that have dramatically increased sales of other companies titles. The first trend Milestone avoided was the movement toward gimmicky covers, a trend that proved excessively popular in the early 1990s. Other companies, including industry leaders Marvel, DC, and especially Image, boosted their sales to collectors through the use of embossed, die-cut, foil-enhanced, holographic, and other cover variations. In a desperate attempt to find novel gimmicks one publisher even shot a bullet through stacks of his comics and then sold the "bullet hole" books as limited edition collector's issues. Milestone's goal of concentrating on quality storytelling rather than gimmicky features—substance rather than flash—may have made them less competitive and less appealing to an audience seeking to collect the next hot thing.

The second highly visible industry trend that Milestone has avoided participating in is the Bad Girl phenomenon. Alluding to the Good Girl art of the late 1940s and early 1950s, the Bad Girl trend refers to the currently popular practice of depicting extremely large-breasted superheroines in skintight costumes and sexually suggestive poses. Books like DC's Catwoman, Topp's Lady Rawhide, Crusade Comics' Shi, Malibu's Mantra, Eternity Comics' Lady Death, and Harris Comics' Vengeance of Vampirella have all shot to the top of the charts primarily thanks to the sex appeal of their leading heroines. Milestone has steadfastly refused to participate in the Bad Girl trend despite the fact that it means some readers will spend their comic book allowance on other titles. Unwilling to follow the current trend of exploiting sexy female heroes, Milestone has been praised by some critics for bringing "many credible female characters to the comic world, with Rocket, star of Icon, in the forefront. In fact the general consensus is that Icon is clearly Rocket's book" (Rimmels 1995, 36). In fact the frustration of sales hampered by not conforming to popular comic trends like the Bad Girl phase was apparent in Dwayne McDuffie's editorial regarding the censorship of *Static's* anniversary cover, the one that DC

Comics objected to because condoms were included in the illustration: "Here's the sad part, if I had commissioned a cover where Daisy was wearing a thong and kicking one leg high in the air so everybody could get a really good look at her crotch, or if she had her back to the camera and her spine arched at an improbable angle to accentuate her ass, or if her enormous breasts, miraculously immune to the effects of gravity, were positioned so you couldn't quite tell whether those shadows were her nipples, there would be no problem. Problem? Heck, we'd probably have a 'hot book' on our hands" (from *Static* #25, 1995).

Far from a blank slate that audiences can play with and interpret in any way they choose, Milestone comic books both intentionally and incidentally restrict and inform the readings that fans make of the text. The fan's reading is shaped by a complex web of associated, extratextual factors before he or she even opens the comic book. Impressions of Milestone as the black comics company, impressions of Milestone as an attempt at "revolutionary" politics, knowledge of Milestone as under the wing of DC Comics, and awareness of genre conventions and popular industry trends are all part of the cultural baggage that the Milestone books carry with them. The unique status of the Milestone line means that they are understood by fans as encoded with certain properties that inform, define, and restrict the range of possible interpretations that the readers can make. And all of these perceptions that impinge on the actual enjoyment of the Milestone narratives are further constricted by a reader's degree of involvement in the culture of comic book fandom. It is through the realm of fandom that some of the most interesting modes of negotiated readings are performed. Comics fandom operates on certain principles that involve levels of interaction with not just the text and other fans but also with the creators themselves. Before continuing with the social structure of fandom and how it influence readers' perceptions of the texts, chapters 4, 5, and 6 will deal with individual Milestone fans and how they relate to the comics within a limited range of culturally defined possibilities.

3

Comic Book Fandom

The practice of media fandom provides a highly visible and intensely concentrated example of how people interpret, internalize, and use popular texts in their everyday lives. Fans are extraordinarily interested and often active textual participants, and many of them organize into loosely structured interpretive communities based on a shared fascination for a specific text, genre, or medium. Comic book fandom is one of the most popular and best organized of media fan cultures. A reader's degree of participation in fan culture is a strong marker of his or her personal involvement with the text and of how the properties of the text are mediated according to certain presuppositions. Fan cultures, particularly ones as formalized as comic book fandom, are influenced by rules and conventions, both textual and extratextual, that shape and perpetuate a fan's reading of a media text. In this chapter I want to sketch a portrait of the world of the comics fan and outline how some of the formal aspects of comic book fandom operate as a cultural economy, as a system in which the readers can invest and accumulate cultural capital and which effects textual understanding. By considering how the cultural phenomenon of fandom involves fans in both textual and social experiences, it becomes possible to approach an understanding of how comic fans use texts, such as the Milestone titles, to develop a sense of self in cooperation with others via a negotiated narrative meaning.

While the central focus of my research has been the comic books published by Milestone, I want to make clear that I also intend this study as a consideration of comics fandom more generally. It would be impossible, and pointless, to separate Milestone fans from the wider range of comic book fans. By considering comic book fandom in general we can better understand the position of the Milestone books and readers, and by looking at those readers expressly we can better understand the elements of the overall culture of fandom. Within the world of comic book fans there is a great variety of tastes and reading habits, and while most readers do prefer certain series over others they almost never specialize to the point of reading only one series exclusively. Comics fans usually follow a number of different characters or titles from a variety of publishers, or they may collect the work of individual writers or artists. The audience for Milestone must be understood as an audience devoted to comics generally and to (black) superhero comic books specifically.

"This Is Not a Clubhouse!" declares the emphatic, handwritten sign taped to the front door of The Black Knight, a comics, cards, and collectibles store. But on any given Saturday or weekday afternoon a clubhouse is exactly what The Black Knight looks like. The corner entrance to the store is often blocked by up to a dozen young males drinking pop, hanging from their mountain bikes, rocking on their skateboards, and discussing comic books. During peak hours The Black Knight's owner, or one of his two teenage employees, routinely points to the sign and reminds the group to move around to the side of the building or else risk being banned from the store. It's common knowledge that no one has ever really been banned, but after some mock bravado everyone complies with the request in order to avoid straining their valuable relationship with the store's owner. Inside, the small store is often crowded, particularly on Wednesday afternoons when the week's shipment of new comic books arrive. High on the walls are an array of colorful promotional posters featuring a seemingly endless number of brawny men and busty women in skintight costumes striking heroic poses. Each poster promises a breathtaking universe of must-have action that the reader just can't afford to miss: "Blasting your way in February," "Roaring your way in April," "Screaming your way in December," and so on. Hung just beyond reach, on the walls not decorated by posters, are Mylar-bagged comic books with sticker prices ranging from ten dollars to ninety-five dollars. Many of these highly sought after back issues are "hot" titles, only a few weeks old but already worth five or ten times their original cover price.[1] The few really rare comics worth upwards of one hundred dollars are locked away in the glass display cabinet that serves as a front counter, beside such other valuables as a few miscellaneous pieces of original artwork, a couple of books signed by their authors, and rare trading cards—the assorted Holy Grails in the world of fandom.

Manning the cash register is The Black Knight's owner, Dave, a large man in his early thirties who is nearly always dressed in jeans and one of the Spider-Man T-shirts from his extensive personal collection. Dave, like most comics store owners, is friendly and personable with his regular customers. He chats enthusiastically with each as he rings up their weekly purchases and usually recommends an upcoming comic book or two that the buyer might be interested in. During the busiest store hours Dave almost mechanically alternates between conversing with some of the regulars about recent books and future story lines and gruffly reminding some of the younger clientele not to block other peoples' access to the new comics displayed alphabetically from *Animal Man* to *Zen Intergalactic Ninja* on the homemade magazine stand. The customers on any given day, though predominantly male, are a diverse lot. Most of them stand relatively mute in front of the display of new comics while their eyes scan the titles and flashy cover art; they frequently reach out to extract a book from its pile for a quick flip through or for a better look at the cover work. Some of the browsers decide at a glance whether or not they'll be adding the book to their list of purchases, while others read almost the entire story before making up their mind, despite the handwritten sign, above the display, reminding customers: "This Is Not a Library! If You Want to Read It, *Buy* It!" Among those considering what comics to buy are a few kids under seven years old who have been brought to the store by older siblings or sometimes by mothers who tend to wait impatiently by the counter, pocketbook in hand. Peering over the heads of the youngest patrons are the preteen and young teenage boys of every shape and size that make up the bulk of the crowd. Mixed in with the group is a scattering of older men mostly in their twenties and early thirties but occasionally ranging upwards to senior citizens. Most of these adult comic book fans dress casually, but on occasion suits and ties do sometimes appear. In addition to the mothers, young women do at times venture into the crowd. A few of these women actually read comic books themselves but most are wives or girlfriends who don't seem to share any real enthusiasm for the four-color worlds on display.

Once they have made their selections, some of the customers move away from the display rack and enter into discussions about the comics industry with friends or acquaintances. Others go on to search the cardboard bins lined up at table height down the center and along the back walls of the store, looking for inexpensive back issues to fill holes in their collections. Quite a few simply proceed to the cash register and pick up the books that have been specially held for them if they are members.[2] Then sheepishly duck out after only a few perfunctory words with Dave. This is part of the most noticeable and regular routine of comic fandom. It happens in much the same way every week in comic book stores around the world. Of course the exact make up of a store's clientele varies by region and by the emphasis on what type of comics a store stocks, but the same pattern consistently holds true. These men (and women) are loosely united in the makeshift community of comic book fandom. Some are active participants while others are passive, remaining on the edge of social interaction and preferring a solitary pursuit of their hobby. In fact, industry professionals have estimated that the hard-core comic book fans, those who live and breathe comic books, although the most noticeable constituency, actually constitute only 10 to 20 percent of the total audience. Yet still it is the devoted fan who is the lifeblood of the industry, guaranteeing sales, influencing trends, supporting small publishers, and providing a constant source of energy and feedback. The distinction between a comic book fan and an occasional reader is a difficult one to make. Many within the community feel that only those who actively participate in the formal workings of comic book consumption—shopping at specialty stores, developing a collection, attending conventions, etc.—can be called fans. But although this most identifiable portion of the audience for comic books is the source for most of the research in this study, I have found it hard not to consider individuals who regularly buy comics at the corner convenience store as "fans." Despite avoiding active, consuming practices such as discussing the stories with other readers or even saving the comic books, these seemingly uncommitted readers, some of whose responses I include in this study, often manifest a distinctly involved sense of self, via the comic narrative, that can rival even the most devout of hard-core fans.

An exact profile of the comic book fan community in North America is a difficult one to sketch. Due to the extremely competitive nature of the comics industry, the major publishers and distributors are reluctant to disclose any detailed information on sales or audience research. As Calvin Reid has noted in the trade journal *Publishers' Weekly*, the two big publishers, Marvel and DC, are "notoriously tightlipped about sales figures" (1990, 22). Despite this reluctance to divulge exact numbers it is possible to estimate the size and nature of the comic book reading community in North America. Weekly or monthly sales figures alone are an inaccurate measure of audience size. According to comics retailers, a customer's regular weekly purchases can be anywhere from a lone book to over twenty issues, often with multiple copies of certain titles being bought by a single collector/investor. Conversely, it is impossible for sales statistics to account for readers who share or trade books amongst themselves. By assuming the conservative figure of 20 million comics sold monthly divided by an average of sixteen copies per customer, Patrick Parsons has estimated the size of the domestic North American comic audience at about 1.25 million (1991, 77). But industry professionals and trade papers routinely posit the shifting audience size as much larger, from 4 to 6 million at any given time.

Since its emergence in the 1930s the comic book audience has always been viewed as an audience of children. Various studies of comic book reading habits conducted over the past six decades have indicated that until the 1970s the overwhelming majority of comics readers were children between the ages of seven and eleven (see Muhlen 1949; Lyness 1952; Lyle and Hoffman 1971). The advent of the Marvel Age, increased prices, changes in the distribution format, and the rise of formalized structures of media fandom in the 1970s and 1980s resulted in the loss of many younger readers, and the average age of the remaining readers increased to between six and seventeen years, with a mean age of about twelve (Christman 1984, 110). A mid-1980s study of comics specialty stores conducted by *Variety* indicated the customers' age range to be between sixteen and twenty-four, with a mean age around eighteen (Bierbaum 1987, 42). Currently, such industry leaders as DC Comics advertise available promotional space in their books with the copy—next to an image of Superman soaring high above Metropolis—declaring "Buy the Power of Comics! Millions of Boys 7–17."

According to the staff I questioned at twenty comic book outlets located in heavily populated lower- and middle-income urban areas, the general readership can be broken down into three main categories. There is the traditional preadolescent group aged six to eleven, the core audience of adolescents between eleven and seventeen years of age, and the adult market of consumers from eighteen up, with a heavy concentration in the early twenties. Comics retailers often distinguish between the age groups based on the type of comic books they prefer. Joe, a twenty-two-year-old part-time sales clerk and a student at a creative arts college, described the difference between the audience segments: "The young kids go for the cartoony books like the Disney stuff and easy-to-read superhero titles like the Batman and X-Men books based on the animated [television] series. The older kids are into all the flashy superhero stuff, Image and Marvel books, some of the independents who hop on the bandwagon of every trend once its declared "hot." And the older readers, the college guys, usually go in for the *Sandman* type of book.[3] But mostly I'd have to say *everybody* buys superhero books in one form or another, even if the older guys don't like to admit it."

The most easily recognizable fact about the comic book audience in the 1990s is that it is overwhelmingly male. Bierbaum's 1987 study of comic book stores indicated that with even the most generous of estimates only 6 to 10 percent of customers are female. Likewise, none of the over thirty retail store managers I spoke with estimated their clientele to consist of more than 10 percent women. Walk into a comic book store or a comics convention at any given time and you would be hard pressed to find more than a handful of women. If comic fandom is a clubhouse, the club would at first glance seem to be "The He-Man Woman Haters' Club" from the old *Little Rascals* film shorts. I do not mean to imply that female comic book fandom is any less important or intriguing than the activities of male fans. Quite the contrary, in fact, as a minority of the core audience female fans represent the possibility of some very interesting differences in reading styles. Here, I only want to point out that, statistically, feminine interests and concerns have been skewed to the periphery of the comic book industry. As will be discussed in later chapters, the masculine preoccupations of the industry and its surrounding fandom are the most significant elements in comics' social role and symbolic use in identity formation.

Traditionally, comic book readers have always generally been a predominantly white and masculine audience. Historically such socioeconomic factors as low childhood literacy rates and lower household incomes limited the means and abilities for children of ethnic minorities to participate in comics reading. Over the years though, children from nonwhite backgrounds increasingly found themselves drawn to the world of comics. As the African American industry professionals from Milestone and Ania declared in the preceding chapter, it was their childhood involvement with comic books that lead to their choosing careers as writers, artists, and editors. Likewise, many of the current top industry talents, such as Jim Lee *(Wild C.A.T.S.)*, Brandon Choi *(Gen 13)*, and Bernard Chang *(The Second Life of Dr. Mirage)*, often credit their early years as die-hard comic book fans for their success. Currently, however, even the most cursory survey of any fan gathering in North America still reveals an relatively white majority. Yet, by most accounts, the subculture of comic book fandom is quickly becoming a more ethnically diverse community as the range of products increases thanks to micropublishing systems such as direct distribution. Of the over twenty comic book specialty stores that I polled throughout ethnically diverse neighborhoods in the Greater Toronto Area, the racial mixture ranged from one retailer's estimate that 70 percent of his customers were white, 20 percent Asian, and 10 percent black to another's estimated distribution of only 40 percent white, 30 percent Asian, and 30 percent black. Of the 128 fans I interviewed or spoke with for this research, 50 percent were white, 32 percent were black, 14 percent were West Asian, and 4 percent were Hispanic or East Asian (see appendix for more details).

When I first began approaching comic book readers and declared that I was interested in talking to fans in general, and fans of the Milestone books in particular, many people were reluctant to identify themselves as comic book fans. To be a "fan" in Western culture is considered by some to be part of a dubious category of social misfits. And to be a comic book fan, one seems to run the risk of being stereotyped as an awkward, pimply faced geek. "I'm no fanboy," one-fifteen-year-old male maintained despite his Batman baseball cap and an armful of new comics. "I just like to read them. It's not like I get geeked out over them or anything." The stereotype of comic book fans as nerdy adolescents with little or no social skills and an almost pathological obsession with superhero power fantasies is a contentious point for many comics enthusiasts, contentious because it is an image not without some factual basis. While very few comics consumers described themselves as fanboys—a term that Roger Sabin defines in *Adult Comics: An Introduction* as "contemptuous . . . implying attitudes that [are] anal retentive, adolescent and emotionally arrested" (1993, 68)—most agreed that the stereotype had a grounding in reality and were quick to point out others who *really* were comics nerds. "See that guy over there?" a thirteen year old asked me as he pointed to an overweight teenager perusing the racks at Yesteryear's Heroes. "*He* is your typical comics geek. Probably no friends, no life. He's here every new comics day and he never misses a convention." When I asked how my informant knew all this about the other customer if he had never spoken to him, he said without a hint of irony, "Because I always see him here and I almost always bump into him at the cons."

Confronted with the idea of the nerdy, nit-picking fan, many readers seek to distance themselves from the stereotype. When I asked one comics aficionado to describe a typical fan he painted this portrait: "I'm not one, but let's face it: a lot of the fans are real geeks, you know, nerdy, pimply, either really skinny or fat. They definitely don't know how to dress: Bi-way jeans and shoes, bad haircuts, T-shirts that don't fit, the whole geek uniform. [He laughed.] And for girls, forget it! These are definitely not your average high school jock type. Most have never been near a girl. Maybe that's why they go for all these cartoon babes in skimpy costumes, something to jerk off to until they work up the courage to buy a *Playboy*. Of course there are lots of normal comics fans around, but its the damn geeks everyone thinks of when you tell people you're into comics." Commenting on the negative stereotype of the comics fan, another reader in his mid-teens suggested that the character of Jerome from the recent novel *What They Did to Princess Paragon* by Robert Rodi was an exaggerated but also painfully realistic lampoon. Consider this passage describing Jerome's first visit to a comic book convention:

[N]early *everywhere* at the convention there was a misfit of some recognizable type. Jerome had never seen such a number of them, stuffed into ill-fitting clothing, peering out at the world from beneath stringy or pubic-fuzzy hair.

The sight rendered him happy beyond measure.

At long last, he had found a crowd of people among whom he could hold his head high! After so many years of skulking about in the shadows, here was an opportunity to walk where he willed. For no one here would look on *him* with ridicule, any more than he would so look on them. This was his home port, his paradise found—nothing less than geek Valhalla.

As he walked through the enormous exhibition hall the convention staffers called the dealers' room, he saw himself reflected again and again in the form of large, perspiring persons who sifted determinedly through cardboard file boxes filled with musty-smelling antique comic books, searching, no doubt, for the elusive issues they needed to complete their already bloated collections. They could also be seen buying science-fiction movie posters, portfolios of fantasy artwork, old pulp novels, pirated videotapes of Japanese cartoons, and more. It was filled with treasures, this brightly lit, wonderful world, this dealers' room; and, most exciting of all, these outcasts who inhabited it, these gun-shy specimens, these refugees from the caprices of culture and class, were stopping everywhere and *talking to each other*. They had formed a society to replace the one they didn't fit. (1995, 111–12)

Although carried to a comical extreme, Rodi's description is an accurate summation of the stereotype of comics fans: social and physical misfits, "nerds" who are overly devoted to their colorful objects of fascination and who have opted out of mainstream culture in preference for a world of their own making, populated only by fictional heroes and like-minded enthusiasts.

The negative stereotype of fans as immature, socially awkward "fanatics" is not limited to comic book buffs. In her article "Fandom as Pathology," Joli Jenson points out that both academics and the popular media have often characterized fandom as "excessive, bordering on deranged, behavior" (1992, 9). Jenson goes on to discuss two particular fan types, the obsessed individual and the individual in a hysterical crowd, as constructed images of deviance, as disreputable forms of the "other" that the rest of society uses as a marker to distinguish their own behavior as "normal." Indeed, the notion of the deranged fan as a lethal lunatic has become one of the most pervasive notions of our society's fascination with media figures in the late twentieth century. The infamous legacy of murderous fans like Charles Manson (a Beatles fan), John Hinkley (a Jodie Foster fan), and Dwight Chapman (a John Lennon fan) is joined by what seem to be almost weekly reports about demented fans stalking celebrities as diverse as Michael J. Fox, Cindy Crawford, David Letterman, and Anne Murray. The image of the violent delusional fan has even become the subject of Hollywood films such as *The King of Comedy* (1983), *Misery* (1990), and the appropriately entitled *The Fan* (1986). Likewise, the fan swept up in the emotion and the mob mentality of the hysterical crowd is a familiar concept played out most commonly by the young women who have screamed, cried, and fainted over the years at the rock concerts of Elvis, the Beatles, David Cassidy, the Bay City Rollers, and the New Kids on the Block, to name but a few. And these collective mobs of fans have turned dangerous on more than one occasion. Remember the disaster at the Who's Cincinnati concert, where eleven people were trampled to death, and any number of sporting events, particularly European football matches where fan rivalry reaches fevered and often violent, sometimes deadly, heights.

But unlike the image of the potentially dangerous fan, the stereotype of the comic book devotee falls into the tradition of the silly and juvenile media buff. Comic book fans are regarded in much the same way that *Star Trek* fans are. The well-researched community of *Star Trek* fandom has often been criticized by the media and scholars alike (see Tulloch and Jenkins 1995; Jenkins 1992; Bacon-Smith 1992; Penley 1991) as a collection of " 'kooks' obsessed with trivia, celebrities, and collectibles; as misfits and 'crazies'; as 'a lot of over-weight women, a lot of divorced and single women'; as childish adults; in short as people who have little or no 'life' apart from their fascination with this particular program" (Jenkins 1992, 11). Change "overweight, divorced, and single women" to "overweight *or* underweight, adolescent, and nerdy boys," and "program" to "comic books" and the same derogatory description would apply to the standard perception of comics fandom. "When I told some of the guys at school that I was still into superhero comics they really started to ride me," one high school senior told me. "They called me a little kid, a geek, a loser, a nerd boy . . . asked if I really believed in Superman and Wonder Woman, if I could memorize all the stories I'd ever read, stuff like that. I denied it all of course, told them I just collected as an investment. I didn't want them to think I was a fanboy, but like all the other people you see here today [at a comic book store] I have, uh, sorta committed all this weird information to memory. But those guys just wouldn't understand. It doesn't mean I'm a geek about it like some fans, I'm just really into comics." The stereotype of geeky fanboys and not quite grown-up adult men, social misfits all, feverishly devoted to the exploits of two-dimensional fictional heroes, memorizing worthless facts, such as the issue in which Marvel's character Wolverine first appeared and who drew the most issues of Hawkman, is an image that most comic book fans admit exists, but always in those around them, never in themselves.

I do not mean to suggest that the negative aspects of the comic book fan stereotype are true and that most fans live in a sense of denial about their own practices. Instead, I want to point out that there are varying levels of fandom from the most extreme personification of the stereotype to those who appear quite removed from the more active participation in the subcultural practices. In their study of soap opera fans, Harrington and Bielby (1995) distinguish between "fanship" as an individual activity and "fandom" as organized fan activity. This distinction is a useful one because it clarifies the degrees of social involvement that every enthusiast might partake in. There is a vast difference between the fan who reads a comic book for private pleasure and a fan for whom reading the book is only the first step in the process of participating in various interrelated fan events. There is also a vast difference in the discursive cues that these two, and countless other, types of readers have at their disposal for interpreting, personalizing, and making sense of the story in the course of their everyday life. At the other end of the spectrum from the fan as fanatic is someone like John, an eighteen-year-old college student who receives his comics through mail-order subscription. "I've always liked comics. I think they're a great medium for telling stories that television and literature can't handle. But I never go to the comics specialty stores, even though there's one right down the street from where I work. I don't want to get caught up in that whole fan thing, you know, caring about what's hot and what's not, who drew what . . . I'll pick up a fanzine every now and then just to see if there is anything new I might be interested in. I guess I would still have to call myself a fan, but I really just want to read my stories on my own." Although a comic book fan, John is part of the less noticeable comics audience, preferring not to participate in many of the formal aspects of comics fandom, aspects that influence how certain readers interpret and use the stories.

In his discussion of British comic book enthusiasts who read *2000 AD,* featuring the popular character Judge Dredd, Martin Barker argues that "the image of the 'fan' is not some social/mental 'stereotype' which actual fans feel insulted by. Rather, it is a *real site* which the conditions of the comics industry have created and encouraged." If, as Barker believes, the fan is in part a construct of the industry, it is a carefully crafted image molded from the conjoining of readers' fascinations and the publishers' economic needs. Barker continues, "Go to a convention—or just read about going—and experience the careful management of the possible encounters between readers and creators. Watch the comics press news, and see the magnification of new hero authors to Homeric heights. The image of the 'fan,' I would argue, is a cartoon drawn from the *actual* social relationships allowed by the dominant production forms in the present-day comics industry" (1993, 179–80). While I would not want to deny Barker's observation that the comic book producers "manage" the relationship between the producers and the fans, at least to some extent, for financial reasons, I do think he has overestimated the publishers' position as the creators of fandom. In fact, comic book fandom was originally initiated by the readers, who then affected some of the elements of production, including systems of distribution, the resale market, and creator recognition. Moreover, the subculture of fandom operates for readers well beyond the purview of the producers, in daily encounters with friends at school or in the comics stores; and in some cases the practices of comics fandom actually work against the interests of the publishers, for example, when fan opinions elevate a "troublesome" artist to star status or when fans circulate slash fiction that takes excessive liberties with established characters. Contrary to Barker's perception that fandom is a subject position created by the industry, these meetings between audience and industry are mutually interdependent in that they shape the very identity and perception of fans as a subculture and validate many of the formal aspects of comic book fandom.

Given that many comic book fans either describe themselves as outsiders or feel the burden of the "nerdy fanboy" stereotype (approximately 80 percent of the fans I spoke with reported feelings of social awkwardness around nonfans, at school or at home), it is not surprising that they often turn to fandom as a way to bolster their perceptions of self-worth. The world of comics fandom allows readers to explicate their familiarity with the texts, it justifies their passion for the medium, it provides a form of social approval for their behavior, and it helps structure their interpretations of the texts. I would like to emphasize a point I have made elsewhere (see Brown forthcoming), namely, that the understanding of comics and the practice of comic book fandom is greatly influenced by the way the social value of the text is constructed according to the principles of what Bourdieu has referred to, on a general level, as cultural economy.

As Fiske (1992) argues, the culture of media fandoms is associated with the tastes of the disempowered, of people who are subordinated by the socioeconomic system that determines the status of individuals within the general community. The institutionalized image of fans as social misfits devoted to accumulating worthless information about "crass" entertainments has caused fandom to be devalued as one of the basest and most superficial aspects of popular culture. But comic fandom, and the practice of comic book collecting in particular, is evidence of the complex and structured way that avid participants of popular culture construct a meaningful sense of self. They create a culture that simultaneously resists the tyranny of high culture, which dictates what cultural commodities should be considered "art," and forms what Fiske calls a "shadow cultural economy" that mimics bourgeois standards (1992, 30). Fiske's term is derived from Bourdieu's metaphor of culture as an economic system divided along the twin poles of cultural and economic capital. Bourdieu's theory provides an apt language for discussing how people attempt to invest in and accumulate qualities that are perceived as valuable within a culture. Like our capitalist economy, the cultural system distributes its resources on a selective basis to create a non-fiscal distinction between the privileged and the deprived. The system ascribes value to certain "tastes" and devalues others. Typically, the tastes that are privileged are those associated with the higher classes. Dominant tastes are seen as superior by most members of Western culture because the ruling class naturalizes their tastes through the control of institutions such as universities and other school systems, museums, and art galleries. High culture is socially and institutionally legitimated as the "official" culture, distinguishing between the "haves" and the "have nots." Thus, like economic capital, one can *invest* in an education or *invest* in a good suit to better one's chances of advancing socially and economically up the ladder of official culture.

In his magnum opus, *Distinction: A Social Critique of the Judgment of Taste* (1984), Bourdieu crafts a detailed analysis of social hierarchy in contemporary France. He builds from the basic notion that "good" taste, social status, and economic position are intricately related. "To the socially recognized hierarchy of the arts, and within each of them, of genres, schools or periods, corresponds a social hierarchy of the consumers. This predisposes tastes to function as markers of 'class'" (1984, 1–2). By considering both cultural tastes and economic status as measurable capital, Bourdieu constructs a two-dimensional graph onto which he maps social/hierarchical space (fig. 3.1). The north-south axis measures the amount of capital (economic *and* cultural) that one pos-

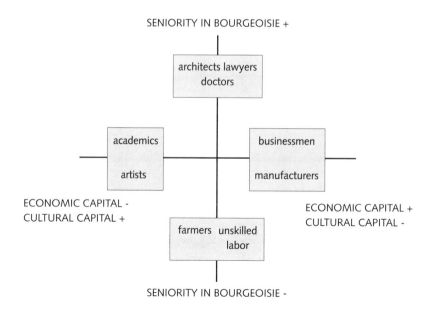

3.1 *Model of cultural and economic capital*

sesses, and the east-west axis measures the type of capital (economic or cultural).

Fiske emphasizes two limitations of Bourdieu's model. The first is Bourdieu's narrow focus on economics and class as the discriminating features of social position. Other discriminatory features such as sex, ethnicity, and age need to be included in the model. Fiske's second criticism is that Bourdieu makes the mistake of underestimating the complexity of proletarian culture. The model is primarily concerned with social stratification amongst the "haves" since the "have nots" are assumed to have no capital with which to negotiate their social position. This view ignores the power of the subordinated to construct their own semiotic texts from, and often—at least according to the current populist trend in cultural studies—in opposition to, the original texts provided by the cultural industries. It is easy to see how people disempowered by sex, ethnicity, and, in the case of most comic fans, age would fall somewhere in the southern hemisphere of Bourdieu's model. But by looking closely at the complex system of meanings that constitutes the culture of comics fandom we can see how the traditionally disempowered act to bolster their social position within the community of fans. Bourdieu's rules for gaining prestige within the general culture are mimicked by popular culture, allowing members of fan communities to accumulate, within the subculture, an equivalent to the forms of social status and self-esteem that accompany cultural capital. While many of the comic book fans I spoke with were from traditional middle-class backgrounds, they still relied on their expertise as fans to boost their self-esteem. Though not disempowered in the economic sense of the term, as Bourdieu would see it, most of the younger comic book readers are disempowered within their families by virtue of their age, and dozens of these young fans also complained of being social outcasts at school (certainly not an uncommon feeling among adolescents). But an outcast in one social situation can become an admired authority figure in another.

Despite the swelling ranks of adults within the comic fan community, most people still perceive the medium as childish. They believe that comics consist of immature, simple stories and "cartoony" art. This condescending view is, in fact, far from the truth. Modern comics deal with highly complex issues in mature and innovative ways (see the analyses by Berger 1978; Barker 1989; Witek 1989), and as was discussed early in this chapter, the age range of comic book readers has grown over the past two decades to include a significant number of adolescent and adult readers. But the stereotypical perception of comic books as a childish medium with childish enthusiasts is a form of criticism common to all popular fan cultures. Such notable fandoms as those associated with Star Trek, The Rocky Horror Picture Show, or even Harlequin Romances

are characterized in the popular imagination as childish, as feeble-minded enthusiasts or arrested adolescents. The problem is that fan cultures challenge
what the bourgeois have institutionalized as natural and universal standards of
"good taste." As Bourdieu tells us, the economy of culture is so powerful that
any aesthetic tastes not conforming to the established norms of high culture
are devalued to the point of being socially unacceptable. Any practices that do
not adhere to the dictates of "good taste" are taken as markers of an individual's inferiority. Fans and their subject of enthusiasm are necessarily looked
down upon by the greater society because their aesthetic preferences amount
to a disruption of, and threat to, dominant cultural hierarchies.

Because pursuing a leisure activity that is in "bad taste" is considered by
teachers and parents alike—prime representatives of the powers-that-be for
young fans—to be detrimental to one's development, society often adopts a
paternalistic attitude of wanting to save fans from the harmful effects of popular media. There is a moral backlash that accompanies all new and suspect
forms of entertainment, from the early pulp novels and turn-of-the-century
movies to modern music videos and role-playing games (for a detailed discussion of various media and moral panics see Starker 1989). In his study of television science fiction fandom, Jenkins points out that "materials viewed as
undesirable within a particular aesthetic are often accused of harmful social
effects or negative influences upon their consumers. Aesthetic preferences are
imposed through legislation and public pressure; for example, in the cause of
protecting children from the 'corrupting' influence of undesired cultural materials. Those who enjoy such texts are seen as intellectually debased, psy-
chologically suspect, or emotionally immature" (1992, 16–17). This moral
condemnation of undesirable aesthetics and institutionalized regulation of the
medium is particularly clear in the history of comics. The criticism of comics,
under the guise of protecting children from the corrupting influence of the
medium, was almost solely responsible for the drastic decline in sales and the
near death of the industry in the 1950s. To this day, even though the self-
imposed censorship of the Comics Magazine Association of America has been
voluntarily adhered to by all the major publishers since 1954, the medium is
still occasionally attacked by the moral right, who have recently closed comic
shops in several U.S. cities, accusing them of selling obscene literature. Likewise, such books as John Fulce's simple-minded denunciation of modern
comics, *Comic Books Exposed: Seduction of the Innocent Revisited* (1990)—
published by the same people responsible for other great classics of fundamen-
talist paranoia, such as *The Lucifer Connection,* Lord! Why Is My Child A
Rebel? and Backward Masking Unmasked: Satanic Messages Hidden in Rock
Music—charge the comic book industry with corrupting innocent children.

Many of the comic book fans that I have spoken with complained that authority figures, primarily parents and teachers, constantly ridiculed their reading of comics as immature behavior and detrimental to improving literacy levels. Andrew, a twelve-year-old honor student, complained that his teacher had a narrow-minded understanding of acceptable reading material. "Every Wednesday in my advanced English class," Andrew explained, "we have what's called a 'silent reading' period where everyone has to bring a book to read for pleasure. The problem is that Mr. Lewis always checks what you're reading, and if it isn't considered worthy you're given a penalty and sent to the library to get a real book. So one day I brought in my copy of *Maus* to read and I got in real shit from Mr. Lewis. He said, 'That's just a comic book,' and that I'd never learn to appreciate the classics if I only read picture books. Well, that really pissed me off because I do read the classics. I've already read Gilgamesh, Beowulf, some Dickens, some Sherlock Holmes, and stuff. Meanwhile the people around me are still reading The Hardy Boys and Nancy Drew. I explained to him that *Maus* was a serious book about the Holocaust and had won all kinds of awards, but he didn't care . . . sent me to the library to get something real to read." I heard similar stories about concerned parents. "I have to hide my comic books from my Mom," one shy comics fan of about fourteen claimed. "She doesn't like me reading them 'cause she thinks I'll never learn to read really well. I told her I've stopped reading comics but she's still suspicious, checks my room sometimes, looks in my closet. Maybe if I just sat around and watched TV like my sister she wouldn't worry about me becoming illiterate."

The legacy of the Wertham comics scare still haunts the fan community, as do the stereotypes of comics as childish and readers as immature nerds. The problem with comic fandom gaining legitimacy within contemporary North American society is that it contradicts the standards of "good taste." Ironically, fandom seems to offend dominant cultural standards by applying the same rules of appreciation to popular texts that are supposed to be reserved for elite texts. John, a thirteen year old who helped me locate rare comic books on several different occasions, seemed bewildered that his father, a successful businessman, resented John's dedication to comic art. "My Dad loves art," John explained. "He has a large collection of paintings, and he pays a fortune for them. But when I brought home some original comic art that I bought at a con he said it was a waste of money. What a hypocrite, when he buys art because it's by a famous artist that's okay, but when I buy stuff from a comic artist he thinks its a joke." In fact, John's knowledge of comic book artists, their styles, techniques, and influences, not to mention a piece's fiscal value and chance of appreciation, would likely rival any university-trained critic of "legitimate" art. As Bourdieu notes, "[T]he most intolerable thing for those who regard themselves as the possessors of legitimate culture is the sacrilegious reuniting of tastes which [good] taste dictates shall be separated" (1980, 253). The general public regards the acute attention that fans pay to comic books as inappropriate for simple, mass-produced, disposable texts. The close scrutinizing, collecting, analyzing, rereading, and resulting accumulation of knowledge is deemed acceptable for a serious work of art but ridiculous for a mass medium. Yet it is by mirroring these very practices of the official cultural economy that members of the fan community seek to bolster their cultural standing within their own circle of social contact.

For example, Kevin, an extremely knowledgeable fourteen-year-old comic book fan who first helped me find my way through the ritual of bargaining with dealers at conventions, told me that he felt like other fans listened to his opinions but that outside of fandom he was socially awkward. "It's taken a while," Kevin explained as he looked through a small pile of second-rate original artwork being sold by a local inker who needed the money to pay his back rent, "but among the other fans I know, I'm considered a real authority on collecting. Even the guy who owns the store I usually get my books from is amazed by how I can tell who drew what just by looking and how I can remember all kinds of little details from old storylines—you know, like the name of the law firm that Icon works at, or what Wolverine's favorite beer is." Kevin continued talking as we moved on to a corner table where the dealer was selling laminated versions of the publishers' promotional posters. "At school, uh, I don't know; I sorta don't really fit in with a large group of people. I've got lots of friends and stuff, but when I'm with other comic book fans I'm the one they come to for advice. I like that. It makes me feel good." For Kevin this sense of accomplishment, this sense of an elevated status in comparison to his position in other social situations, is achieved through his mastery of attributes valued within the cultural economy of comics fandom. Specifically, Kevin spoke of his ability to identify the work of significant creators and to recite from memory information that helps to illuminate the importance of certain story lines. Kevin also spoke proudly of the praise he receives for accurately assessing the value of individual comic books as well as entire collections, and for knowing which books will increase in value due to artistic merit and shifts in market interests. In short, a comic book fan like Kevin is able to gain cultural capital within the fandom community by adopting manners of connoisseurship that parallel those valued by official culture.

Many of these critical skills that can boost subcultural capital for knowledgeable fans like Kevin are based on the comic book itself as a revered form of material culture. Comic fandom is rather unique in relation to other popular culture fan communities because it is almost exclusively centered around a physical, possessable text. For *Star Trek, The Rocky Horror Picture Show,* or Grateful Dead fans, it is the experience of viewing the show, hearing the band, or participating in ritual consumption that is of prime importance. And while reading the comic is obviously fundamental to comic fans on an individual basis, it is the possession of the actual comic that acts as the focal point for the entire community. Other fan cultures can own a New Kids on the Block album or videotape all the episodes of *The X-Files,* they can even purchase all the T-shirts, dolls, and posters they want, but none of it carries the same ability to substantiate fan authenticity in the way that owning a copy of *Wolverine* #1 does. In discussing comic books as popular icons, Harold Schecter goes so far as to claim that it is the physical book that is of prime importance. "When a Batman fan sees a mint-condition copy of *Detective Comics* #1 in a display case, he doesn't want to take it out and read it," Schecter argues. "But, for the true devotee, there is a special potency—magic, luminosity, call it what you will—about the original. It's enough for him just to stand nearby and gaze at it, to be able to go home and tell his friends—veneration in his voice—that he actually saw a copy of *Detective* #1. Some comic books have so much of this potency that they endow their possessors with mana, so that, at the comic book conventions, the owners of especially rare issues are themselves regarded with a certain sense of awe" (1978, 264). The awe that such noteworthy collectors are often regarded with, despite Schecter's claim for a magical transfer of mana from a rare comic book to its owner, is due more to the owner's earned reputation as a skillful fan. The awe Schecter describes is understandable when we consider the ability of canonical texts to endow their possessors with cultural status. A fan's comic book collection only reflects well upon the collector if it proves his ability to exercise cultural knowledge in making discriminating choices of what is, and what will be, valuable. Knowledge, acquired through detailed observation and participation in fan activities like conventions and fanzine consumption, and the ability to use that knowledge properly to collect worthwhile titles, amounts to the symbolic, or the immaterial, capital of the cultural economy of comic fandom. The comic book itself represents the physical currency, the material substantiation of the fan's subcultural skill and participation.

Collecting is an important marker of status within official culture. It signifies the ability to distinguish between objects of worth and worthlessness, a knowledge of important canonical features, and a substantiation of "good taste." Elite collecting is based upon the ability to discriminate and thus to acquire the exceptional rather than the common. First editions are more important than reprints, originals more than copies, old more than new. Collecting by fans, on

the other hand, is often seen to be "inclusive rather than exclusive: the emphasis is not so much on acquiring a few good (and thus expensive) objects as
upon accumulating as many as possible. The individual objects are therefore
often cheap, devalued by the official culture, and mass-produced. The distinc-
tiveness lies in the extent of the collection rather than in their uniqueness or
authenticity as cultural objects (Fiske 1992, 44). This may apply to most media
fan communities, but for comic fandom, which is based so intently upon the
collection of primary texts, it is not so much the size of the collection as its
uniqueness and its inclusion of canonized comics that counts. "Collecting the
entire run of, say, *Prime* or *Static* is relatively easy to do if you're willing to
spend the bucks," an eighteen-year-old fan told me during a regional Toronto
convention. "The books will be out there, somewhere. But the real skill comes
from being able to collect what is going to be valuable when it first comes out,
or at least when you don't have to pay much more than cover for it. That's the
sign of someone who knows what they're doing when it comes to comics."

   To amass cultural capital within the comic community, the fan must build
an extensive knowledge of the industry. The fan strives to become, as Larry,
the successful comics negotiator at the Chicago super con, was described by
his friends: "the master of his domain." Fans are what Bourdieu refers to as
"autodidactics," individuals who are self-taught in an effort to raise their status
within the subculture as a compensation for their lack of cultural capital and
the economic capital that often comes with it in mainstream society. By reading
and collecting comics for an amount of time, by participating in conventions,
and by reading various fanzines, fans develop an ability to discriminate between different writers, different versions of a character, and, most commonly,
between different artists. Indeed, the shift in comic book connoisseurship from
concentrating on characters to concentrating on creators as markers of quality
worth collecting has had a profound effect on the structure of the industry
since the late 1980s. The ardent fan learns which creators and character combi-
nations result in the best comics and which comics will be valuable in the future
because they include the first appearance of a writer, artist, or character who
will likely become popular. Conversely, many fans can tell at a glance which
comics are destined to flop. If a fan is consistently right, then he gains status
among other fans and his collection exists as verification of his knowledge
about comic culture.

   One of the condemnations of popular culture leveled by critics such as Allan
Bloom (1987) and Eric Donald Hirsch (1987) is that it is canonless. For Bloom,
the move from canonized literary texts to mass culture is one of the central
problems causing the erosion of Western culture. "The failure to read good
books," Bloom argues, "both enfeebles the vision and strengthens our most

fatal tendency—the belief that the here and now is all there is" (1987, 64). Contrary to popular culture, the argument goes, elite culture arises from an appreciation of established canons. It professes that certain works of "art" are monumentally significant in the historical development of culture and that the significance of individual works lies in the authoritative presence of a single creator. This is juxtaposed with the belief that popular culture is repetitive, formulaic fluff and all works are anonymously produced and uncritically consumed. But the necessarily discriminatory skills of the comic collector disprove this narrow view of media texts. The ability to discriminate between significant and insignificant comic books creates a very specific canon. Comics historian Thomas Inge outlines the "variety of factors that determine which comic books are the most desired by collectors": (a) original issues of popular titles, (b) the work of particular creators, (c) the titles of a specific publisher, and (d) complete runs of favorite characters (1984, 9–11). These strategies of comic collecting are identical to those of high culture. Like official cultural practices, comic fandom recognizes historically significant events such as the first appearance of Batman in *Detective Comics* #27 or the engagement of Superman to Lois Lane in *Adventures of Superman* #50. And increasingly, the author/artist as creator has become an especially important marker of canonical value. While fans with a moderate understanding of why some comics become valuable can easily discern that a landmark issue like *The Death of Superman* is significant, it takes an experienced eye to tell that a particular artist or writer has what it takes.

The cultural economy of comic fandom is based on the ability to acquire canonical texts, as determined by either plot or creator significance. By possessing these comics, the reader substantiates his participation in fandom and builds his knowledge of creators, characters, and storylines. As I said earlier, comic fandom is unique, unlike the fan cultures that exist around other popular media, because it is so fundamentally based on the serial, possessable text. It is also unique in that it has taken on a directly economic guise. As the popular press is fond of reporting, rare and significant comic books are worth a lot of money. *Action Comics* #1 with the first appearance of Superman is worth between $100,000 and $120,000, and *Detective Comics* #27 with the first Batman story can fetch anywhere from $110,000 to $125,000. Even contemporary comics, like the four-issue *A Death in the Family* series, where Robin was killed as the result of a 1-900 phone survey, can sky rocket from a $1.85 cover price to over $100 in a matter of hours. The market value of comics is carefully monitored via weekly, monthly, and annual fanzine price guides. Like any other market the prices are based on supply and demand.

The irony of this justification is that the entire comic book market is an unintentional parody of high culture while at the same time retaining many of the principles and rules inherent in the high-culture model. The real value of the comic is not monetary but cultural. In other words, although the monetary value of a single issue may rise to $40 within the first month of it's release, the $40 is really incidental in comparison to the status one can achieve for quickly recognizing the quality of the comic on the day it is released. Like the high-culture world of art collecting, value is a relative term. It requires cultural knowledge of the creator, a historical sense of tradition, a knowledge of generic conventions, and a recognition of the avant-garde to determine the "hard" value of a work. And as the bourgeoisie scoff at the nouveau riche who can afford to buy fine art but can't really appreciate it, comic fans condemn buyers who are in it just for the money. A fan letter reprinted in the letters-to-the-editor page of *Spawn* #9 in March 1993 sums up the attitude toward nonfan "collectors": "[T]he day Jason and I purchased *Spawn* #7, we bore witness to the strange phenomenon of brain-washed consumers. It was hard to watch and understand. Three middle-aged professionals walked into the store we frequent and picked the shelves clean like a vulture would a corpse. They bought everything from *Alpha Flight* to *Youngblood*. They were impartial about their purchases, everything was sucked into the ever-growing stack of comics. Over $70 was spent by each of them and they happily walked away with their prize catches of the week, beaming tidings of joy over their investment—but what is their investment? We could guarantee over 75% of the merchandise would not be looked at but merely shoved into polyurethane bags to sit and rot on the chance the market might increase its value."

For a real fan the comic cannot just be bought. It must be understood and enjoyed. The economic aspects of collecting are false. Simply acquiring the books is the act of a heartless villain: an investor. The fan collects because he loves the medium and the stories that are told. As Steve Geppi, the president of Diamond Comics Distributors, wrote in a special issue of *Wizard,* celebrating the one hundred most collectible comics, "I found myself automatically listing comic books which have achieved a significant dollar value. Well, I'm not sure if the books I list here will necessarily fall into the category of elite comic investments; but I do know these books are special, and collectible for the best reason of all: they are the stuff which childhood dreams are made of" (1993, 6). Thus, to truly understand the logic of fandom we must realize that many of the claims about a comic book's monetary value are posturing. The dollar figure attached to each comic in the price guide is an indication of its cultural value not its monetary value. "Truth be known," one of the Comics Cavern regulars whispered to me as we left the store one sunny spring afternoon, glancing over his shoulder, wary of prying ears, "I know how we all just told you what great investments comics are, but don't put too much stock in that coming from this bunch; they, we, are all fans, not investors. There isn't one of us that would part with his comics for any amount of money." First and foremost fans are fans because they share a love of the tales told in comics.

If comic book fans have "formed a society to replace the one they didn't fit," as Robert Rodi suggests in his humorous novel, then it is a society clearly organized around several key formal structures. Among the more concrete and visible of these formal structures are the comics specialty store, the comic book convention, and the array of amateur and professionally produced fan magazines. Aside from the actual texts themselves, the comic book specialty store is one of the prime elements of fan culture. Emerging first in the 1970s as an offshoot of head shops and specialty book stores, the comics shop really expanded to cater to the growing niche market in the early 1980s as a result of the advent of direct distribution. There were approximately four hundred comics shops in the United States by the end of the 1970s; the number has now reached over five thousand in the United States alone, with thousands more in Canada, Britain, and the rest of the world (Fost 1991, 16). Comic book specialty stores, like The Black Knight mentioned above, deal almost exclusively in comic books and related objects of fan interest such as role-playing games, action figures, posters, collector's cards, and science fiction and/or horror literature. These stores provide a focal point for the entire culture of comic fandom. They mediate between the readers and the publishers, the fans and the industry professionals, and they give the fans who might otherwise feel secluded in their entertainment pursuits a place to meet and express their common interests.

Although each comic book shop is unique, there is a certain atmosphere common to all of them. By their very nature they are rather insular, a distinct enclave for fans and run by fans. Most of the stores were established not by outside retailers looking to capitalize on a new market but from inside the realm of comic fandom by longtime enthusiasts risking their own capital in order to develop stores designed to satisfy their own needs and those of fellow fans. Without fail, every one of the specialty store owners whom I spoke with claimed to have been a fan long before becoming an entrepreneur. "I was always into comics, even when it wasn't cool to be, and opening up my own store just seemed like the perfect thing to do," the thirty-something owner and sole employee of the midtown Cape 'n Cowl store remarked. "Now I get to do what I love: talk to other fans, read all the comics I want, and pay the rent at the same time. It's great!" Others, like Ken, the co-owner of Magical Realms, a comics and rare science fiction bookstore located in a middle-class suburb of Toronto, saw it as a chance to be more than a fan, to be a little closer to the professional side of the relationship. "I always wanted to draw comics when I was a kid. I'd try to imitate Mike Grell or Neal Adam's style but I wasn't really good enough," Ken remembered. "I still work on some local photocopied fanzine stuff once in a while, but I'm happy working at the store. It's as close as I'll ever get to being a pro, but I do feel like I'm privy to a lot more of the insider industry stuff than I ever would be as just a fan." Even those retailers who are not independent entrepreneurs but rather managers or franchise owners of individual stores in large chains like The Silver Snail or 1,000,000 Comics claimed to have entered the business through their love of comics. John, who manages 1,000,000 Comics on Toronto's busy Yonge Street, said, "I worked here part-time while I was going to university for economics. Then when I graduated I just couldn't face a suit-and-tie, nine-to-five job, so I asked myself what did I really want to do. And this is it. I love comics and I'm in charge of my own business. Not bad, eh?"

Although the business and the social structure at every store is remarkably similar, each store has distinct qualities based on stock preferences, location, and the personalities involved. For example, among the over thirty comic book specialty stores in the Toronto area a few of the best-known ones are identified by their unique atmospheres. The Silver Snail outlet in the heart of Toronto's bohemian Queen West District is generally considered the premier comic book store in the city. Across the street from the popular Black Bull biker bar and an outdoor T-shirt and jewelry market, The Silver Snail is located between a trendy used clothing store and an environmentally responsible head shop. The Silver Snail's flashy new storefront window has a large built-in display area that promotes a different theme every couple of weeks with life-size cutouts or mannequins of characters like those from Neil Gaiman's *Sandman* series, favored by the neighborhood's Goth population. Inside, the store is larger than most with distinct areas for new, recent, and back issues as well as for graphic novels, books about comics, books on art, alternative magazines, toys, sculptures, and an entire second floor for games and role-playing-related merchandise. Fans come from as far away as the suburbs to shop at The Silver Snail, because, as one enthusiastic young customer explained to me—and to his nearby mother, who made the long trip with him every two weeks because she was afraid to let him go downtown on his own—"They got it all here. They're big and they order lots of everything I want, so I know I'll be able to find it all." The Silver Snail's size and large staff ensure that customers can easily find most recent mainstream titles in sufficient enough quantities to avoid annoyingly quick sellouts. Overall, The Silver Snail is seen as a store with a bit of everything for both conservative and alternative tastes. But the store's efficacy is also regarded by some as a lack of charm. "I come here because I like the area and can get what I want, but it's a little too professional for my tastes," a customer in his early twenties remarked. "It doesn't have that feel of a neighborhood shop anymore . . . It's too big, too clean. Uh, I sometimes miss the type of store where you recognize the same faces all the time and everyone knows you by name."

Almost the antithesis of The Silver Snail is a fan favorite, The Comics Cavern, located in a residential area of middle-class suburban Mississauga. A family business, the store is owned and run primarily by twenty-four-year-old David, his mother, and some friends. David opened the store over ten years ago as an evening and weekend venture while he was still in high school. The Comics Cavern is actually a small house converted into a cramped retail store with minimal floor space. The narrow center display rack for new and recent comics is nearly overshadowed by the mismatched, overstuffed cardboard file boxes that line the counters and floors along three of the walls in the small store. Along the fourth wall is the narrow, cluttered display case full of rare items, and any number of young fans can be found at any given time hovered around this counter. "It's a local hangout, a home away from home for some of us," one adolescent customer told me while he and a friend competed to see who could find the best erotic poses in the newest issues of Image's *Gen 13* and Marvel's *X-Men*. "Some owners," he explained, "don't like you hanging around too long, but David's cool." Catering to a very specific clientele of personal friends and a core group of members from the two nearby high schools, The Comics Cavern is an extremely insular place where unfamiliar customers are often met with indifference or disdain from the regulars, despite David's polite encouragement. The fans who frequent this store define themselves as members of a distinct in-group and are wary of outsiders who might look down upon or trivialize their interests.

Another type of store, the alternative comic book shop, is typified in Toronto by The Beguiling. Ranked by the *Comics Journal* as one of the top five comic book stores in North America, The Beguiling is a two-level store located among the small restaurants, specialty book stores, and rare video outlets in the avant-garde area known as Mirvish Village. On the first level is a wide assortment of scholarly and pseudo-scholarly books about popular culture and the media, hard-to-find European erotic graphic novels by cult favorites like Moebius and Milo Manera, and coffee-table art books on such controversial soft core pornography topics as gay and lesbian photography and stylized sadomasochistic paintings. On the second level are the new and recent-issue comic books that include most of the mainstream superhero-type books but also include numerous "adult-oriented" books from the alternative and underground presses.

Side by side with the newest Batman and Spider-Man books are such mature-themed comics as Chester Brown's satirical black comedy *Yummy Fur,* Dan Clowes absurdly exaggerated portrayal of urban life in *Eightball,* Peter Bagge's aggressively paranoid *Hate,* and Harvey Pekar's popular autobiographical series about blue-collar life in Cleveland, *American Splendor.* In addition to these and other mostly satirical/critical series are the other more sexually overt mature comic books, from the glossy, high-quality *Penthouse Comix* to the eroticized cartoonishness of *Omaha the Cat Dancer* and *Cherry* to the very explicit work of various gay, lesbian, and bondage-oriented titles like *Drawn and Quarterly, 2 Hot Girls on a Hot Summer Night, Women on Top, The Art of Spanking,* and *Horny Biker Slut.* The explicit illustration of sex appears to be a dominant concern for the alternative comics at The Beguiling. Accordingly, the customers at The Beguiling are, on average, older than comics readers at more traditional stores. The Beguiling's emphasis on alternative subject matter creates an environment different from other stores and allows adult readers to continue participation in fan culture at the same time that they expand their reading material beyond that geared for children and adolescents. The Beguiling also permits the customers to perceive a certain amount of distance between themselves and the stereotype of all fans as arrested adolescents.

In summary, the tightly knit but highly competitive network of comic book specialty stores is for many readers the heart and soul of fandom as a cultural activity. As a focal point for comics fandom the specialty store provides a unique service. Not only does the store guarantee a large assortment of the dozens of new comic books released each week and a large catalogue of back issues, it also acts as a conduit for fan-related information. The store provides insider gossip from the publishers and distributors about upcoming projects and controversial developments. For example, months before Milestone Media publicly announced that its series *Xombi* and *The Shadow Cabinet* would be discontinued due to poor sales, I was warned of their inevitable demise by Gordon, the owner of Capital City Comics. "I know you are interested in the Milestone stuff," Gordon explained when I asked how he knew the books were about to be cancelled. "I heard some rumblings last week from the guy I order my books from, and I thought you might want to know. I haven't told anyone else yet, so that should kinda give you a leg up on some of these young guys who are always giving you advice." In effect, Gordon was offering more than just idle gossip or good advice, he was giving me privileged information—a form of subcultural currency. By letting me know something that some of my young informants were not yet aware of, Gordon was selectively attempting to raise my standing within the hierarchy of his store.

The specialty stores also control the ordering and reserving of much sought after materials and are the main source of information about comic book conventions, personal appearances. and fan clubs. Many of the stores also act to promote and develop the writing and illustrating talents of fans trying to break into the industry. Numerous stores provide wall space for sample drawings by customers and some provide an informal network of contacts, introducing aspiring writers and illustrators to each other and, on rare occasions, to professional talent scouts. More than a couple of aspiring artists told me that they wanted to post their work on the store's walls in the hopes of being discovered. The "discovery theory" is, I suspect, nothing more than comic fandom's version of an urban legend. No one personally knew anybody who had been discovered through the stores, but everyone was certain that it had happened. Of course there are dozens of examples that the fans recirculate to emphasize the fluidity between the ranks of amateur, aspiring artists and the real thing. "I had my doubts," a sixteen year old told me, "until I heard about how Norm Breyfogle [the artist for Ultraverse's flagship title *Prime*] had been discovered when some guy at DC saw his stuff on a store wall." Unfortunately, the accuracy of this discovery story is doubtful as Breyfogle himself is cited in the fan press as having gone through many of the regular channels to become a professional artist. Interestingly enough, in support of the discovery theory, a clerk at Yesteryear's Heroes produced an issue of *The Batman Family*, an anthology-style Batman title from the 1970s, which reproduced artwork submitted by fans, including one piece from a young Norman Breyfogle.

As a result of the various activities undertaken at comic book specialty stores, an informal sort of hierarchy is often observed by the patrons. The owners are afforded the most status and respect because they are in a sense the gatekeepers of the fan community. The owners of these small shops are privy to valuable information, often linking the reader to the publishers. In a sense the owner's status and his access to information and materials make him a broker of cultural capital. Just as Gordon of Capital City Comics was able to offer me a bit of symbolic currency which I could use in my dealings with the fans who frequented his store, other owners can help readers establish or confirm status. Given this gatekeeping function, it is not surprising that many fans went out of their way to develop friendly relationships with the owners of their local comic book stores. Dave, of The Black Knight, recalled one high-school-aged member who brought him a greeting card every holiday and then complained vehemently when Dave had not reserved a limited edition comic for him. "The kid was all pissed off at me 'cause I didn't pull a book that he hadn't ordered," Dave explained sarcastically. "All his friends had been smart enough to order the book ahead of time, but he figured since he had brought me these cards that I should automatically get him books that would turn out to be hot."

The owners are also typically the most devoted fans with the longest history of comics involvement. They have spent decades reading and collecting comics, and they represent for many fans the next best thing to becoming a professional comic book writer or artist, they have managed to take their passion for comics and turn it into a full-time profession.

Next in status to the owners are the stores' staff members, who, in addition to fulfilling many of the same functions as the owners but to a lesser extent, are often aspiring comics creators themselves. Usually in their late teens or twenties, many comic shop employees are longtime fans who have made a conscious decision to pursue careers as comic book professionals and work part-time in the stores as a way to support themselves while honing their craftsmanship as writers or artists. "It's the perfect way to bide my time while I'm working on developing my style, and I get to take advantage of all this stuff I know about comics that is no good for any other job," Steve, a nineteen-year-old employee of Cosmic Adventures observed. "And it's a really sympathetic environment to work in. I can keep up with all the industry changes and get feedback on my work from some of the customers who really know their stuff." As semipros, or at least talented wanna-bes, these staff members are often regarded as minor celebrities and their views and opinions about comic books are respected accordingly. Similar to the status of specialty store employees are the regular fans who devote much of their time to the pursuit of comics fandom and hopefully to a career as industry professionals. A small step down from the store's staff, because they are not seen as capable of affecting anyone's access to new comics or fan-based events, are the fans who have willfully displayed not only their knowledge of comics but also their ability to write or draw them. Moving down the hierarchical ladder of fandom, one's expertise and involvement with comics collecting and fan activities becomes the marker for a position. Leaving aside individual charisma for the moment, those who have participated in comics fandom the longest or with the most intensity are accorded the most status, while those who are new to the experience or who seem to have only a casual, undeveloped interest in comics are granted little respect. One informant succinctly expressed the importance of subcultural knowledge in relation to acceptance at fan conventions: "In academics it's 'publish or perish,' right? Well, at a comics con it's 'know or don't go.' "

But just how do the young comic book enthusiasts amass detailed information on the current and historical aspects of the industry? For many a quick wealth of knowledge is gleamed from the various comic book fanzines that are readily available at almost any comics specialty store and at some magazine newsstands. As a point of clarification, the term "fanzine" is customarily used within various fandom cultures to denote independent, noncommercial, ama-

teur publications produced by fans for fans. The low-budget, often photocopied 'zines are a haven for fan criticism, fan-authored original stories, and
artwork and have played a critical role in bringing lesser-known creators to the
attention of a wider audience (see Sanjek 1990). In *Over Fifty Years of American Comic Books* (1991), comics historian Ron Goulart traces the origin of the
comic book fanzine to Ted White's 1952 publication of *The Story of Superman.*
And 1953 saw the start of the fanzine Fantasy Comics and a slate of other
fanzines dedicated to EC Comics, including The EC Fan Bulletin, Concept, EC
Scoop, Graham Backers, and Potrezbie. In the 1960s several now-legendary
fans produced what the *Price Guide* refers to as "the first true comics fanzines." Dick Lupoff headed up Xero, dedicated to comics and science fiction;
Jerry Bails and Roy Thomas began publishing Alter Ego; and Don and Maggie
Thompson started their long careers with Comic Art. Then, as Goulart puts it,
"Comics collectors and fans got their bible in 1970, when Robert M. Overstreet published the first edition of his *Comic Book Price Guide*" (1991, 316).
Known now simply as "the guide," Overstreet's annual publication is a three-
hundred-plus-page book with articles about the history of comics and fandom,
special topics such as women in comics or how to restore damaged books, and
a detailed list of recommended prices for every comic book ever published.

Currently, what are still commonly referred to as fanzines are in effect more
akin to professional magazines. Although still produced by publishers with their
roots in organized fandom, and ostensibly still for the fans, the bulk of the
magazines are glossy, professional journals distributed for profit and promotional purposes. Numerous small-circulation comic book fanzines still exist in
the true sense of the word, featuring fan-authored art, stories, and criticism,
but the most popular and influential fanzines in the 1990s are *Wizard: The
Guide to Comics, Comics Scene,* and *Overstreet's The Fan.* Each of these
monthly publications is dominated by lengthy interviews with industry professionals about their current work and upcoming projects. They also include small
news items about each of the publishers, commentary about trends and related
issues such as the development of comic book characters for film and television, tips on how to draw or write comics, and regular contests featuring the
best of fan art. Though informative, up-to-date, and attractively packaged,
some fans consider this new breed of professional fanzines an oxymoron.
"Yeah, I read 'em once in a while, probably more than I should," confessed
Scott, an eighteen-year-old regular at The Black Knight, while flipping through
the latest issue of *The Fan.* "You can't really call them fanzines, but everybody
does. They're more like advertising features for the big companies. Look, every
one of them has the same stuff this month—an interview with John Bryne
about his taking over Wonder Woman, Frank Miller bitching about censorship,

something about one of the Bad Girl comics—all the same stuff that you get in the companies' own promotional newsletters. It's interesting, but they really just exist to help sell more comics; that's why the pros are willing to give them so many interviews and draw some covers for them." At the other extreme, there do exist comics magazines concerned more with issues and less with promoting sales, such as the long-running *Comics Journal: The Magazine of News and Criticism,* which does not shy away from controversial topics like creators' rights, censorship, and the juvenile disposition of comic books.

What the current crop of popular fanzines may lack in criticism they make up for with the sheer volume of information each magazine contains, information that devoted fans can use to organize their collecting or to add to their interpretation of certain stories. "When I first bought Hardware I was sort of looking at it as Milestone's version of Batman—you know, lone avenger, high-tech gizmos, no super powers," a recent convert to the Milestone comic books explained. "But then I was reading in one of the fanzines, I think it was *Comics Scene,* about the development of the company and how McDuffie and Cowan had met while working on Marvel's *Deathlok* . . . and then it dawned on me—duh—Hardware was more like Deathlok, with a reliance on machines and an alienation from his body. The stories took on a whole new light for me after that." With their access to the top professionals and the ever-changing fan favorites, these fanzines also seem to close the gap between the readers and the creators. In addition to the frequent interviews and the occasional celebrity columns, the magazines often contain features like "A Day in the Life of Todd McFarlane" and contests where the winner is drawn into an actual comic book or gets to work for a professional studio. "I always send in my best stuff to the 'zine contests," an aspiring sixteen-year-old illustrator told me. "I'm just waiting for the day when I get a phone call from one of the big name guys asking me to fill in for them for a while. It happens all the time. Last month in *Wizard,* Jim Lee chose the top three pieces of fan art and the first one was so good that he said right in the magazine he was ready to give the guy some work if he could get out to San Francisco on his own."

Over the last two or three years comic book readers have begun to rely on electronic bulletin boards (BBSs) as a new form of communication. Indeed, in the 1990s comic books have become increasingly high-tech with experimental marketing ventures including interactive comics software and CD-ROM comic discs (see Jensen 1994). A surprisingly large number of the readers I spoke with claimed to use the comics BBSs at least once a week to discuss stories, gossip, and comics-related topics. Logically, this segment of comic book readers is heavily skewed toward those from higher-income households as internet communication is dependent on having regular access to a computer and modem.

Part of the popularity of comic book BBSs is likely due to the fact that they allow readers who do not want to be perceived as stereotypical fans to still partake in a discussion of their interests. "Over the computer is a great way to discuss comics with other fans," one middle-aged reader explained. "That way I can talk to people who read the same books, hear their opinions, clarify points, find out what's coming up if they've heard anything I haven't. And best of all, nobody knows who I am on the internet. I'd be too embarrassed at my age to hang out at a convention talking comics with teenage boys." The largest and best organized of the BBSs are the comic book forums located on the American Online, CompuServe, and Genie systems. The World Wide Web also has hundreds of professional and amateur sites devoted to every conceivable aspect of the comics.[4] Each of these forums includes a long list of discussion topics that subscribers can log onto, including almost every comic book title and related areas such as "Casting Comic Book Movies," where fans can suggest who would best portray certain characters if a comic were turned into a feature film, or "Collector's Corner," where fans from across the country help each other locate hard-to-find back issues. Like the traditional fanzine, the BBSs also feature categories for fans to submit their own stories and artwork for discussion and downloading by other fans.

One of the main attractions of the computerized BBSs for fans is that they provide another link of communication between the readers and the comic book creators. Industry professionals often make guest appearances on the large networks to discuss their past and future projects. Fans can ask unmediated questions, offer suggestions, point out failings, and sometimes even lobby for work. Other professionals, like Milestone Media's editor in chief Dwayne McDuffie, habitually log onto the system for enthusiastic chats with the readers. "I've always been into computers so I thought that the internet would be a great way to stay in touch with our fans and have a little fun at the same time," McDuffie said. "[I]t's great to hear what people think about the stories as soon as they hit the stands, and the feedback is important—not definitive, mind you, because a lot of the fans who are active on the Boards are older and have different interests from our core audience—but it does let us know when we've really struck gold and when we've really blown it." As an added bonus, some of the publishers will offer free previews of story lines and art work for subscribers to download. Occasionally, comments regarding the work are solicited by the publishers directly; and indirectly, the potential popularity of the comic is indicated by the amount of attention it attracts and how often an image or story is downloaded.

In addition to commercial publications, fan networking, and the local comic specialty store, the comic book convention, "comicon," or simply "con" is another major focal point of modern fan culture. Cons range in size from the monthly regional ones that attract anywhere from a few hundred to a few thousand fans to the annual "super cons" that last from two to fourteen days and attract tens of thousands of fans from around the world. The bible of comic book collectors, *The Overstreet Price Guide,* describes cons as an event where

Dealers, collectors, fans, whatever they call themselves can be found trading, selling, and buying the adventures of their favorite characters for hours on end. Additionally if at all possible, cons have guests of honor, usually professionals in the field of comic art, either writers, artists, or editors. The committees put together panels for the con attendees where the assembled pros talk about certain areas of comics, most of the time fielding questions from the assembled audience. At cons one can usually find displays of various and sundry things, usually original art. There might be radio listening rooms; there is most certainly a daily showing of different movies, usually science fiction or horror type. Of course there is always the chance to get together with friends at cons and just talk about comics; one also has a good opportunity to make new friends who have similar interests and with whom one can correspond after the con. (Overstreet 1989, A-53)

As Overstreet's description indicates, cons often appeal to a much wider range of fandom than just the comic book enthusiast, they also incorporate film and paperback literature fans and role-playing gamers. What must be kept in mind is that devoted fans tend to participate in several fan communities at the same time. Thus, the cultural negotiation that is conducted within the comic fan community can be somewhat extrapolated to include fans of other media and other genres. The con is seen by many fans as an individual's final point of entry into the social order of comic culture. Because the cons are the largest and the most dynamic experience possible in comics fandom many of the fans refuse to consider anyone who has not attended a con as a fan at all. In fact, no matter how knowledgeable a fan may be, he is open to the criticism of being a "con virgin" until he has experienced a major convention. The con is a place for fans to accumulate and demonstrate their cultural knowledge of comics. It is the market place of fandom's cultural economics.

According to comics historian Ron Goulart (1991), the earliest American comic book conventions were modest affairs held in privately owned lofts in New York City's Greenwich Village around the mid-1960s. By 1968 local enthusiasm for the events had apparently grown to the point where Phil Seuling (who was also instrumental in developing the direct distribution market) was able to organize the first annual Comic Art Convention, a four-day event held at the New York Statler Hilton and featuring such notable talents as Bill Everett, Jack Kirby, Jim Steranko, Gardner Fox, Gil Kane, and Joe Kubert. Borrowing from the established tradition of science fiction conventions (see Sanders

1991), North American comic cons—and also by the early 1970s British and European cons—quickly expanded into a lucrative business with several organizations competing to sponsor large cons in major cities and regional cons in smaller towns. Following Seuling's lead, most conventions feature appearances by industry professionals (with the size and status of the event reflected by the popularity of the guest attendees), discussion panels focusing on diverse comics-related themes, from "how to break into the industry" to "who is faster, Superman or the Flash?" and of course numerous dealers with back issues and rare comic books for sale. Today the largest and most respected American super cons are held each summer in San Diego and Chicago, each featuring top-name talents for autograph signings and attracting thousands of enthusiasts from around the world. In France, where comics have attained a higher degree of respectability among the general public than in North America, for a week every January the town of Angouleme is given over to a celebration of comics that attracts a staggering three hundred thousand people and has been described as "the Cannes of Comics." If the comics specialty store has become the church of comic book fans, the super cons have become their Mecca.

A super con, such as the twentieth anniversary of the Chicago Comic Book Convention, which took place over Independence Day weekend in the summer of 1995, is similar to a regional con but with every activity heightened to almost hysterical extremes. As an unaccustomed attendee to the Chicago convention, which was held in the expansive Rosemont Convention Center, I was initially surprised by the sheer volume of people and activities. Making my way from the overcrowded parking lot, through the lobby, and into the long line of visitors waiting to pay their admission and pick up a complimentary bag of assorted freebies, I was constantly surrounded by small groups of mostly adolescent males eager to scout out the various galleries. Some of the conventioneers were better prepared for the experience than others. Standing in line, I noticed that one young teenager in a group of five was dragging with him a dolly stacked with three large and obviously well-loaded cardboard comics storage boxes, while his friends each carried only one small spiral-bound notepad. "It's only my second time at the con," Jerry, the box carrier, explained, "so it's going to be my job to hold onto everybody's comics, the ones we brought for trading and signings and stuff, while these guys do all the running around to get the best prices on issues we need . . . I'm sorta the command central." Other visitors were armed with backpacks or briefcases full of comics and up-to-date price guides, video recorders, pocket cameras, art portfolios, and money belts. It seemed that everyone going to the con was prepared, with the exception of a few bewildered looking parents and girlfriends.

Inside, the con was divided into distinct areas for publishers' promotional booths, independent artists and small press tables, the dealers' gallery, and separate rooms for film screenings and discussion panels. Dominating the main hall were the elaborate display booths set up by Marvel, DC Comics, Dark Horse, Malibu, and the other major publishers. Each booth was a colorful design, with Marvel's and DC's featuring elaborate panels and tubing structured around oversized video screens playing clips from movies and television shows based on their characters. The main purpose of these fanciful publishers' booths is to promote their upcoming projects and to raise their recognition factor among the fans. To this end, the publishers vie for the attention of convention goers by giving away thousands of glossy posters, buttons, trading cards, and even free samples of some of their comic books. In addition to the give aways, the publishers present some of their best-known talents for autograph sessions at various times throughout the convention. Depending on the popularity of the creator, fans will line up for hours for the chance to have a book signed, artwork critiqued, or even just to exchange a few words of encouragement or criticism. Along with the opportunity to talk to some of the creators, the publishers' booths often seek fan approval and/or feedback on upcoming story lines by providing color-photocopied samples of comic books still in development that won't be seen by the general public for months.

The possible exchange of ideas and information between the publishers and the readers at the conventions is regarded by many fans as a unique possibility for actually helping to shape the stories they love. For example, at the Milestone table within the DC Comics booth, Mike, a sixteen-year-old fan, was able to argue his case to a DC public relations representative regarding the apparent impending departure of the main character Augustus Freeman, aka the alien Argus, from the *Icon* series. "They've been hinting about Icon's leaving Earth for the last few months now . . . and when I read that bit from a future story that shows him saying good-bye to Rocket and going back to his own planet, I though, Oh shit! They can't do that, can they?" complained Mike. "So I told the guy at the desk that I'd be real upset if they changed the book that much. And he told me that the series is supposed to be about Icon as a concept not as a specific character and that they were going to be experimenting with the idea of using Rocket and maybe some others as an icon. That may all be okay, I said, but it's just not the same without the Icon in the story. So we talked about it for a while, and he said that he would pass along my comments because other people said the same thing today, so maybe they'll have to rethink what they're going to do." Now it is not likely that the individual comments made by Mike or any of the other fans would directly affect a story line already put into development, nor is it likely that *Icon* writer Dwayne McDuffie ever really intended to remove the character permanently (and as it turns out, the character of Augustus Freeman returns to Earth as Icon after being away for only a few issues); but the general opinions of the fans are expressed, and they do ultimately influence the creator's understanding of the book. Most importantly, many of the fans feel that they are involved to some extent in the construction of the comics they read and are encouraged by this general aura of contribution that abounds at the cons to try further communication with the writers and artists of their favorite series.

The most active part of any convention is in the area reserved for the dealers' tables. Dozens to hundreds of comic book retailers from near and far rent four-by-twelve-foot tables from which to hawk their old and new comics, cards, and collectibles. At the Chicago comicon, just inside the doors to the hectic dealers' hall, I found Brian, the "command central" for his friends. At first glance—to the uninitiated—the auditorium looks like an overcrowded market with people fighting to get the stalls' owners to barter with them, barkers shouting about the price and quality of their merchandise, and masses of people pouring through the bins looking for that one special find. "We've been doing pretty good so far," Brian informed me. "We've already gotten most of the easy-to-find stuff at decent prices, like this issue of Wolverine I wanted that Larry got for seven dollars . . . He really soars at these kind of things. They're all out now looking through the bins for the really tough stuff." A few minutes later Larry returned and asked Brian if any of the others had found a good price for the Evil Ernie books featuring the early appearances of Lady Death. They hadn't, so Larry dashed off and then quickly reappeared with three mint comics, which he smugly told us he only paid a total of fifteen dollars for. "You really gotta know what you're doing at a con like this," he explained. "It's not like at the store where you're a regular and you can, more or less, trust the guy not to screw you on the price. Here you gotta know when they're jackin' up the price and telling you it's so hot, so you gotta buy it right away and shit. I like it [the con] 'cause I know the prices in the guides, and I know what the books are really worth and which ones are hot but not worth a lot of cash 'cause they're easy to find. I can usually talk them down once they realize I know what I'm doing." Larry ran off again as soon as he had finished clarifying how he managed to so prodigiously navigate the dealers. "Cool, huh?" Brian asked. "He's like the master of his domain this year."

But despite the flurry of events, as both Overstreet's instructional and Rodi's fictional descriptions indicate, the con is perhaps most importantly a place where fans can meet and talk. Some fans even go so far as to exchange addresses in order to further their discussions of common interests. Visitors freely exchange information and opinions with one another in an environment where they know they are safe from ridicule. "I love coming to events like this," a man in his early twenties told me. "I can really talk about the stuff I enjoy, without feeling like the other person is looking at me like I'm some kind of childish weirdo." Safe from the scorn of the outside world, a mundane world that legendary Marvel publisher Stan Lee refers to as populated by nonbelievers, fans are able to interact and thus often shift their perception of the comics themselves. Consider the two preadolescent white males I found stocking up on back issues of Milestone's *Hardware.* "We both like Static a lot and had read Hardware once or twice before during the crossovers," they explained, "but we always thought that, hey, if you want to read an Iron Man story you might as well have the original and not a rip-off. But we were talking to this older black guy at lunch—I think maybe he was a dealer or worked for one of them or something—anyway, he was telling us about how cool Hardware is now and how it's gotten away from the suit thing and into a lot of interesting stuff. So we thought that if the guy could get us hyped up by just talking about the book we better pick up some of the issues he recommended and give it another shot. Now I'm going to read it as more than just an Iron Man/Deathlok clone."

Comic book fandom is a loosely organized experience that is capable of affecting how individual readers interpret the fictional narratives. A reader's awareness of a specific text's place within the lexicon of the hundreds of different titles published every month colors his definition of that book. Fan-derived familiarity with the medium, the genre, the publisher, the writer, the artist, past story lines, behind-the-scenes gossip, and so on all come into play when reading a comic book. Even for those less visible comic book enthusiasts who participate in the individual realm of fanship rather than the communal realm of fandom, the associated knowledge and cultural rules of the fan subculture play an influential role. Whether the individual/private comic book reader agrees with, mimics, or refutes the activities of active fandom he can hardly ignore its dominant presence. The conventionalized aspects of comic book consumption often combine with each reader's unique social position to produce an informed and negotiated reading, informed of both transtextual facts (e.g., the character's back story or similar events in other comic books) and extratextual facts (e.g., historical genre references, knowledge of the creative team, or monetary value of the comic), negotiated in the sense that all of the different influences and contingencies are interpreted in relation to one another.

One of the most unusual aspects of comic book fandom is the degree of integration that exists between the fans and the small industry of professionals, or perhaps, more importantly, that this is always perceived by the fans to exist and thus directly influences their reading of the comics. Even if an individual reader has never attempted or experienced any form of contact with the pro-ducers, he is aware that this integration plays a factor and he feels that his interests, or those of other fans with similar concerns, are taken into account. Media fandom ethnographers in the cultural studies tradition have predomi-nantly linked fan subcultures to notions of marginality, disempowerment, resis-tance, and opposition. As Harrington and Bielby point out, "Henry Jenkin's poachers, Constance Penley's slashers, and Camille Bacon-Smith's fanziners, for example, are groups that ostensibly organize as alternatives to marginalized social status" (1995, 181). While comic book fans may be ridiculed and mar-ginalized as geeky fanboys by society at large, their existence is for the most part encouraged by the creators and publishers. Through contact at conven-tions and comic book specialty stores and with fanzines, electronic bulletin boards and, monthly letters-to-the-editor columns, readers can feel like active participators in the medium's construction. For comic book fans, interpretation of meaning does not necessitate a counter-hegemonic stance against mono-lithic ideologies but often a form of negotiated understanding. The exact meanings that the readers make from the texts are as diverse as the readers themselves but are also informed by the specific properties of comic book con-sumption. In the next two chapters I want to look further at the process of comic book reading as it is informed by the social infrastructure of the fan culture and also look closely at some of the actual Milestone readers and the properties that they bring with them to the text.

4

The Readers

Whereas the last chapter focused on comic book fandom as an organized activity premised on certain subcultural conventions, this chapter will address a sample of actual comic book readers. The comic book fans discussed here were chosen because they come from a variety of cultural and economic backgrounds and because they exhibit some of the most important recurring characteristics that I encountered over the course of my research; specifically, they express a sense of continuity between themselves and the comics' creators and they are experienced in a variety of the social aspects that define comic book fandom, aspects such as attending conferences and frequenting comic book specialty stores. The readers profiled here also situate their reading of comic books in relation to other media that explore common themes, hero-oriented video games, action movies, and such, all of which reveals the fans' interest in "masculine" pursuits and in comic book characters as models of masculinity. In a broader sense, this chapter is also about the need for audience studies to address how young males interact with the media in ways that do not invalidate their pleasures, under the assumption that they, unlike female consumers, are more willingly indoctrinated into a patriarchal, hegemonic standard.

As a media audience, the majority of individuals who participate in comic book fandom are clearly distinguishable by age and gender. Unquestionably, the largest bulk of comic book fans are males between the ages of eight and twenty-two. In fact, these two defining features—young age and male gender—are crucial for understanding the type of connections that exist between the readers and the media texts. The relationship between young people and the media is a constant concern. One of the fundamental beliefs of our culture is that children are innocents, susceptible to the corrupting influences of the world around them. The agents of that feared corruption have changed over the centuries from literacy and free speech to the most familiar and the most contemporary of villains: the mass media. The image of a wide-eyed child held spellbound by television, hypnotized by violent video games, or writhing in sexual ecstasy to popular music is never far from the discourse on children and the media. This popular image, a precise, symbolic shorthand, has often been used to alarming effect in relation to the supposed corrupting influence of comic books (see, for example, figs. 4.1 and 4.2). Ironically, where we fear this undivided and rapturous attention to the media on the premise that it is "doing things" to young minds, it is the same sort of devoted attention that we would reward children for if it occurred in school. Of course we usually do not think of education as brainwashing; school is good, but popular culture is different— popular culture is *bad*.

"Many parents I know have similar feelings," wrote David Denby in a re-cent cover story for the *New Yorker*, "and quite a few are surprised by the depths of their ambivalence and in some cases misery on the subject . . . upset by the way popular culture in all its forms has invaded their homes, and the habits, manners, and souls of their children . . . And a few parents I know have given themselves over to bitter rage and are locked in an unwinnable struggle to shut out pop culture and the life of the streets—the two are now indistin-guishable—from their children's experience" (1996, 48). Despite Denby's inac-

4.1   A 1950s child reading a comic book. "Boy reading Menace," Associated Press, September 30, 1954 (World Wide Photos).

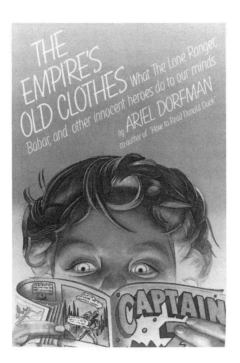

4.2   The Empire's Old Clothes

curate conflation of popular culture and the life of the streets—the two are by their very definitions separate facets of the modern urban experience—he does explicitly voice a fairly common conservative and neoliberal concern that is usually dressed up by politicians in the rhetoric of reestablishing an idealistic culture of "family values." That these romanticized, good old family values never really existed in the first place is irrelevant to the social and political agenda of saving innocent children from the evils of the media machine. Under the guise of protecting innocent young children, adults have always looked for scapegoats, outside forces to which we can point and say, "See, that's the real problem. That's what is making our kids different from us!" Our society's current fears about rap and hip-hop music, the *Mighty Morphin Power Rangers* and *Sailor Moon* television programs, and the unknown evils of the internet are not new; they are merely a modern version of the same fears that previous generations expressed about the printing press, newspaper, and radio (see Starker 1989). It should be clear by now that the comic book industry has been subjected to the same sort of accusations which are leveled at all media for supposedly corrupting young, innocent minds.

The fear that the media are doing terrible things to our children has lead to countless projects, each trying to study how the media affect young consumers. More than with any other audience group, when it comes to children and the media the stilted old model of the hypodermic needle is brought into play. The hypodermic model is a crude theory of media effects; it assumes that a whole array of harmful values and ideas are directly injected into a passive audience. On almost any given day in North America one can pick up a newspaper and find some article about the dangers of the media or some parent's fear that the media are really behind what is "wrong with kids today." Thus, most research into the topic of media and children can be roughly lumped together under the heading of *effects* research. The other side of the coin, the side that has been largely ignored, the side that might shine a much more revealing light on the place of media in late-twentieth-century culture, would be research concerned with the way that children relate to and use the media. As David Buckingham writes in the introduction to *Reading Audiences: Young People and the Media,* one of the few works to directly confront these issues, "[T]here has been very little attempt to investigate the ways in which young people use these media, and the meanings and pleasures they derive from them" (1993b, 5). This is precisely the premise of my research here, to investigate the way that young male readers use a particular set of comic books to construct meanings and to derive personal and social pleasures.

Much of the work centered on youth and media use, whether it follows the hypodermic model or not, is also concerned with exploring the gender divisions that seem so apparent in children's media. Youth-oriented media texts are generally regarded as extremely effective agents of socialization, particularly when it comes to teaching the roles and the standards of culturally appropriate gender behavior. For the most part, the media teach little girls to be passive, frail, dependent, and beauty conscious, while, conversely, the media teach little boys to be active, tough, independent, and aggressive. *Think Barbie versus G.I. Joe.* Although different media are criticized for different reasons, the gender divide is represented fairly evenly throughout. As far as reading is concerned, this gender-based division is both constructed by and reflected in the traditional split between girls' and boys' literature. For girls there are romances, melodramas, and other relationship-based stories, while for boys there are science fiction, military, and other action-adventure stories. In her historical survey of the gender differences in children's literature, Elizabeth Segel points out that adults impose and foster gendered divisions in reading preferences: "The publisher commissioning paperback romance for girls and marketing science fiction for boys, as well as Aunt Lou selecting a fairy tale collection for Susie and a dinosaur book for Sam, are part of a powerful system that operates to channel books to or away from children according to their gender" (1986, 165). Where the books deemed suitable for girls dealt with interpersonal relationships and domestic elements, Segal argues, the books for boys were the exact opposite: "The boys' book was, above all, an escape from domesticity and from the female domination of the domestic world . . . Boys' books are the epitome of freedom in part because they are an escape from women, the chief agents of socialization in the culture" (171). Although Segel does not mention comic books specifically, they are still a clear example of this socialized gender division. For girls there are such popular romance-oriented series as *Young Romance, Archie,* and, in Britain, *Jackie,* while the comics for boys, the ones that dominate the market, take as their chief concern costumed superheroes, secret agents, cowboys, and detectives.

This institutionalized split in reading types has long-lasting effects beyond the genders' traditional preferences for different literary genres. In essence, boys and girls are socialized to read for different things and in different ways. The argument, put forth most succinctly in the collection *Gender and Reading,* is that men learn to read from a goal-oriented perspective whereas women learn to read from a more social perspective (Flynn and Schweickart 1986, in particular see the chapters by Flynn, Schibanoff, Suleimen, Fetterly, and Bleich),. Just as some popular linguists, such as Deborah Tannen (1994), characterize men's speech as "report" talk—direct, functional—and women's speech as "rapport" talk—social, supportive—there is a similar demarcation of men's and women's reading patterns. Men are seen as reading on a more individualistic basis, following an authorial voice and attending to the narrative as a linear form of communication, as a chain of information, all in an attempt to get the story straight. Women, on the other hand, are thought by such analysts as the ones cited above from *Gender and Reading* to read primarily as a social experience. They perceive the narrative not as a chain of events but as a world to be entered and explored; often untethered by the singular voice of the author, they are more reflective and engage with the book in a sort of dialogue or conversation in which they can be active contributors. As David Bleich found in his study of gender-based reading patterns, women relate to a narrative "as if it were an atmosphere or an experience . . . without strict regard for the literal warrant of the text, but with more regard for the affective sense of the human relationships in the story" (1986, 256). In this regard, the male type of reading has been institutionalized as the proper or academic way to read a text, while the female type of reading has remained on the periphery as a less legitimate form of reading. Because women's pleasure in reading has been marginalized, both in the way they read and what they read, they have often resorted to creating their pleasures where they can within the text. Women's reading has been characterized through its necessity to rewrite the texts in ways that serve women's own interests in the face of a male-dominated culture, for example, in imaginatively developing romantic subplots or concentrating on the lives of minor characters. This gender division in reading has gone a long way in explaining the practices of a number of female fan communities that actively relate to media texts. The female reader and the media fan, whether male or female, both read the text as a social world in which they can be involved.

The female reader of media texts, the female fan, has become remarkably visible over the course of the last two decades. A wide range of studies have explored the ways that the media socialize women and the ways that women use the media for their own ends. Female comic book readers are no exception to this trend. There have been an impressive number of studies which have taken young female readers and romance comics as their subject. Unfortunately, most of them are concerned with British comic books; still their findings can shed quite a bit of light on how girls relate to comic books generally. Among the most notable has been Angela McRobbie's ongoing research on *Jackie* and its readers (1981, 1982a, 1991); this has been joined by other similar studies of girls and their comics by Walkerdine (1984), Willinsky and Hunniford (1986), Frazer (1987), and Moss (1993). It is not my intention to review this body of work here (for a discussion of this work on romance comics see Barker 1989, chaps. 7, 8, and 10). I have not done research explicitly on female comic book readers, nor on romance comics. In fact, romance comics have all but disappeared on the North American market and would be extremely difficult to study today. What I do want to point out by mentioning these studies is that they outnumber any comparable works on male comic book readers, despite the much larger number of boys who read comic books. This bias seems especially curious since the entire comic book medium, in both North America and Great Britain, is primarily geared toward its established male audience.

The work conducted by McRobbie, Walkerdine, Frazer, Moss, and others about girls who read romance comics is premised on a feminist approach that seeks to expose the presentation of limiting gender-based stereotypes *and* to validate female pleasures in media use. This focus is similar to many of the ethnographic-based accounts emerging from the field of cultural studies in the last decade and a half. When, in her 1980 essay "Settling Accounts with Subcultures: A Feminist Critique," McRobbie first accused Paul Willis (1977) and Dick Hebdige (1979) of ignoring female members of working-class subcultures in favor of emphasizing masculine activity, she defined an agenda of feminist research that would come to dominate cultural studies. McRobbie effectively argued that by concentrating solely on the male members of Willis's working-class "Lads" and Hebdige's "Punks," both studies, in effect, contributed to the hegemonic norm that devalues and silences feminine subjectivity. As cultural studies' ethnographic project shifted from youth subcultures to media audiences it became an increasingly fertile ground for feminist scholars to cultivate. The convergence of female media users as subject, ethnography as method, and feminism as theory has proven a perfect fit for demonstrating one of the central political theses of feminism, which is to show, as Sherry Ortner has put it, "how practice reproduces the system, and how the system may be changed by practice" (1984, 154). In other words, feminist-based research on media audiences has repeatedly justified women's pleasure in relation to such traditionally "female" genres as soap operas and romantic fiction by illustrating the various ways that they use the texts to understand and to counter the female position within a misogynistic culture.

Thus, due to the politically and personally motivated enthusiasm of feminist scholars and the wealth of fascinating female audience groups, the most notable cultural studies works in the 1980s and early 1990s have generally been those which concentrated on how women use media texts strategically in their daily lives. Among these are the landmark studies conducted by Brundson (1981), Hobson (1982), Modleski (1984), Radway (1984), Ang (1985), Walkerdine (1990), Lewis (1990), Bacon-Smith (1992), and D'Acci (1994), to name just a few. Since women have long occupied positions of social subordination on several levels—within the home, at work, in media representation—these academic studies of women audiences have been tantamount to an emancipation of female pleasures and textual practices. It has become common wisdom in the field that women can, and do, draw their own meanings from popular culture rather than automatically accepting patriarchal/hegemonic ideology, no matter how blatant or appealing the package seems to be. While these studies (and numerous others similar to them) clearly demonstrate the ways that audiences actively resist or evade being hegemonically situated by mass media texts, I am always struck by how narrowly defined the field has become in their wake. Given the diversity and the sheer number of media texts that women must contend with in Western culture, the repeated investigation of the female audiences for soap operas, romantic fiction, and *Star Trek* seems rather limiting.

Moreover, aside from the dogged investigation of a few core media genres, I am concerned that this emphasis on female audiences validates the agency of one gender at the expense of another. As Ien Ang has recently pointed out, "[M]ost research that sets out to examine gender and media consumption has concentrated exclusively on *women* audiences" (1996, 177, italics in original;

also see van Zoonen 1991). The unequal investigation of female audiences might also run the risk of perpetuating some of the very misconceptions that feminist theory originally set out to resolve. Firstly, by extrapolating from the activities of a select group of fans to the media consumption of women in general, the individualities of different lived experiences is effaced for women. And secondly, the repeated emphasis on exclusively female audience members can become problematical if women are then dialogically constructed as the *other* sex, the one that needs investigation, the one that is deviant, thus leaving men as the norm, as the yardstick against which women are measured. But my main trepidation about the lack of men's audience studies is that where women have been emancipated from the assumption of ideological *dupism,* men have been more or less ignored because their pleasures are seen not to be in need of rescuing, as the dominant beliefs seem to serve their interests. The danger is that this split along gender lines tends to authenticate the harmful assumption that male audiences are beneath careful consideration, and to confirm the belief that all men simply read along with the text and gladly let themselves be indoctrinated into a self-serving, hegemonic order. Where female pleasures in media use have been validated, there has been, by exclusion, a parallel invalidation of male pleasures. I do not think that any of the feminist-based research on audiences meant to reduce gendered media use to the level of *women as active resisters* and *men as complicit dupes,* but there has been a tendency for the overall understanding of audiences to drift into this sort of essentialism.

In fact, until very recently, there has been little investigation of male audiences. What we do know about male audiences is primarily centered on the consumption practices of homosexual men. It is interesting work, but polemically it unintentionally aligns gay men with women (an alignment that has frustrated the gay movement for decades) and marks them as deviant others. Martin Barker echoed some of the concerns I express here when he wrote of the female audience bias in cultural studies: "I am interested in the *absence of any equivalent* [studies outlining how women negotiate dominant constructions of femininity] *for men and boys.* It is curious to ask why it is nigh on impossible to imagine a parallel study of, say, soft porn, violent adventure or sports stories, arguing that men's pleasure in these genres is not evidence of their textual subordination or ideological construction; rather it reveals the ways in which men have to negotiate with dominant constructions of masculinity—or even of femininity—and through fantasy cope with the stresses and demands of living out those constructions" (1993, 160, italics in original). Barker is right to point out that there has been a notable absence of any equivalent studies of liberating media use for men or boys. Things are, perhaps, changing in the 1990s with scholars like Ang and Hermes calling for more equilateral research: "we would argue that it is now time to develop a mode of understanding that does more justice to variability and precariousness in the ways in which gender identities—feminine and masculine subjectivities—are constructed in the practices of everyday life in which media consumption is subsumed" (1991, 142). There is a growing field of literature concerned with *images of men* in the mainstream media, especially in films (see Cohan and Hark 1993; Bingham 1994a), but not much has been written about men as active negotiators of cultural texts.

The kind of emancipatory work performed on behalf of female audiences is almost unthinkable for male audiences because male audiences are seen, almost by definition, as not requiring any justification for their pursuits. Since Western culture is still rooted in a decidedly patriarchal system, masculine subject positions are still regarded as unassailable positions which merely reproduce hegemonic standards. Where recent feminist theorists have gone so far as to find subversive and empowering traits in what were previously regarded as some of the most conformist of gender-specific behavior, such as women's use of cosmetic surgery (Davis 1991) and makeup (Radner 1989), it is hard to imagine resistance-based theories applied to specifically "male" activities. As perhaps the most obvious of "men's media use," pornography is a good example of the a priori limitations that male-oriented audience studies might face, limitations that a similar female audience study would not face. To my knowledge, Andrew Ross's (1989) call for a similar audience-based study of pornography as a traditional "men's genre" has never been answered. Perhaps the closest we have come are such autobiographical accounts of academic and presumably liberal men found in texts like *Men Confront Pornography* (Kimmel 1989). It is almost impossible to imagine an audience-based study of men using pornography that might in any way parallel past studies of women using romantic fiction. In fact, the only audience-based studies, of which I am aware, that justify pornography use as a source of personal liberation and political agency have been conducted with women (see Loach 1993) and with gay men (see Burger 1995). Any straight men who use pornography, the assumption seems to be, must be doing so in a self-serving manner that exploits women and perpetuates patriarchal norms. I am aware that there have been a number of pro-pornography writings, by both men and women, that argue for positive aspects of male pornography use; but these have always remained in the realm of the *theoretical*, perhaps because writers are apprehensive of the obvious and the writings are hard to defend against the criticisms—"Of course real men *say* they don't use pornography in a sexist manner!"—that an audience study would be subjected to.

I feel that disadvantaging how real male audiences use media texts which

are commonly defined as "men's genres" is to run the risk of merely perpetuating gender stereotypes. Just as feminine subjectivities should never be assumed, neither should masculine ones. Mainstream masculinity is not a stable,
consistent position against which other subject positions can be deconstructed.
If it has been regarded as a foundation, then it is time that that foundation is
addressed. Since this study is a consideration of how a masculine audience
relates to a traditionally masculine media text, it is important to look at some
of the specific readers upon whom my research is based and to look at some
of the ways that they approach texts of masculinity.

I met all but a very few of the fans I spoke with over the course of this
study through comic book specialty stores and at comic book conventions. The
readers discussed in this chapter are no exception. In every case I was first
introduced to these fans by the owners, or by one of the employees, at the
various stores where the fans are members. Like comic book fans often joke,
membership has its privileges. But where they mean privileges such as substantial discounts in the cover price of a comic or access to the dealer's information
about upcoming books, for me the privilege translated into access to the members. These retailers were extremely helpful for putting me in contact with
individual fans. Usually the people working at the specialty stores were able to
introduce me to some of their customers during peak hours on Saturdays and
Wednesdays (when the week's shipment of new comics arrive). On other occasions they would go out of their way to arrange for me to meet Milestone fans
at prearranged times in the store or at conventions. This system of using the
store owners and staff as intermediaries proved more fruitful than when I initially approached comic book fans on my own. I found all of the fans more
willing to talk with me after the "gatekeepers" had given me an endorsement.

As I mentioned in the introduction, most of the interviewing for this study
was done on an informal basis. In the first few encounters I tried to administer
a verbal questionnaire, but all of the potential informants were disinterested in
this type of approach. They would suddenly turn quiet when only a few minutes before they had been boisterously arguing some small point of comics lore
with friends. When I switched to a conversational style the readers were more
willing to expand on their relationship to comic fandom. Suddenly, many of
them seemed to feel like they were "on solid ground." As one formerly reluctant informant put it, "When I'm talking comics I'm the authority." The following readers were all particularly forthcoming individuals. They do not, of
course, represent the full vicissitude of comic fandom. Comic fandom is a very
large and diverse subculture with distinct pockets of interest each fully deserv-
ing of their own study. For example, within comic fandom one could consider
various intersections, such as female readers of underground comics or adult

readers of Japanese comics meant for children. But the readers discussed here are fairly representative of the audience for mainstream superhero comics generally and Milestone comic books in particular. Each of the readers chosen for this chapter also gave voice to different areas which proved important to understanding the way fans relate to the Milestone books.

I met the first two Milestone readers, Darnell and Bruce, at the annual Chicago Comics Convention. Though both are African American fourteen year olds who live in the same downtown Chicago neighborhood and attend the same high school, they appear to be exact physical and social opposites. Darnell is tall for his age, heavily muscled, and conventionally handsome. Bruce, on the other hand, conforms to the most cartoonish of fandom stereotypes: awkward, overweight, thick glasses, bad haircut, and dressed nearly head to toe in clothes featuring the likenesses of various superhero characters. They are an odd pair to be travelling together at a comics con. Bruce admitted, "We're good friends but not all the time; at school we never hang together or nothin'." "Yeah," Darnell added, "It's not like we dis' each other when we're with our other friends, but we just kinda don't have that much else in common. We hang with different people." The only thing these two occasional friends seem to have in common is a lifelong passion for superhero comics.

Darnell has been reading comics for as long as he can remember. He describes his reading habits overall as "voracious" but confesses that over the last two years he has been reading fewer and fewer comics. "I've been busy with other stuff . . . like my sports, and I got a girlfriend now that I spend a lot of time with. She don't know about my being into comics at all . . . she thinks I'm at a baseball practice right now." Not only does Darnell keep his comic book reading a secret from his girlfriend but he also has not told anyone on his football or baseball teams about his hobby for fear that his friends will ridicule him (even though he is the captain of both teams and seems very self-confident and charismatic). "People just don't get it," Darnell explained. "They think comics are just for little kids and geeks, that if you still like them there has to be something wrong with you. It just ain't worth the grief to let them all know, I don't want my girlfriend to think she has hooked up with some Momma's boy loser. Besides [he looked sideways at Bruce, who was laughing at his insecurities], I'm more like the anti-Superman, you know, unlike mild-mannered Clark Kent, who is really Superman. I'm more like super-Darnell, who has this hidden comic book fan side as his secret identity."

For Darnell his continued enjoyment of comics is becoming increasingly problematic. He is at that stage of adolescence when he feels he needs to be careful about how his peers perceive him. Darnell's concern about his girlfriend and/or his teammates finding out that he is a closet comic book fan influences his friendship with Bruce: "It's not like I'm embarrassed of hanging out with Bruce at conventions like this, or of getting together to swap comics or anything; it's just that he doesn't fit in with the rest of my life. I'm into other things right now and I don't have as much time to obsess over comics as Bruce does. But he's pretty cool in his own way. anyhow; he's got lots of friends that I don't know, too. It's not like anyone at school really picks on him . . . Besides, if they did, I'd kick their ass. It does look kinda weird to people already; I mean, lots of them know we are friends but they don't really know why. It's a secret what we do together, but I guess I'll have to confess soon or get out of comics altogether because I don't want people thinking we're fags or something." Though Darnell intended his comment about his secret relationship with Bruce and his hidden passion for comics being mistaken for homosexuality as a joke, it does suggest a concern with presenting a proper masculine persona, a concern which parallels what is perhaps the most fundamental feature of superhero comics: their explicit function as role models for young male readers.

In fact, although Darnell is self-conscious about his continued interest in superhero comic books, he is clear that for him part of their allure is the characters' status as unqualified role models. "The other day in English class we had to write a short piece on who our favorite role model is. I think my teacher was really surprised that I didn't pick a football player or a baseball player or any other athlete; she just assumed that because I'm a jock all my heroes would be famous sports stars. I didn't go that way though. I chose Batman as my favorite role model and wrote about him and all the good things he stands for." For Darnell, characters like Batman represent an untarnished heroic model that far exceeds any real-life personalities. "Lets face it," he explained, "most of the millionaire sports stars that they market as role models are actually full of problems—sooner or later it always comes out that they have huge drug habits or that they beat their wives or that they really couldn't give a shit about the fans. But with characters like Batman and Icon you never have that problem . . . and because they are fictional you know you never will."

In a very self-aware manner Darnell continues to read comics for the values embodied in his favorite characters. "Honesty," "self-sacrifice," "upholding justice," and "defending the less fortunate" were all features that he identified as essential to his being attracted to a character. "These just aren't things you find with sports heroes. So a guy runs for a bunch of yards in a game, or hits a couple of home runs, it doesn't really make them a hero in my books. At the end of the day they're getting a big fat pay check. Let me see them doing some charity work that isn't just for good public relations and then maybe I'll call them a role model. Don't get me wrong. I'm sure a lot of them are great guys, but to make them out as perfect role models is asking too much of any real person. If I want a perfect person to try and live up to, I'd pick Icon any day." For Darnell the altruism and the strict moral code observed by the fictional heroes is an ideal to strive for in his own life. "I know they aren't real, and I know it is impossible to live my life like that. But I figure why not set the bar really high; then if I even get partway there I'll be doing great."

Where Darnell is able to pinpoint his current interest in superhero comic books in relation to the ideal role models represented by the fictional characters, for his friend Bruce this sort of precision is not as simple. Bruce is, by his own enthusiastic admission, completely caught up in the world of comics and comic book fandom. Although he has favorite characters who form the foundation of his interest in comics, he is equally enamoured of the culture of fandom. He faithfully attends every convention in the Chicago area and frequents three different comic book specialty stores on a regular basis and dozens of others at irregular intervals. He is an avid collector who proudly mentions his extensive collection to anyone who cares to listen (he currently has twenty full comic book boxes at home, each holding approximately one hundred comics). Bruce tries to wear at least one piece of clothing every day with a comics character on it. He says he cannot remember when or why he started reading comic books; it has always been a part of his life and he believes it always will be. Unlike his friend Darnell, Bruce is passionate about his involvement with comics and doesn't care who knows it.

Bruce is so active in the Chicago area comics community that most of the store owners know him by name and many of the younger fans will ask him to recommend back issues that they might enjoy. In fact, it is not just a cliche when Bruce announces, "Comics are my life." He does organize his school activities and social life around reading comics, going to the shops, and attending the conventions. But Bruce is also quick to point out that his passion has a purpose:

I plan to make comics my life's work. I figure I know so much about them it has to be what I'm meant to do. The only difference is where a lot of these guys here [at the convention] want to become professional artists or writers, I intend to open up my own mega-store in just a couple of years. I've worked in a couple of stores, and Lord knows I've been a customer in enough of them to know what will really work. I know what books to order and how many so that I don't over extend my operating costs. I already have enough back issues in my personal collection to stock a good-size store and I think I've got a good enough reputation that I'd attract some serious customers right off the bat. Yep, when everyone else drones off to community college in a couple of years I'm going to be getting a youth business loan to open up my own store. I just don't have a really cool name for it yet.

For Bruce then, his attentive reading and rereading of comics, his tracking of "hot" books and price changes, his familiarity with the careers of specific writers and artists, and his interest in market trends is focused around his desire not just to enjoy the stories but also to succeed in the business side of fandom. It is impossible to tell if his career plans will work out, or even if they are really plans or just a rationale for what outsiders might consider a ridiculous devotion to comic books. Darnell teases Bruce that his dream of opening his own comics store is merely an excuse to "geek out" over comics and not be ridiculed for spending so much time and money on them.

"Maybe I am a stereotypical fanboy," Bruce admitted. "Personally, I don't see that as a bad thing, and if others do, so what? Fuck 'em. It's what I like to do and if they have a problem with it tough luck." Bruce embraces his immersion in comics fandom. In many ways he sees himself as romantically nonconformist in comparison to his peers. "I at least have the convictions to like what I like and not care what everyone else thinks. A lot of people at school aren't really into the music they buy or the movies they go to; they just do it because their friends do, 'cause they think it will make them look cool. I buy comics cause I like them—end of story." Bruce is so involved with his passion for comics, including his activities within the world of fandom, that it constitutes a defining feature of his self-image. He is known at school and in his neighborhood as "the comics guy" and that suits him fine.

It doesn't come as much of a surprise that Bruce's favorite comic book of the moment is Milestone's *Static.* Even Bruce admits that the parallels between himself and the character Virgil Hawkins/Static are what initially drew him to the book. "Yeah, yeah, of course I love the series. The hero is a black teenager from a major city who is into comics and role-playing games and is sometimes considered odd by some of the jerks at school. The only difference between Virgil and me is that he got lucky and woke up with superpowers one day. Doubt that's going to happen to me, but there is definitely that-wouldn't-it-be-cool factor when I'm reading the book. I could handle having electrical powers." In fact, the wouldn't-it-be-cool factor is obviously fundamental to the enjoyment experienced by many comic book fans right through adolescence. The identification that is fundamental to the readers who imagine themselves as supermen through the stories is especially apparent with Bruce in the case of Static. Rather than a generic everyman of the Clark Kent variety, the character of Virgil Hawkins so closely parallels Bruce's real-life situation and personality that it facilitates his fantasies of empowerment.

Unlike Darnell's attention to the values embodied by characters like Icon as ideal standards of personal conduct to strive for, Bruce relates to Virgil Hawkins/Static on a more immediate level. "When I'm reading *Static* it's like I'm right in there with the story. I lose sight of the art and the ads and the writers and just sort of play along. It's a lot of fun! I imagine what I would do in the situations if I had powers like Static's. It's like role playing but cooler because you're not limited by the roll of the dice. And, quite honestly, some of the solutions I come up with are even cooler than the ones Static does." Where for Darnell the characters represent a future goal, for Bruce they, especially Static, represent a fantastical identity that he can imagine occupying right now. Though reading for slightly different things, these two friends both consciously relate to comics as ways to shape their own identities.

Thomas is seventeen years old. He lives in a middle-class suburban home with his parents and his two younger brothers, Dave, fifteen, and Peter, eleven. Both of Thomas's parents are first generation immigrants. His father is a contractor from Jamaica, and his mother, originally from northern Africa, works part-time in an auto parts office. Thomas has a lot of close friends, many of whom do not share his enthusiasm for comic books and a few who do. "Some of my friends who aren't into comic books tease me sometimes," Thomas explained. "But the rest of us just ignore them. So long as I enjoy them I'm not going to give up collecting any of my favorite titles."

Thomas began reading comic books as a school activity when he was in second grade and has always associated comics with learning. Although Thomas now refuses to mix his enthusiasm for comics with school for fear that high school teachers might ridicule his choice of reading materials, he does attribute his good grades to the reading skills he developed from comic books. Like almost all of the high school kids who are still serious comic book fans, Thomas has always seen his interest in comics as more worthy than interests of his non-comic-book-reading friends because it involves *reading*. For Thomas, reading comics is a sign of his intelligence.

We had a really cool teacher [in second grade]. He always kept lots of books around the classroom for us to read. A lot of these were comic books and he encouraged us to read them. I always thought it was so cool that he would let us read comics in school; not a lot of teachers would allow that. In fact, I remember him letting me take some of the comics home so that I could become a better reader. It's not that I was stupid or anything, I just wasn't all that great a reader. I think I was bored by all those little kiddie books they made us read most of the time. Anyway, I really got into the comics he had and began reading them every day. By the end of the year I tested the highest in the class for reading skills. I was reading stuff that was meant for kids in the fifth grade. While all the other kids were just playing video games or listening to music, I was *reading* things. I don't care what people may say about comics being stupid, they're not. In fact. they're a lot more sophisticated than some of the stuff they used to make us read. If I'm a good student, and I am, it's 'cause of comics.

After his initial introduction to comics, Thomas gradually began to pursue comic books outside of the classroom as well. Initially, he recalls, he pestered his parents to buy him comics from the corner drugstore, and then when he was a little older he took to spending most of his allowance on Marvel Comics at Four Colour Worlds, a comic book specialty store that opened not far from his home. For Thomas the specialty store was his first foray into the world of comics fandom, a world which he had read about in the letters columns of his favorite series but had never experienced firsthand. The discovery of other individuals with a similar devotion to comic books further ensconced Thomas's interest in the medium and refigured his relationship with comics from an individual pursuit to a social experience.

I couldn't believe it. I had been buying comics at the Mac's Milk near my school, but the pickings were pretty slim. They had a fair number of DCs and a few Marvels, but some weeks they would have four issues of *The Amazing Spider-Man* all at the same time and then you wouldn't see another one for a couple of months. There were lots of times that I would read a cliff-hanger and then never be able to find the next issue to find out what happened. Then my dad told me about a new store called Four Colour Worlds, which opened up not far from our house. I was in awe! All these new comics every week without missing an issue. It was great! Plus they were all at U.S. cover price, which was a real bonus.1 John [the store's owner] really knew his stuff. He started pulling books for me before I even knew what it meant, and he introduced me to a few of the other fans who were into the same titles I was. Man, it was great to talk to other guys who were into comics. We would run into each other at the store every Saturday and shoot the shit about the comics we had read the week before . . . you know, which ones were good, which ones sucked, who the best artist was, could Wolverine beat up the Hulk, stuff like that. It changed the way I read comics; now I had to be more careful 'cause I knew I'd be talking about them with other fans and I wanted to make sure I got it right.

For Thomas, getting it "right" seems to mean understanding the story in its full complexity. He needs to comprehend all of the narrative possibilities so that he can discuss not just that single story, but, as he puts it, ". . . everything that everyone else might see, including what the writer meant, what it might mean for future stories, what I would do in a situation like that, or what other characters might do." Thomas's reading of the text is now influenced by extra-textual factors that emerge from his growing involvement in fandom.

Thomas kept his comic books in pristine condition even before discovering the world of fandom through his local comic book store. He never folded them, tore them, or discarded them the way many young comics readers do before they adopt the collector's mentality that is so prevalent in comics fandom. Today, Thomas has an impressive collection of mint-condition comic books, all safely bagged with acid-free backing boards and stored in a dozen long cardboard boxes. Though he has never actually counted them all, Thomas estimates his collection to consist of about a thousand comics. He desperately wants his parents to buy a home computer so that he can list all his comics in a specially designed database which would allow him to keep an accurate account of their value, ostensibly for insurance purposes but also, he confides, for bragging rights. For a time Thomas achieved a great deal of status within the small community of fans who frequented Four Colour Worlds:

One time, not long after I got to know him, John paid me to help him man a booth at a local comic con. My friends were pretty impressed because you really gotta know your stuff to do that and not get ripped off. All these guys are trying to shit you and tell you that that book isn't worth the sticker price, but I knew what I was doing—knew when to sell a comic below guide price, when to sell it above.2 By this time I was spending more time talking about the books than I was reading them and I realized some people thought me a real authority. I still remember the time this guy, Scott, asked me to explain an issue of *The Uncanny X-Men* to him. It is a complicated series, so it was understandable. He wanted to make sure he had gotten all the references to other stories, so he confirmed it all with me. I enjoyed that, it was the first time someone came to me because I was an expert on something.

In fact, I first made contact with Thomas through a clerk at Four Colour Worlds, which is a relatively small, family-run comics store. Until recently, Thomas was very active as a fan, even tried his hand at writing original comic book stories, and became known to the store's regular customers as a friendly and knowledgeable comics expert. Thomas, like most regular comic book readers, detests the stereotype of fans as ''geeky losers.'' But he also will admit to being a fairly hard-core fan. ''Three or four years ago I was much more into it than I am now. I would never miss an issue of any of my titles, no matter how broke I was, and I went to just about every con my friends and I could get to.'' Currently, Thomas has eased up on his comic book collecting because he is busy with a part-time job at a local gas station, a job he took, in part, to help support his increasingly expensive comic book habit. Still, he is always one of the first customers at the store each week when the comics arrive, and he attends at least two of the larger local comic cons a year. One of his goals is a pilgrimage to either the San Diego or the Chicago annual convention. Thomas says, ''[I want] to just go, with lots of money in my pockets and just, you know, totally geek out for a couple of days.''

While Thomas's original passion was for the comics published by Marvel, especially *Spider-Man* and all the X-something titles, he now favors ''more mature comics, like *The Sandman, Preacher*, and most of the other Vertigo titles.'' He claims to have left behind the popular superhero type of books. Those are what his younger brothers are reading now. Although there is no real evidence to back it up, Thomas fits the profile of older fans who, most retailers and comic book professionals believe, grow out of superhero fare by the age of sixteen. The sole exception to Thomas's recent embargo on super-hero comic books are those published by Milestone Media, all of which he lists among his favorite ongoing series. As Thomas explains it, his first criterion for continuing to buy any series is that it must be a "quality" title, the story must be well told and well illustrated and thus have the potential to increase in value. Thomas attributes his initial attraction to Milestone to his perception of these qualities in the Milestone books coupled with his interest in seeing substantial black characters in comics. In many ways his curiosity about Milestone may have been racially based; but, like many serious comic book fans, Thomas is quick to point out that regardless of the character's skin color he would drop the books if the stories did not meet the standards of quality that he is always watchful for since becoming involved in fandom. "As a fan who happens to be black, I couldn't resist picking up the first Milestone books after I read about them in a magazine. They're a little uneven in quality but I never miss *Icon* or *Hardware* or *Static*, and I used to really like *Xombi* before it got cancelled. They've really won me over. The stories are generally strong, although Static has gotten a little weak lately, and the art is occasionally great. I've been a fan of Dwayne McDuffie since he was writing at Marvel. McDuffie really cares about what we fans think; I mean, I've seen him pick up on things in the letter columns and include them in stories just a few months later. I've even 'talked' with him over my friend's computer during one of those American Online chat-special things. That was so cool; we really talked about what was going on in Icon."

The fact that the books had to win him over before he would add them to his *must-have* list was important to Thomas, because he takes his skills as a fan and a collector very seriously. His skills are, after all, what gain him some re-spect in the eyes of his comic book friends, not to mention his younger broth-ers. He was not willing to buy the books solely on the premise that they featured black characters. The color of the characters or the creators is not as important to Thomas as the quality of the work and the fact that the creators are sensitive to the input of fans. "Man, if I bought them *just* because they were black," Thomas explained, "that would be insulting, that would be to-kenism just as much as when Marvel and DC and everybody thought they *had* to have at least one black superhero running around." Thomas points to the fact that as a black man he was willing to give both *Purge* and *Ebony Warrior* a chance, but as a serious fan he could not justify any loyalty to series that fell well below his personal standards of quality. "It's not that they weren't trying; they get an A for effort, but the books just weren't up to snuff—spelling mis-takes, confusing art—not my style." While Thomas feels he should be supportive of positive images of black characters in comics, those characters must first be acceptable according to his fan-derived principles of quality, originality, and collectability.

In recent years, Thomas has supplemented his passion for comics with a detailed interest in other media. As with almost all of the other comics fans I met, comic books are only one of several areas of popular culture with which Thomas is involved. Unlike when he first began reading comics and looked down on other kids for being involved with non-reading-based hobbies, Thomas now sees comics as one example of his many areas of media expertise. He is also a serious fan of rap music, video games, and independent films. In fact, Thomas has become such a serious film buff that his future goal is admission to a college with a good animation program. Not surprisingly, Thomas often uses cinematic comparisons when describing comics: "I can just picture Static as a big budget movie, maybe starring that kid who was in *Fresh*. Get him to grow some dreds and he'd be great. The special effects would have to be cool, like in that *X-Files* episode where the guy was sort of a human lightning rod. I can picture it now. Of course I'd be the ideal director—ha, ha—but all the flying stuff can be done now in really believable ways and the costumes could be like those kevlar suits they use in the *Batman* movies."

Thomas now sees his relation to comics primarily through the lens of a film fan. "I still enjoy the adventure of books like *Icon* and *Static*—the wouldn't it be cool if I could fly and do all that superhero stuff kind of fantasies—but I look at them more like little movies . . . you know, like action movies but with costumes. I'm more into realistic heroes now, the kind you see in action movies. I know, I know, they're not realistic either, but they are probably more likely to happen than finding a magical old sword that turns me into a Greek god or something." Moreover, Thomas cites this preference for more *realistic* heroes as the reason for preferring the Milestone characters over other currently popular superheroes. "Too much of the stuff out there right now is a joke. I look at my brothers' books and they're all these ridiculously large guys, and women with *huge* tits, all running around with guns the size of cannons. I mean, come on! At least with Milestone the heroes are a little more realistic; they have the kind of personalities and the kind of problems that could really happen."

Steve is a relative newcomer to the world of comic books. He is ten and estimates that he has only been reading comics for about two years. Before getting his first comic book from a friend at school, Steve's only experience with superhero fiction was the *Batman* movies and such Saturday morning kids programs as *The Teenage Mutant Ninja Turtles*, *The X-Men*, *The Mighty*

Morphin Power Rangers, and *Batman: The Animated Series*. Steve lives with his mother, Sarah, a restaurant manager, and his older sister, Judy, in a two-bedroom apartment on the outskirts of New York City. Steve's father left when he was three years old and they have not heard from him since.

Steve knows that his mother does not approve of his reading comic books. She thinks it will hurt his grades. She also fears that it will keep him from meeting more children and from getting out of the apartment more. Although he is blessed with a good sense of humor and is very polite, Steve is also an extremely shy boy. He has few close friends, avoids social activities, and is most content when he can find some privacy in the small apartment and closet himself away to read for a few hours. Steve's use of comic books fits well with his solitary tendencies. One day he proudly informed me that he has never read a comic book just once, he always reads it right through two times in a row and then rereads and rereads favorite scenes until he has them memorized. Then, if he owns the book, he will often reread the entire story again on later dates. "I read my comic books a lot. You could pick any comic I have and I can tell you exactly what it's about. I used to read them so much that they would fall apart. The staples would fall out or I'd bend the covers back until the whole book stayed rolled up like a tube when I put it away. Now I'm more careful, I try not to put creases in the comic or to tear the pages. I want to have a good collection in case I sell it one day. I even put them in bags when I get the chance. But I still read them at least twenty times before I buy another comic."

Like many comic book fans, particularly those who are in the younger half of the spectrum (from about five to twelve), any superhero comic is of interest to Steve. Most fans limit themselves to a specific genre, in this case the superhero genre, but read a wide variety of comics within that category. No comic book is read in isolation; it is always measured in comparison to other books which are deemed similar in some way, either due to the characters or the creators. Since he is a fairly new fan there is an incredible wealth of back issues out there that Steve is desperate to read. The family budget is limited, so Steve tries to borrow as many comics as possible from among a small group of classmates whom he knows are regular comic books buyers, and he makes sure to commit the stories to memory before he returns them. Contrary to his mother's fear that comic book reading will isolate Steve from friends his own age, it actually has helped him create a new circle of friends. "I especially like *Spawn* and *Superman* and *Static*, but I don't really care. I mean I'll read any superhero stories that I can. Sometimes, if I have some Christmas money or birthday money, I just go through the discount bins looking for the cheapest books they have. There are a couple of guys in my class who read a lot of comic books, so I get them to lend me their books when they're done with them. I'm real careful with those. It's a lot of fun to read the same stories that someone you know has already read. We talk about them and argue about who the coolest characters are. Some of the other guys think it's a waste of time, but they're stupid. Most of my friends now are into comics, too."

Steve does, of course, prefer some characters over others, and he places *Static* high on his list of favorites. For Steve, his enjoyment of *Static* is directly associated with his ability to identify with the character. Steve would often make comparisons between what he sees as deficiencies in his own life and the social shortcomings that are so broadly depicted in the meek alter egos of the comic book superheroes. "If I had to choose . . . I guess I like Static the best. He's great. He has really cool electrical powers, he's funny, and he's not some boy-millionaire like Tim Drake [aka the current Robin] with a Batman to teach him stuff. I guess it's 'cause Static is closest to me. I mean, I'm not black or nothing, but I live in the same sort of house that Virgil [Static's secret identity] does, and he doesn't really fit in at school either. I don't think it's his powers though; I mean, every hero has some kind of special power and lots of them would be more fun than Static's. It'd be great to have a suit like Ironman's or to be able to stretch like Mr. Fantastic, but Static always knows what to say. That's kinda the coolest part. I'm more like Virgil; he's cool but nobody sees it until he becomes Static."

The way Steve often emphasized the parallels he perceives between his own life and that of the costumed characters he reads about makes him a textbook example of how superhero comics are *supposed* to work. He identifies with the downtrodden, mild-mannered, Clark Kent side of the characters and fantasizes about becoming a Superman. "Yeah, there are times," Steve explained, when I asked him which characters he feels the closest to, "even when I'm sitting in class, just daydreaming, when I think how great it would be if I really had electrical powers like Static, and I could fly around saving people and having people notice me, especially having the girls really notice me." For Steve, the typical superhero transformation from wimp to he-man is not simply a fantasy of power, it is also a fantasy of *attention*. As a preadolescent male it is not surprising that part of Steve's comics-inspired fantasy is to be noticed by the girls in his class. Don't most heterosexual boys approaching puberty dream of receiving more attention from the girls around them? At its most rudimentary level, in comic book terms, we might think of Clark Kent's eternal longing to be noticed by Lois Lane.

Steve's fantasy of receiving attention from the girls in his class may be one common to many young males. But Steve's comic-book-influenced fantasies of attention also expresse a need to be perceived *apart* from women, specifically his mother and sister. To Steve, comic book reading is an assertion of his own identity, of a *masculine* identity which helps him carve out his own space in a female-dominated home. Steve uses his comic books and the fantasies they inspire as a way of asserting his own autonomy. They are a critical tool in his attempts to define masculine activities and behaviors. "I think one of the reasons I like comics so much right now is because my mom and my sister hate them. I always have to watch what they want on TV, listen to the music they want to listen to, and stuff. Neither one of them likes comics, so it's one of the few things that are my own. All my friends who read comics say the same thing; their moms and their sisters think comics are stupid. If anyone in their families get it, it's their fathers or their older brothers. Only guys read comics; it's a man's thing. They are all about guys and they're for guys, so—uh—women wouldn't know how to behave in a comic anyway. They'd probably just panic and stuff. Like my friend David says, 'It's men doing manly things.' "

That the perceived masculinity of the heroes and of the medium is a key to their appeal for Steve is associated by him with the lack of adult males in his life. On three separate occasions Steve expressed a great deal of hostility toward his absent father, a hostility that seemed to revolve around the unfairness of the situation for his mother, who has to work long hours and still watch the family budget very carefully, and around leaving Steve in what he regards as an all-female apartment. Steve has no strong male presence in his life, no father, no uncles, no big brothers, and no male teachers. When I asked Steve if he ever talked to non–comic book fans about the books he reads I got an unexpected response: "Oh yeah, all the time. My mom says I'm driving her crazy when I do that. If my mom is fussing about my clothes not matching or being wrinkled I'll say something like, 'Well, you know, Mom, I don't think Batman would worry too much about *his* clothes.' Or if my sister is asking me about how her hair looks or how her makeup looks, I'll tell her, 'Guys don't care about that. Why should I care what your hair looks like? I don't think Icon would care what his sister's hair looks like.' " Rather than really talking about the comic books with his mother and sister, Steve uses the characters as a reference point for how he should behave and how he should relate to his family. The superhero characters with whom Steve has spent an increasing amount of time are the most convenient blueprint of masculinity available to him on a daily basis. In a sense, I do not think it would be too great an exaggeration to say that, at least metaphorically, the comic book superheroes have taken the place of his absent father.

Jordan is fourteen and has lived in three different cities in the past four years. His father is an army officer; his mother, a homemaker. Unlike most of the comic book fans whom I met, Jordan understands his relationship to the texts on an individual level rather than a social one. While many of the fans, like Steve, may perceive themselves as modestly awkward in social situations such as school or team sports, they still enjoy the alternate social contact that they have established through comics fandom. "Solitary" is a word Jordan often uses to describe his life. As an only child and the perennial new kid in town, Jordan feels that he rarely manages to have the social contact or the close personal bonds he would like with others his own age.

Jordan often takes comfort from his sense of social solitude by "really getting into" his comic books. It isn't that Jordan has no friends—in fact, Jordan is very personable and makes new friends easily—but that his favorite comic book characters are his best and most consistent friends. Jordan first took up comic book reading when he was seven. His dad bought him a dozen or so comic books to read in the car during a particularly traumatic cross-country relocation. "I think my dad just wanted to shut me up for a while, stop me from balling my eyes out, but I remember reading the comics . . . well, mostly *looking*, probably, 'cause I wasn't the greatest reader at that age, and just being mesmerized. Let's see, there was a couple of Spider-Mans and Super-mans, a Batman, a Teenage Mutant Ninja Turtles, and some of the X-titles. They were great. I've still got them in my collection, but they're in pretty rough shape 'cause I just kept reading and reading them." Over the years Jordan has repeatedly turned to his fictional friends for comfort: "No matter what happens, or where we move, they are always there when I need them." For Jordan, the "they" he is referring to as constant friends are both the actual comic books and the familiar characters that he visits within the pages.

As a devoted fan Jordan was able to recount for me many of the specific narratives that he cites as his favorite stories of all time. In some cases he can recite bits of dialogue or captions almost word-for-word. In addition to this precise cataloguing of canonical events, Jordan, like many fans, is also able to flesh out the lives of characters in amazing detail. No event or offhanded comment seems to be too small for attention. He knows, for example, how many buildings Bruce Wayne has donated to Gotham University in the name of his parents. And Jordan has mapped out on several pages of an old spiral-bound notebook all of the events that he knows have happened to Icon since he crash-landed on Earth in 1839. He also has filled in some of the gaps in Icon's history with events that he thinks might have possibly happened. Much of Jordan's identity—the way he sees himself as a person—is bound to the every-day qualities of the comic book characters he favors in that he consciously identifies personalities who he would like to know or who he perceives as similar to himself. In a very tangible way, Jordan seems to be interested in establishing what Ang (1985) has called the "emotional realism" of the characters, the foundational elements that allow readers to understand the text as *ringing true* to their own lives and their perception of the world.

Rather than identifying with the characters merely as role models, Jordan identifies with them as character *types* who appear authentic because they can be fleshed out by his own imagination. "I spend so much time with these guys that it's almost like getting to know them as people. And if you look around, they are like real people. They have whole personalities and I don't want to lose sight of that. It's the little things that make them real, the things that regular fans all know. Adding this stuff about Icon just helps me understand him as a person until more of his personality is revealed in the books. He is the kind of guy I'd probably like to know in real life; he's also sort of like how I'd be if I was in his situation."

Although an avid fan, Jordan has in recent years become a very discriminating collector. His principal criteria of late has been more the artist than the character or the stories. Because Jordan is an aspiring comic book artist, he has decided to closely follow the style of several of his favorite draftsmen. For Jordan, as for many other fans, the artwork in a comic is pivotal to understanding the overall feel of the story. The key distinction Jordan makes is between "scratchy lines" and "clean lines." According to Jordan, scratchy illustrations are "harsher" in tone, using thin pen lines that are not smoothed out by an inker,3 thus leaving a more ragged or angular feel to the illustration, and by extension to the story (see, for example, fig. 2.4 by Denys Cowan in chapter 2). Clean lines, on the other hand, are bolder, smoother, and less detailed, closer to a more cartoonish style and feel. As with most of the longtime fans I spoke with, Jordan stresses his ability to distinguish between individual artists based on the style they typically employ. Topping Jordan's personal list of "hot artists" are M. D. Bright, the artist on Milestone's *Icon* series, and Humberto Ramos, formerly of Milestone's *Hardware* and the current penciller on DC Comics *Impulse*.

I know everybody is into art right now—Todd McFarlane, Jim Lee, Rob Liefeld, Scott Campbell—you just can't get away from all the hype about those guys at Image; but to me they all look the same in a lot of ways, so I'm trying to follow some of the other guys who I think are underrated. My personal favorites right now are Bright and Ramos. They both have really clean lines. I'm moving away from that real scratchy look, which I used to love. When Ramos took over for Cowan on *Hardware* I thought, "Aw, shit!" Cowan's scratchy style was so distinctive I thought the art would just go down the tubes, but it didn't. If anything, it looked even better with Ramos; it had an almost graphic-design feel to it. Where M. D. Bright's work is clean in a really classic sense of superhero art, Ramos work is really stylized, kind of like Manga or Anime,4 except I can still tell the characters apart.

In a sense, Jordan's growing interest in the illustrators is a further step in the social contact he feels with the comic books themselves. The artists are, he says, "like people I actually know, I mean I read about them, what they're up to, and I check out their work every month." Furthermore, Jordan describes "the ultimate highlight of [his] life" as the day he met M. D. Bright at a convention.

I was at this big con in the states with some old friends . . . They had relatives there. It was great. We were getting some really good prices on stuff and checking out the artists' alley, where guys doing these little local books try to sell you their original art or promote their own books. I met M. D. Bright on the second day and it was amazing. He's a pretty cool guy; didn't try to shuffle me off or anything. He signed a copy of one of my *Icon* books and one from an old *Falcon* series he drew years ago that I had just bought at the con. I told him he was my favorite artist and he said it was good to meet people who could really give him some feedback on what he had been drawing . . . He took a quick look at a couple of the things I had brought from my portfolio and said I showed some promise, but that I had to work on my panel transitions5 more than just my figure drawings.6 He gave me some good tips and I was flying after meeting him. What a buzz . . . and I look for those things when I read his books now, to see how he does transitions and face expressions.

For Jordan, the creators are as much heroes as the cape-wearing characters they draw. The comics themselves provide a link between Jordan as an isolated fan who would love to become a professional artist one day and the world of current comics professionals.

Todd is eleven and a devoted fan of the Milestone line of comic books. He lives with his mother and grandparents in a small, government-subsidized home on the northern fringe of Toronto. Todd's mother, Janine, is frequently ill, and her bad health has cost her a number of part-time jobs over the last couple of years. His father lives across town, and Todd spends two weekends a month visiting him. Todd has mixed emotions about his parents' divorce. On one hand he admits to "loving them both very much," while on the other hand he complains that "their bad relationship, their divorce, is a real pain in the ass for [him]."

Todd's parents are, or rather *were*, an interracial couple. His mother is the daughter of Ukrainian immigrants, and his father, who moved to Toronto from Detroit, is African American. With his diverse cultural background, Todd seems, at times, to be struggling with the choices available to him. His father is very active in local cultural politics and has imbued Todd with a strong sense of black nationalism. "It's kind of weird," Todd explained when I first asked him about his background. "Sometimes, when I think about it, it seems almost strange. Here I am, a black man, trying to learn more about my people and my background, but I live in an all-white house with my mom and her folks. Don't get me wrong, they're great . . . but the house is full of Ukrainian pictures and religious stuff, except for my room where I have posters of Nelson Mandella and Snoop Doggy Dog." Todd feels quite literally trapped between two cultures; this may have something to do with his passion for forms of popular culture that he can readily identify as "black."

For Todd, comic book fandom is only one pursuit among many. Todd is also into rap and hip-hop music, basketball, video games, and action movies and is getting more and more interested in tagging (graffiti art). "My grandparents get mad when they see me spending all my money on CDs and comic books, but it's about things they can't understand. I don't think it's just the money; it's 'cause it's a *black thing*." Todd's embrace of popular culture forms that he defines as "black" is an important element in his continuing attempt to define cultural boundaries within his own life. They act as a mild form of rebellion against his mother's and his grandparents' influence, which he perceives as "white." In this regard the Milestone comic books make perfect sense for Todd, who unlike many of the other readers I spoke with *does* care first and foremost about the race of the characters. For Todd, his current interest in the Milestone books is a chance to renew old pleasures in a way that he feels is more culturally responsible. "I've always liked comics a lot—*Batman, Spider-Man, The X-Men*—but I was getting tired of them. I was getting into other stuff and I kinda stopped readings comics. You know, I was going to some rallies with my dad on the weekends and meeting a lot of other people, learning a lot of different things about black culture. I just didn't want to read about all these white heroes anymore, except that I did give Superman another try, for a little while, when I heard that Shaquille O'Neal is a huge Superman fan. Then I came across some article in *Vibe*7 about all the new African American comic books, and I thought 'Great!' Now I could read comic books—which I still love—and they'd be about black guys and black culture."

In addition to the entire line of Milestone books—"Except *Kobalt*, I hated *Kobalt*, not 'cause he was white but because the whole concept was tired right from day one"—Todd also lists among his favorite comic books a variety of what are generally referred to as underground black comics, including *Killer Ape, Brotherman, L.A. Phoenix,* and *Jonathan Fox*. Todd pointed out, "It's hard to find a lot of the independent titles. At least with Milestone's books I can get them at any comics store, but the other titles are pretty hard to track down. Basically, I'll take whatever black comics I can lay my hands on since there are so few to begin with." That these titles represent a wide range of cultural politics does not concern Todd. Rather than seeing them in a type of opposition, he reads them as a continuum. "I don't care much about the real specifics," Todd says. "If some are in the Malcolm X mode and some are in the Martin Luther King mode, that don't bother me none. It's like the difference between a Spike Lee movie and a John Singleton movie. Sure, they're saying different things . . . but I like them both." For Todd, reading black-oriented comic books, any black-oriented comic books, is a way to reaffirm his own identity despite surroundings that may run counter to his cultural preferences. The comics are a sign, a text that Todd can choose and possess, that clearly represents his efforts to align with his father and a distinct cultural group.

In addition to reading a wide range of black-identified comic books as a continuum, Todd also relates the comics to other media texts. His comparison of the comics to films by Spike Lee and John Singleton is typical of the way that Todd sees comic books as merely one element in a whole constellation of popular culture texts that express his identity along racial lines. Todd compares the comic books he reads to the "energy" he finds in hip-hop music. Both media, he claims, appeal to him on an artistic or sensory level. More concretely, Todd characterizes the topics and themes central to his enjoyment of both the comics and hip-hop as the struggle of black men to succeed in a racist world and of people trying to rise above the conditions they have been forced to live in. For Todd, who approaches the books from a specifically black perspective, the stories found in Milestone are about the black urban experience, whereas for other fans, like Jordan and Thomas, the stories are less culturally specific and more about the eternal struggle of every man. Todd said, "The Milestone books are more energetic than a lot of those tired old white books. You see the same thing in hip-hop, you know. There's just more to it; it's more original and you can just feel the energy . . . It's like African American people have just been waiting to explode in different areas and have all these new ways to look at things. They [Milestone comic books and hip-hop music] are really about the same things. They're both about making your way in a racist world, a world where no matter what you do, no matter how hard you try, people always look at you funny if your skin is different. I like Milestone because they show black people being heroes and succeeding, whether they're from the projects or the burbs."

In more specific terms, Todd often compares the comic books to action films featuring black actors. Though he admits that Jean Claude van Damme and Arnold Schwarzenegger movies are his all-time favorites, Todd also bemoans the lack of successful action films with African American leads.

Thank God for Wesley Snipes! I mean, Arnie and Wham Bam van Damme are great but why is it so hard for people to accept a black action hero? Sure, people always say that guys like Danny Glover and Damon Wayans have done big action movies . . . but, come on, they're always the sidekick. Who's kidding who here? It's good to see them up there, but why not make them the stars. At least you don't have that problem with comics like *Hardware* or *Blood Syndicate* or *Jonathan Fox*. In the comics it's OK for a black guy to be the hero. Things are, I hope, starting to change in movies, too. Now you're getting more Wesley Snipes films and stuff like *Bad Boys*, which actually had two black leads. I still think it has something to do with the comic books 'cause these guys know all about them. Will Smith even has the Milestone books framed on his bedroom wall on *The Fresh Prince of Belair*.

Todd also plays the common fan game of speculating about who would star in the big screen adaptations of favorite comic books. If it were up to Todd, Denzel Washington would be cast as Icon, Jada Pinkett as Rocket, and Eriq La Salle would star as Hardware. "I'm sure that black superhero movies are going to be the next big thing in Hollywood," Todd said. "After *Meteorman* and *Blank-Man* and *Mantis* all bombed 'cause they didn't take black superheroes seriously, I think they're finally going to hit big. With Wesley Snipes doing *The Black Panther*, Lawrence Fishburne doing *Luke Cage*, and—this is so cool—Shaquille O'Neal starring in *Steel*, how can they miss?" For Todd the comic book superheroes represent a launching pad for more widespread yet similar images of black men as heroes. This in turn affects how he looks at the comic books as a core expression of a common theme in black popular culture.

Will, probably the most spirited comic book fan I encountered, is only fourteen years old but knows more about the industry than most fans twice his age. His mother teaches English at a community college and his father is a dentist. They live in a recently remodeled home in an affluent downtown neighborhood. It becomes obvious soon after meeting Will that he is an enthusiastic learner, and his parents point out that he has always done well at school. Recently, Will has been trying to organize a comic book club at school, and I have no doubt that he will be able to put it together despite any administrative obstacles. Will is typical of serious comic book fans in many ways. He collects a wide range of comic book series and related merchandise (e.g., posters, cards, T-shirts); he hangs out at his favorite comics store at least twice a week, usually meeting friends there with whom he may spend hours discussing comics; and he attends every comic book convention within the Greater Toronto Area. Will traces his interest in comics to his father, but he also identifies it as the source of most of his social contact with his peers.

Like many other fans, Will claims to have been introduced to comics through his parents. Often parents who were subsequently amazed by their children's devotion to comics fandom were the ones who started the whole process by buying them the occasional comic as a special gift or an incentive to develop reading skills. For Will, his initiation into the subculture of comics fandom was less casual than it was for many other fans. His father, John, a longtime comics fan himself, introduced Will to comic book fandom at a relatively young age. Will can vaguely recall attending his first comic convention when he was around five. For Will and his dad, comic book collecting has become a real father-and-son activity, a social bond between generations. They share books, often attend conventions together, and shop at the same comics store, although, as his dad reluctantly admits, Will now often goes his separate way, with other fans and friends his own age, and then meets up with his dad again for the ride home.

It's kind of a blur [Will's first convention experience], but I do remember my dad taking me around and showing me some of the people dressed up in costumes and stuff. Even back then I knew I was going to be hooked. It's something my dad and I can share. But I think I'm much more into comics now than Dad ever was. I've got a massive collection of comics and I'm pretty sure I've got the longest "pull list"8 at my store. Actually, just moneywise I'm lucky my dad enjoys them, too. No, I'm just kidding. The best part about it is that we can both talk about the same stuff. My mom thinks were both crazy. A lot of my friends can't talk to their dads at all. Dad also doesn't mind that I spend less of my time with him at cons and stuff. He realizes that I have a lot of friends my own age who are into comics, and we often talk about the stories in ways that my dad doesn't care about anyway. You know, like who's drawing what and why a writer has some character doing something totally different—like when the stories went downhill in *Static* and started to get really stupid and we spent weeks talking about who the new writer was and why they were having trouble. Then my friend Mike told us that he was on the net and saw that the writers were listening to all our [the fans] complaints and promised to change the stories back to the way they originally were. For my dad it's mostly nostalgia, I think, but for us it's more important.

I met Will at one of the smaller regional comic book conventions held near the Toronto International Airport. We were introduced by Dave, the owner of The Black Knight comic book store, with whom I had previously spoken on several occasions and who was well aware of my research interests. Fortunately, I happened by The Black Knight dealer's booth, located in a poorly lit back corner of the convention hall, just as Dave was discussing the potential collectibility of the Milestone titles with Will and two of his friends, Mike and Andy. Both Dave and Will are certain that in a few years the first few Milestone comics will be rare collector's items, while Mike and Andy feel that the Milestone books will never be worth more than a couple of dollars because they do not feature artwork by any of the currently "hot" artists. Dave called me over and introduced us as mutual fans of Milestone (something that retailers often do when they know several of their customers share an interest in a particular character or creator). Will was eager to explain that he had recently added several of the Milestone titles, *Icon, Hardware,* and *Static,* to his list of monthly purchases. "I've added them to my list," Will clarified, "because they're usually really good stories, good in the same way that the real classic superheroes are, or at least *were.* Nowadays even guys like Aquaman and Green Lantern are being screwed around with too much; everybody wants to publish Bad Girls and tough guy heroes. Milestone's books are better than that; they're much more classic."

Will's comic book preferences definitely lean toward the classic style of superhero characters. Will counts such characters as Superman, Batman, Aquaman, Green Lantern, Captain America, the Flash, and Spider-Man among his longtime favorites. Will said, "I know Spider-Man isn't as classic as the other ones, the DC heroes, but he's a modern classic" Will's preference for what he calls "classic" superhero stories and characters is a trait that I found common to most of the Milestone fans. By classic Will means very traditional characterization whereby the heroes are clearly good guys and their adventures conform to the formulaic superhero plot of saving the world from evil supervillains. For Will and many of the other Milestone fans I spoke with, their categorization of the Milestone stories as classical is determined as much by what the comics are not as by what they are. In other words, the Milestone comics are measured in comparison to other contemporary comic books, such as those published by Image or Ania, and found to be much more conventional. Perhaps it is because Will's love of comics was passed along to him by his father that the traditions of the superhero genre are important to him. At times Will seems almost oblivious to the color of a character's skin; what matters most is the degree to which the books conform to the classic, or the core, narrative conventions of the genre. Consider Will's comments about Icon:

I know about the bit of controversy that surrounded Milestone when they first came out. I read in a couple of the 'zines that some people were complaining that Icon was just a black Superman rip-off; though personally I don't know anyone who has ever read the books and still thinks that. But, man, those kinds of comments—What do they mean? I mean, every superhero is like Superman, duh. Where do they think the "super" part of the name comes from? It doesn't mean he's a rip-off or any less of a hero. Like Superman—hey, that's a compliment, not an insult. In fact, what I like about Icon is that he *is* like Superman. Well, not *just* Superman, but all the great comic book heroes. The stories could almost be any one [of the classic heroes]; they are very well done, very much like all the best stories that have become real landmarks in the comic books. I mean, it's the way superhero stories are supposed to be, not just all these Image-style characters running around pounding on each other.

For Will, a traditionalist even at the age of twelve, his perception that the Milestone characters fall into the noble category of classic heroes is of the utmost importance to the interpretive strategies he adopts and the pleasure he finds in reading the *Icon series*.

One of the reasons that Will prefers the traditional superhero types over the newer breed of hard-boiled types is that Will identifies with the strict moral code they convey. "You could do a lot worse than trying to live up to the standards of a superhero," Will explained. "The real heroes are always honest, fight fair, and defend people without powers. They're real men, not just a bunch of well-armed mercenaries who would just as soon shoot you as talk to you." In a very conscious way Will uses the characters he reads about as his model for proper masculine behavior. They present the ideals and he adopts them as his own personal standard of how to act like a real man.

Many of the fans I spoke with were reluctant to label themselves as such, because of all the negative stereotypes associated with the terms "fan" and "fanboy," stereotypes that some of the older readers (primarily those between fourteen and twenty) feel hit rather close to home at times. Will, though, is proud to call himself a fan: "Just call me a geeky fanboy. I don't care. People assume that anyway, so why not flaunt it? I admit I'm not one of the jocks at school, but so what? I've got friends and I'm proud to be known as the biggest comics fan around." Will has invested a lot of his self-esteem and his sense of identity in being the best comic book fan he can be. And, to Will, being the best does not mean just having the largest comics collection of all his friends or knowing the most about the characters, their history, and the creative teams (although all these points play a large part in his definition of being a fan). Being the best fan means being able to use all this accumulated information to form the *correct* reading of the comic book. What Will stresses above all else is his ability to read the comics from an informed position so that he can arrive at what he feels is the correct meaning, in other words, the exact narrative meaning that the creators wanted to communicate. When I suggested that for many people reading is a much more open-ended concept, Will disagreed vehemently: "No, comics always have a real meaning in each story, you just have to know enough, catch all the references and the clues, in order to understand them properly." In this sense, Will very carefully constructs his readings premised on all the associated bits of information he can gleam from the world of fandom.

Thus, for Will, the Milestone books are interpreted intertextually according to all the information he can gather about the creators and intratextually through all the self-referential, genre-based clues he can find. I asked Will how this might affect his reading of a comic book like *Hardware*. He explained that although there was never much in the fanzines about *Hardware* there were numerous other resources that he could draw upon. Will talks to his friends who read *Hardware*, scans the computer chat rooms devoted to the Milestone titles, and pays careful attention to which professionals will be attending comic book conventions in his area so that he can ask them questions if they are involved with the Milestone books or are known friends of Milestone creators. The degree of contact with the creators, whether it's through fanzines or the net or meetings at conventions, is a privileged source of narrative meaning for Will. He sees his role very clearly as the one who strives to decode the text correctly, but as often as possible Will decodes in cooperation with the makers of the text, looking for clues and inside information that may shed light on aspects that he has not yet considered in a story.

I'm right up to date on all my 'zine reading, so I know what all the artists and writers have said about the books long before they actually come out. I know what a guy like John Byrne is trying to do when he takes over *Wonder Woman*, trying to bring her back to her Amazonian roots at the same time that he wants to make her more believable for the nineties. I also know that Byrne did the same thing for Superman about ten years ago, and a few of the Marvel titles before that, so I'm going to be looking to see if he does as good a job as he did before or if he's just using the same old tricks thinking we won't notice if he redoes Wonder Woman in exactly the same way he did Superman.

I still do things like check all the bulletin boards for the comics I buy on a regular basis. I see what other fans think about the books and then go reread them to see if I agree with them. For a comic like *Hardware* it's sometimes hard to find information, but when you do it can really pay off—like when this guy I hadn't met before told me at the store that he figured this weird kind of friendship that's developing between Hardware and Icon is sort of like the Batman and Superman thing over at DC. I hadn't thought of that, but now I can see it. It makes a lot of sense and I'm sure the Milestone guys have picked up on it. Mostly, the Milestone guys are great over the net. The writers and the artists and the editors are always coming on line and answering questions or telling us what they think about the books they are working on. Then I usually have an idea of what exactly they mean in the story.

Will, like many comic book fans, divines the intratextual meaning of a single comic book primarily by how it relates to and retells previous comic book adventures. This theme is an important one and I will be looking at it much greater detail in the next chapter. It becomes almost like a game of detection for Will, who prides himself on being able to recognize an incredible amount of self-referential points: "That's one of the funnest things about Milestone; they're loaded with things only a real fan would notice—*Static* especially, 'cause Virgil is a comic book fan himself . . . so he's always making jokes about superhero banter, or pretending he's Spider-Man or Batman or something." Because Will sees himself as a *real* fan, and sees the books as full of in-jokes that only a real fan could understand, he often takes it upon himself to explain some of the more parodic episodes to other fans who might not be catching the references. I was present when Will was explaining a crossover issue to a bemused friend: "This is hilarious. Did you catch all this? They're making fun of the old *Superboy and the Legion of Superheroes* stories. I mean, they've got the new Superboy and Static and Rocket done up in these cheesy 1950s costumes to make fun of the whole teen-superhero bit; they just call it 'The League of Superteens.' They even make fun of the hairstyles. And check out this, the 'superteens' walk of fame'; that's where the old Legion used to put up statues of dead Legionnaires, so that means that all these Blood Syndicate guys are supposed to be dead. And I love this; look at the names they find on the 'Mission Monitor': Frat Boy, Mall Hair Girl, Dough Boy, even Fanboy."

For Will, more than half the fun of comics is being fan enough to decode all the inter- and intratextual information which adds an extra layer of meaning onto the basic narrative.

Tony is nine years old, the youngest of five children, and has lived in a working-class Italian neighborhood his whole life. His father works construction. His mother manages the house and is primarily responsible for the children. She also occasionally works at a friend's beauty salon when she has the time or when the family needs the money. Tony can often be found hanging around with his friends at the comic book store Hidden Worlds, conveniently located just down the street from his house. It was on a summer afternoon at Hidden Worlds that I first met Tony and, subsequently, his friends Frank, Neil, Jim, and Mark. Actually, it was on Hidden Worlds' back steps that I first met them. The store's owner usually lets them use the small, covered back porch as a meeting place on the condition that they do not leave it messy. This arrangement was reached as a compromise—as a way to keep the kids as customers but also to stop them from clogging up the front entrance to the small store.

Throughout this study I have concentrated on Milestone comics and their fans. Tony and his friends are not Milestone fans. They are die-hard fans of various Image comic book series. I think it is important to include Tony and his friends in this sampling of readers to illustrate a portion of fandom whose interests run counter to those expressed by many of the Milestone fans. In fact, quite a few of the most active comics fans, particularly those between eight and fourteen years old, currently favor the Image style of comic books, indeed, many more than those who favor the Milestone books. While my main interest over the course of this research has been focused on Milestone, I do not want to lose sight of the larger world of comic book consumption. Moreover, because many of the Milestone fans relate to the books on a comparative level, Image fans like Tony, Frank, Neil, Jim, and Mark are consequential because their favored books are some of the ones that other fans read for comparison. The significance of this juxtaposition of Image and Milestone will be dealt with in much greater detail in chapter 6, where I discuss how the comics construct masculinity and how the readers negotiate that construction.

Tony picked up comic book reading where his older brother left off. When Tony's brother, Angelo, turned twelve he decided he was too old to be reading comic books anymore and passed the few remaining books he had laying around the house to Tony. Tony enjoyed the hand-me-down comics and quickly became a regular at Hidden Worlds, where some of his friends from school already picked up their new books each week. From the very beginning Tony and his friends have shared a strong interest in the comics published under the Image banner. Some of their favorite series include *Spawn, Gen 13, Deathblow, Supreme, Youngblood, Prophet, Wetworks,* and *Ripclaw.* "Some weeks," Tony explained, "when a bunch of good books all come out at the same time, we decide to share. It costs too much money for each of us to buy every book we want, so what we do is decide who will buy what and then we read them and pass them around . . . but you get to keep the book you originally bought. It's kind of fun that way; we all sit around out back reading and talking about the new comics." In an informal sense, Tony and his four closest comic book friends are a casual book club. They meet to discuss comics on a weekly basis (either Wednesday or Saturday afternoons), they all read and share the same books, and they agree upon the standards by which they judge certain comics to be better than others.

Every comic book fan has individual preferences for determining which books he likes. For example, with Thomas it is primarily the quality of the writing, for Jordan it is the personal believability of the characters and the style of illustrations, for Todd it is the ethnicity of the characters and the creators, and for Will it is the classical narrative style of the story. For Tony, Frank, Neil, Jim, and Mark the necessary ingredient for a good comic book is not so much the story but the artwork. More specifically, it is the way the characters' bodies are depicted. Tony explained, "We like them big . . . the bigger the better. If I were a superhero I'd want to be built like this [pointing to Badrock, a gargantuan member of *Team Youngblood*]. He's fucking huge. You could beat on anybody if you're this size. Look at the arms; that would be an awesome size to be. Guys like Superman are supposed to be tough but I bet he'd piss himself if he saw someone the size of Badrock or Deathblow coming at him. They are sooo pumped. Who even needs powers? Man, I'd just flex my muscles and everybody would take off." It's clear that Tony and some of his friends fantasize themselves as the Image heroes. In describing the characters, he constantly slips between referring to them and then talking about himself with the properties of the fictional characters. When I asked Tony about this, he replied, "Oh yeah, we are always joking around about who we'd want to be. I usually pick Prophet 'cause he's tough and huge and mysterious and he really kicks ass. That's what I want to be, a real man, you know, just lots of muscles and stuff when I'm bigger. That would be really cool."

Part of this group's use of the Image comics as physical ideals is played out in the way they banter with each other. On several occasions when I saw them together they would playfully insult each other's virility. On one such occasion, when Jim claimed he was going to be as large as Supreme after starting to exercise with weights, the others all laughed at him. "Nah, you're too big a wuss to look like that!" Tony chided him. "Yeah," agreed Mark, "you couldn't be a man like that no matter what you do—ha ha—where as me, I got Death-blow muscles written all over me." "The only thing you got written all over you," Jim responded, while cupping his hand in front of his chest to represent large breasts, "is Lady Death titty muscles!" Certainly there is a decisive perception of gender norms being bantered back and forth here between these boys. Their ideal is to be as manly as Supreme or Deathblow, which is to say as *muscular* as these characters. And parallel to this ideal is the ultimate insult of being too womanly, of being a "wuss" (half wimp, half pussy) or having an exaggerated female form like that of Lady Death. This is a perception that is not isolated to Tony and his friends. Many of the fans I spoke with over the course of this study held similar sentiments. I think this base perception of gender as expressed in the Image comic books and reveled in by Image fans is important, a perception that is markedly different in the Milestone titles, where muscles are *not* the mark of masculinity, and I will be returning to this in much more detail in chapter 6.

Although Tony is the most vocal of the group, the others all agree with his sentiments. In their attention to the extreme body types currently on offer from the likes of Image, Tony, Frank, Neil, Jim, and Mark echo an interest in comic books that I heard from numerous other young fans (approximately 60 percent of the 128 informants). For these fans, unlike many of those who prefer the Milestone books to the Image ones, the comic book characters represent purely *physical* ideals of masculinity. Contrary to fans like Steve, who see characters like Icon and Static as models of masculinity primarily for the way they behave, Tony and his friends find their enjoyment of the comics relates directly to a masculine fantasy of muscles and power. As Neil put it, "I like the Image heroes better because they're huge. Some of these other guys are OK, but let's face it, someone like Batman just isn't man enough to take on somebody like Bloodstrike. Bloodstrike would probably just crush him in a few seconds. None of this 'I don't kill 'cause I'm a good guy' crap—Bloodstrike would fold him in half and put him in the ground. A real man like Bloodstrike, with all those muscles and all those babes he has working for him, that's the way to be a man. Forget the gadgets and the secret weapons; someone gives you a problem, you just let him have it. That'd be cool. That's the way I want it."

By citing real, individual comic book readers my intention is to bring a sense of the fan's own voice to my review. My fear is that by describing specific fans it might seem that I am stressing the solitary nature of reading. In fact, what I want to stress is that for many comic book fans reading is primarily a social act, not a solitary one. As the previous chapter on comic book fandom as a subculture and some of the specific examples mentioned above illustrate, comic book reading must be understood as latently social on a number of different levels. Whether it is Will gaining prestige among other fans for his authoritative readings, Bruce feeling a strong enough affinity with the subculture to consider it a career possibility, Jordan harboring a sense of kinship or continuity with both his favorite characters and his favorite artists, or Tony and his friends sharing, talking, and fantasizing about comic books, it is clear that fans can and do use the texts as a bridge to social contact. To borrow a term from Brian Stock (1983), who discussed how literacy has historically empowered groups and created collectivities with the power to challenge traditions, we might think of comic book fans as a "textual community."

Of course, I do not want to deny that reading, any reading, is done on an individualistic basis. Physically and cognitively, reading is almost always a solitary activity, but at the level of interpretation, social factors often take over. Common sense tells us that for some people reading is doubtless the most individualistic and personal of all forms of media consumption. We may listen to music in crowded clubs, we may attend movies in huge theatres with hundreds of strangers, and we may watch television in our living rooms with friends and family, but reading is always done alone. In her ongoing work on book clubs and other reading groups Elizabeth Long (1985, 1986, 1987) has challenged the dominant perception of reading as a quintessentially solitary pursuit. Long (1992) has argued that by construing textual interpretation as a fundamentally solitary practice the collective nature of reading is suppressed. Accordingly, reading is aligned with the realm of the private and the personal rather than the public and the social. Thus reading as a political activity is neutered because it is perceived as an inconsequential *micro*process, whereas real political change is regarded as occurring only at the level of the collective, in the realm of *macro*processes. What is overlooked by this traditional perception that Long describes is that macrostructure s (e.g., abstract ideological foundations such as democracy, fascism, or misogyny) can only be realized through microprocesses (e.g., reading, listening, watching).

But as the comic book fans that I have discussed above—or the book clubs discussed by Long or, indeed, any of the literary-based textual communities previously mentioned, such as Radway's romance readers—show, reading is seldom as solitary a practice as common sense would have us believe. Due to the fan-based nature of the comic book industry, many of the readers feel, either directly or indirectly, that they are involved in a social practice. Long's description of reading groups is equally applicable to comic book reading practices: "Reading in groups not only offers occasions for explicitly collective textual interpretation, but encourages new forms of association, and nurtures new ideas that are developed in conversation with other people as well as with the books. Reading groups often form because of a subtext of shared values, and the text itself is often a pretext (though an invaluable one) for the conversation through which members engage not only with the authorial "other" but with each other as well" (Long 1992, 194).

It is important to note that even for comic book readers who have little or no direct contact with other fans there can still be a sense of social contact with the books and the characters themselves. In the same way that Jordan feels his favorite comic book heroes are like old friends who are always with him no matter where his family moves, other comic book fans can develop a sort of parasocial relationship with the text. In other words, the text itself takes on the properties of a social being. Consumers no longer simply watch or read the text, they *relate* to it as a friend. In effect, the comic book itself and the characters within it are ascribed fully developed personalities and the fans can develop a type of rapport with them. If developed outside of any larger social context, such as a fandom, this parasocial relationship can develop negative properties (e.g., the much-hyped cases of celebrity stalkers who claim an intimate attachment with actors they have never met in person). This type of relationship can, of course, happen with consumers of any media texts; but that it happens for young males reading traditionally masculine texts is a disruption to many of the gender stereotypes that surround media fandom reading practices.

By focusing on a masculine subculture, one of the things that this study can show is that the gender division in ways of reading (e.g., women read for social reasons, men read for facts) is far from accurate. For many young male readers the comic books satisfy a social function. They read for a sense of community, either with the characters and the narrative world or with other fans. The most obvious examples that I have recounted here are the cases of Jordan and Tony. Jordan does not read for mere narrative fact but for an entire world to which he can escape; he reads the characters as complete people, not as formalized plot conventions. The informal reading group organized by Tony and his friends uses the comics as a bridge to discuss shared interests and to explore their interpretations of particularly masculine fantasies. Both of these reading strategies confound the perception of reading styles demarcated by gender. Moreover, in relation to reading practices, the argument has been made that women are none too subtly forced to imitate male reading strategies in order to succeed in arenas such as academia and business, where only the masculine form of reading is valued. Due to women's forced adaptability, then, they are regarded as cross-readers, or as bi-readers. This strict adherence to binary gender categorization has always seemed ludicrous and limiting to me. It's sort of like forcing the square pegs of culture into the round holes of theory. Rather than seeing male fans as reading in a feminine way, a theoretical trope that continues to devalue non-institutionalized (i.e., non-masculine) reading strategies, we should consider that both men and women are capable of reading from a variety of subject positions, with a variety of intents, and in ways that satisfy a variety of pleasures and needs.

If on one level Jordan's attention to the presence of the creators is indicative of a parasocial element of his reading, it is also on another level an indication of a type of interpretive contract that exists between the creators and the consumers. The formal rules of the comics medium and the superhero genre mean that creators must work with a limited set of signifiers and that the readers are free to understand these signs within a limited range of possible meanings. The most striking example of the fan side of this contractual arrangement is the case of Will. For Will meaning can only be determined through the close attention of formulaic elements and evidence of the creators' intentions. In a way this makes Will a strong example of what has always been described as a "masculine" reading formation; he very clearly searches for a correct reading based on the intention of the writers and artists, but more than this, Will's interpretation is further premised on how these intentions fit within the entire fictional world of comic book superhero stories. It is impossible to overestimate the importance of genre traditions in the interpretive strategies of comic book fans. Readings are based on the necessity of both sides, the creators and the consumers, following the rules of comic book narration. The following chapter will deal with how fans consume the Milestone stories according to the contractual principles of the superhero genre in general and, specifically, in relation to the long and troubled history of black superhero characters, such as those from the era of blaxploitation.

Another theme that becomes apparent, one that I will be taking up in detail in later chapters, is that for many fans the comic book superheroes whom they read and fantasize about represent masculine ideals. Comic book superheroes are clearly among the most straightforward representations of masculinity our culture has to offer. They are powerful, tough, independent, resourceful, and dashing. They are, in short, the epitome of everything our society tells little boys they should be. The comic book model of masculinity asks, What young reader wouldn't rather be a Superman than a mild-mannered Clark Kent, a Spider-Man rather than an awkward Peter Parker, a swashbuckling Static rather than a geeky Virgil Hawkins? A fan like Steve, and there are many fans like Steve, is a prime example of how some boys turn to the comics to construct their understanding of masculine attitudes and behavior. Living in a fatherless household, Steve uses the superheroes as a model of masculinity and as a way to separate himself from the female dominance he feels while living with his mother and his sister. He even goes so far as to cite his fictional heroes as standards that he tries to live up to when it comes to little things like his mother still picking out his clothes for him. In a similar way Will looks to his favorite superhero characters as a model of moral masculinity. For Will they represent an ideal of conduct; they show how a real man behaves, and it is a standard against which he can compare his own life. All too often boys are presented with a confusing barrage of images in our culture, all trying to tell them how to be a man. For many young boys, like the readers presented here, the task of sorting through the ambiguous flotsam of masculinity to discern what it means to be a man is not a simple one. Where other cultural texts may be vague, the comic books can always be counted on to clearly mark out the boundaries of masculinity.

Contingent upon these characters being read as a masculine ideal is the fact that they also represent a fantasy of identification. In fact, "fantasy" is a term that the fans I spoke with mentioned over and over again. If there is any one thing that all the members of comic book fandom have in common it is that they have an immense emotional involvement with the characters they follow. They have invested a great deal of themselves in their imaginative identification with their favorite superheroes. While Darnell is explicit about his preference for comic book heroes as role models that, idealistically, far exceed any real-life sports "heroes," there is a sense among many of the readers that the fictional characters are not merely role models to be emulated; they are subject positions to be occupied through fantasy. In this case they are particularly masculine positions endowed with particularly satisfying strengths and weaknesses, powers and adventures. Symbolically, they are masculine subjectivities that the readers can identify with for a time and experiment with in a fantasy of alternative positions and ways of dealing with conflicts or dilemmas. The importance of these masculine fantasies cannot be overstated and will be taken up in much greater detail in later chapters. Consider the way Ang describes the role of fantasy in her discussion of women and melodrama: "Fantasy is an imagined scene in which the fantasizing subject is the protagonist, and in which alternative, imaginary scenarios for the subject's real life are evoked . . . the pleasure of fantasy lies in its offering the subject an opportunity to take up positions which she [or he] could not assume in real life; through fantasy she [or he] can move beyond the structural constraints of everyday life and explore other, more desirable situations, identities, lives" (Ang 1996, 92–93).

Ang's description is perhaps even more applicable to young boys reading superhero comics than it is to grown women watching melodrama. The women may be playfully experimenting, but many of the boys are actively searching for alternative positions that can help them make sense of their world and their place in it. The fantasy opens up new modes of masculinity. It does not matter if the fantasy of costumed men with incredible powers is realistic or not. It does not matter if the characters have the same skin color as the reader. What matters is that the fans can explore worlds of imagination, playing with different roles, trying on different masks.

5

Reading Race and Genre

I'm not really sure why, but I still love just sitting back and reading, I mean really *reading,* my comics. It's not that I don't read anything else, 'cause I do, but there is always something exciting about the feel of the paper and the energy in the stories. I'll read my favorite comics over and over again. I've got some Luke Cage and other early Marvels from when I was a kid that I've pretty well memorized by now. And it's kind of weird— when I read comics I find that even though I'm really into the story I'm always thinking, in the back of my head, how it compares to other stuff. You know . . . other comic books, other books, movies I've seen, even some of the music I listen to—it all sort of just gels in my head sometimes.

—James, a twenty-four-year-old comic book fan

I walked out of the air-conditioned lobby of the Holiday Inn located on the edge of a long strip of hotels adjacent to Pearson International Airport. The Holiday Inn was hosting one of Toronto's largest annual comic book conventions. After two hours of squeezing my way through the crowds of fans milling around the dealers' tables looking for deals and rare Golden Age books, I needed a breath of fresh air.

It was cooler out on the back steps, but the sun was much brighter than the perpetually dimmed lights of the hotel lobby. My eyes took a minute to adjust. A group of four teenagers, two white, two East Indian, were leaning against the wall to the left of the tinted glass doors I had just come through. They were comparing shopping lists and debating who had gotten the best deals so far. One of them, who looked to be the oldest at about seventeen, pulled a stack of at least thirty comic books out of a square, tattered briefcase. The others started laughing as he divided them into two piles. One pile for those he had paid for and the other for those he had slipped into his case when the dealer wasn't looking.

To the right of the doorway sat a black child of about twelve. His yellow plastic bag of assorted complimentary "goodies"—coupons, buttons, gaming cards, and numerous comics shop flyers—was on the grass beside him. He was reading the most recent issue of *Static.* He looked up at me with an expression of mild annoyance when my approaching shadow fell across the comic he was reading. I interrupted him, to be precise, just as Static was to save a crowd of onlookers from disaster during a riot in Dakota's new Utopia theme park.

"Can I help you?" he asked suspiciously.

"Maybe." I explained my interest in Milestone comics and he heard me out patiently.

"Yeah, I'm a big Milestone fan. They're almost the only thing I read on a regular basis anymore." He got to his feet slowly.

"I even did this myself," he said as he pulled a wrinkled black windbreaker out of the backpack he had been sitting on. He showed me the sleeves of the jacket. On one was a four-inch hand-drawn picture of Icon striking a heroic, mid-flight pose. On the other was a similarly sketchy picture of Buck Wild, Milestone's parody of funky 1970s hero Luke Cage. "Pretty good, huh? I'm going to be a pro one day."

I was surprised to see Buck Wild given the same amount of attention as Icon. I asked him to explain the jacket.

"You mean why not Rocket or Hardware or something, right?"

"I guess."

"Well," he started to explain as he proudly slipped into the jacket despite it being far too warm to need it, "when I first read the stories with Buck in them I thought they were kinda weird, making fun of all those old superheroes. I mean, I thought it was funny but it seemed kinda out of place, you know, right after Rocket found out she was pregnant and all."

He began to pack up the rest of his stuff in his bag, saying his mother should be picking him up soon.

"But then I was telling my dad about it, and he said he remembered Shaft and Superfly and guys like that from movies when he was younger, and that they may seem stupid now but he used to think they were the coolest. So I don't know; I started thinking about it—how guys like Icon owe a lot to guys like Luke Cage and stuff. It just seemed right to put them both on my jacket. He's also real fun to draw."

He waved to a freshly washed minivan that had turned into the hotel's circular driveway.

"That's my mom. Gotta go."

"So do you mean they're sort of the same?" I asked quickly.

"No, not the same. But—hmm—you gotta know one in order to understand the other, I guess."

Unfortunately, he sauntered off to the van with his backpack hanging off his right shoulder and his yellow plastic bag on his left side dragging across the curb before I could ask any more questions.

Reading, as the quotation above stresses, is a fundamental element—and naturally enough a crucial element—of the comic-book-consuming experience. Not so coincidentally, "reading" is probably the most widely used term in media studies as both a literal and metaphorical catchphrase for what audiences do with texts—be they books, films, television programs, music, clothing, or anything, or rather *everything*, else that is open to interpretation. Within media studies, the pendulum has swung from the original mass-culture critics' view, whereby readers were seen to be always and totally hegemonically incorporated by the reading process, to the opposite extreme, characterized by the likes of Fiske and Chambers, that steadfastly admits every individual reader's proficiency and ability to "construct [his or her] own readings" and to "read against the grain." What I want to explore here are some of the ways that Milestone readers understand these comic books not solely from the position of passive sheep nor solely as diligently resisting readers, but rather as culturally situated individuals who interpret the text in relation to associated extratextual influences. In other words, for a great many of the fans I spoke with (whether they were Milestone enthusiasts or not) comic book reading is a core activity that crystallizes an entire cluster of interests and values.

In this chapter I want to explore two of the subcultural modes of evaluation, modes that fans use specifically to interpret the stories published by Milestone. Since comic book fans are rarely ever fans of just one publisher or just one type of comic, they relate to each individual book as part of a whole. That is to say, they understand a given text by how it relates to other comics, both historical and contemporary ones, and how it differs from those same texts. In the case of Milestone, the first of two very important and interrelated factors addressed in this chapter is how the stories conform to established genre conventions, including how they incorporate innovations to the core superhero formula. The second point of comparison discussed in this chapter is the fans' understanding of Milestone's characters as a reworking of the earlier blaxploitation stereotypes found in superhero comics.

Because the comic book is a medium primarily directed at children and adolescents, the essential issue for most studies of the industry has always been about the possible harmful effects the comics might have on young readers.

Frederic Wertham's infamous *Seduction of the Innocent* (1954) and the Kef-auver Senate hearings in the early 1950s are only two of the most notorious examples. More recently, articles such as Tan and Scuggs's "Does Exposure to Comic Book Violence Lead to Aggression in Children?" (1980) and Shetterly's "Graphic Comics Stir Controversy: Is Censoring Violence, Sex, and "Immoral-ity" in Comic Books the Answer?" (1991) revisit the air of comics paranoia in a modern context. Likewise, a recent wave of police morality-squad raids on comic book specialty stores[1] and the occasional *Hard Copy* television expose on the evil influence of comics on defenseless children revisit the comic-book-burning days of the 1950s. Interestingly enough, *Hard Copy's* episode which aired in the early fall of 1995 accused comic book writer/artist Todd McFarlane of promoting racist beliefs in his best-selling series *Spawn*. The program fo-cused on an issue that involved flashbacks of a black man being lynched, yet the reporters and an outraged psychologist totally ignored the fact that the hero, Spawn, is himself a black man and that most, if not all, of the readers familiar with the series recognized the story as what McFarlane intended: as a warning *against* racism. It would seem that the often uninformed pattern of criticism against comics is still alive in the 1990s. Moreover, this type of misun-derstanding based on a quick glance by censorious watchdogs at a single comic book page actually works against the medium's potential ability to address real-world evils like racism. Issues such as racism, the watchdogs claim, are too serious for the colored page. Rather, comic books should stick to the appropri-ately childish fare of supervillains and criminal geniuses. But the actual fans, those who really looked at the issue of *Spawn* that seemed so inflammatory, had no problem with the story—not because they were being brainwashed by racist propaganda, but because they were adept enough readers to understand the story as a whole rather than as an isolated, single-panel racist image.

I want to explicitly stress the point often forgotten by the critics, the cen-sors, the concerned parents' groups, and the religious right, that for those who read comics, even the most die-hard of fans, the books are only one of count-less possible sources that might influence their understanding of social roles and cultural values. It should be obvious that readers come to a text as already socially constituted individuals, each of whom possess a unique filter through which to interpret the book, a filter shaped by their infinitely varied life experi-ences. The comic book is but one strand in a complex web of potentially influ-ential social and personal forces. Yet, clusters of interests and values shared by particular groups are real, especially for a group with as strong a common interest as comic book fans. Often it is out of similar social, economic, or his-torical backgrounds that otherwise diverse peoples will seek out particular entertainments. That comic book fans enjoy a wide range of associated entertainments, all with a decidedly youthful and masculine bent—from video games to action movies—reveals that the comics themselves, however primary a text they seem to be to the individual reader, are perhaps best understood as a central key to a larger world of subcultural values. Indeed, it would be impossible to study a cultural product as complex and symbolically loaded as the Milestone comic books by merely looking at the primary texts themselves. To isolate the texts as the sole bearers of their meaning(s) would be to deny how they function intertextually in the lives of the readers.

In order to understand how popular texts operate across the possible diversity of social and ideological relations, it is necessary, as Bennett and Woollacott have argued, to "abandon the assumption that texts, in themselves, constitute the place where the business of culture is conducted, or that they can be construed as the sources of meanings or effects which can be deduced from an analysis of their formal properties" (1987, 59). This is not to say that the text should be abandoned altogether. In rejecting the traditional text-centered approach I would not want to go so far as to posit all meaning as residing in the audience. Rather, the text should be understood as a central site around which cultural ideologies are formed by readers in relation to intra-, inter-, and extratextual references. In other words, it must be kept in mind that any cultural text is, to some degree, always a preconstituted object, just as every reader is always subject to an individual, preconceived frame of reference. It is this shifting mass of cultural relations that I am interested in here. Some of the most consistent readings made by comic book fans seem to be heavily negotiated according not just to their own personal and social backgrounds (extratextual), which are obvious influencing factors anyway, but also according to their knowledge of comic books and the superhero genre (intratextual) and their interest in related mass-media texts associated with black popular culture (intertextual).

With the Milestone books, too, we can see how the comics operate for many readers not in compliance with, or in opposition to, the text alone but in relation to other popular media. When discussing their favorite comic books, most of the readers I spoke with went beyond commenting on this single medium to include, among other things, their interests in action movies, arcade games, and various forms of popular music. "When I read comics," James claims, in the citation above, "I'm always thinking, in the back of my head, how it compares to other stuff." For many readers, especially those involved however tangentially in the subculture of comics fandom, the books are not merely read in isolation; rather their meaning is always at least partially derived from how they "compare to other stuff." This common practice of reading in relation to other media texts is an open-ended concept. The limitless differences in personal and social situations experienced by every individual reader mean that there can quite literally be as many *readings* as there are readers. Yet, there are certain related interests that seem to be shared by a great number of comics fans, interests that help to inform their understanding of the books. The next chapter will address separate but interrelated themes, regarding how the Milestone books are read by many young men in relation to contemporary action movies and television programs featuring black heroes and as a modified and potentially progressive ideal of masculinity. But first, in this chapter, I want to focus on a couple of the more loosely organized aspects that characterize how some fans receive the Milestone books in relation to (1) the overall genre of comic book superheroes and (2) other comic books featuring black superheroes, particularly the blaxploitation titles from the 1970s. All of these points of comparison tend to key on the visible ethnicity of the characters as a defining aspect that sets them apart from other more traditionally Waspish comic book heroes. This emphasis on the blackness of the Milestone heroes is accumulatively read by some fans as yet another mask, another layer of the costumed identity worn by the heroes. Understood from the fans' point of view, the Milestone books facilitate a reading in relation to other superhero characters, a reading that reworks the position and the possibilities of heroic African American figures.

In different terms, we might also think of comic book reading as the satisfying of a contract, a contract which is fulfilled when the writers and the artists manage to captivate the needs and the fantasies of the fans; and the fans have learned how to demand that their expectations be met. It is a fact that the comic book world is a small one where the producers and the consumers can speak to each other directly. This contact has allowed the publishers to discern the tastes and pleasures of their audience, and it has allowed the fans to establish a symbolic system which appeals to their desires. For fans the comic book is more than just a static, one-dimensional text, it is a cherished orchestration of symbols and signs and meanings that are interpreted through a shared knowledge. The creators work within a given sign system to tell a story that is both unique and familiar. Moreover, the readers learn to work out these stories in specific ways according to their own personal preferences and more formalized standards of evaluation. The formula becomes a sort of meeting place for the creators and the readers to negotiate individual stories. The contract, as Martin Barker sees it, "involves an agreement that a text will talk to us in ways we recognize" (1989, 261). Thus, the first step in relating to the comics text, in negotiating the contract between the creators and the consumers, is learning what to expect and how to read the sign system properly.

It seems obvious that popular culture and media fans approach the reading of texts in a different way than do academics. Where scholars may tend to concentrate on the stylistic and structural features of a literary work, fan groups have generally been found to refrain from evaluating a text on such artificial formalities and instead focus on the free play of the narrative's meaning, the believability of characters, and the satisfaction of the fantasy (see Radway 1984; Jenkins 1992). This practice of reading for a sense of identification with the story and the characters rather than for vaulted artistic merits led Elizabeth Long to conclude in her study of recreational reading groups that "It is more fruitful, then, to examine reading as a culturally embedded and potentially variable set of attitudes and practices than to conflate cultural classification with textual evaluation as does the traditional categorization of reading habits" (1987, 307). I would agree with Long that the culturally interpreted meaning of the text is of prime importance for media fans, and thus should be of prime importance to any critics approaching the texts; but it is also important to note that comic book fans as readers seem to differ from other fan groups in their attention to the formal stylistic conventions of the medium. Indeed, the basic ability to read a comic page properly is what many fans use as the essential distinction between themselves and what they often refer to as "the nonbelievers." Within the shadow cultural economy created by comics fandom the fundamental capacity to read comic books is just the first, but also the most essential, step in valued interpretive skills.

The importance of reading ability, at its most fundamental level, was made clear to me by a group of three young fans when I first began to talk with readers about their interpretive practices. I had a rather discouraging time approaching some of the fans at the first local convention I attended—one of Toronto's smaller monthly comic book gatherings held this time in the lower concourse of the Hilton Hotel. Armed with a tape recorder and a small note pad rather than a bag full of comics, I must have seemed out of place to the droves of young enthusiasts pouring through the back-issue bins, haggling with dealers over the value of certain *wall* comics (the unusually rare and valuable comics displayed on walls behind the makeshift booths), and discussing the validity of a collection of *ash-can* comics.[2] As I approached people throughout the afternoon many were more than willing to indulge my questions, while others quickly excused themselves from conversation once they found out I wasn't a newspaper or television reporter. It seemed like everyone wanted to be the token fan who would appear on the local news telecast of the *de rigueur* human-interest bit on "those silly fans who pay hundreds of dollars for a single comic book." Late in the day, in a stairwell outside the main dealers' hall, I found three eleven-year-old boys who initially regarded me with some suspicion, but who finally explained to me that many fans do not like talking with anyone they perceive as a nonfan. Rather than being snobbish or exclusionary, they argued, some fans avoid discussion with anyone who appears unaware of the world of comics simply because it is too hard to explain the meaning of the books.

"I won't talk about comics with anybody else unless I know they're into them . . . not even with some of my other friends 'cause they don't even know how to read them," Michael, the tallest of the three friends, explained while adjusting the strap on the new X-Men baseball cap he had just bought. "Yeah," chirped in Eric and John in unison, which seemed appropriate since I had at first mistaken them for twins in their matching Spawn T-shirts and black Los Angeles Kings baseball caps. "Some people are just so stupid when it comes to reading comic books," Eric continued. "They don't know whether to look at the pictures and then the words, or read all the words first." "He's right," confirmed Michael, really warming to the topic and, I think, the chance to lecture to an adult. "Lots of people get totally confused when they look at a comic book. My mom, for instance, is really pretty cool about my collecting comics. She calls it—ugh—my little hobby and even tried reading a few of my favorites one time just to see what I was into. But she drove me crazy with questions—not about the characters or the stories or anything, but about which words went with which panels. She was reading them all mixed up and they didn't make any sense to her. I finally had to take them away from her and tried to explain the stories . . . but she never did get it." "Nothing," Eric said, "is as annoying as someone who can't even read a comic. That's why a lot of people here may not want to talk to you if they think you aren't a real fan." "No kidding," John added without even lifting his eyes from the new *X-Force* comic he had just removed from a protective Mylar bag. "There's no point in talking to somebody at a con if they're illiterate!" Clearly there is a sharp distinction to be made by fans about an individual's ability to understand comics based on what the fans see as the most fundamental level of reading. In this case reading is seen as being grounded in technical skills which differ from main stream culture's larger, standard sense of literacy.

Comic book literacy is in fact quite different from what we usually think of as literacy. Put simply, the comic book medium's unique and highly stylized combination of printed words and sequentially ordered drawings expands the concept of "reading" beyond the conventional, literary sense of the term. I had my first glimpse of how confusing comic book reading is for individuals unfamiliar with the medium's conventions several years before the fans above expressed their frustration with the inability of outsiders to read comics properly. When I had students read Frank Miller's acclaimed graphic novel *Batman:*

The Dark Knight Returns for an introductory course in popular culture studies, I was astounded by the number of people who claimed that the text was completely unintelligible to them for pages at a time. Many of the students complained that they did not know whether to read the captions or the dialogue first, to look at all the images, or indeed what order the images were supposed to be in. After numerous failed explanations about the unrestricted formations of comic book reading, I was forced to pair up the students who were having comprehension problems with those in the class who were more comic book literate and could help guide the inexperienced through the book page by page, panel by panel. While some students learned with a little guidance how to interpret the semantic conventions of the graphic novel, others were never able to master what they regarded as a confusing collage of images and words. It also quickly became apparent during in-class discussions that only the students who were adept comic book readers could move beyond the narrative style to consider the book as a cultural text ripe with a revisioning of Reagan-era American mythologies. In effect, the reader's familiarity with the technical styles and conventions, a familiarity that allows him or her to read the book's narrative in the literal sense, is analogous to the fan's "reading" of the book in the wider, more metaphorical sense as a cultural text.

Figure 5.1, from *Hardware* #29 (1995), is an example of a contemporary comic book page. The composition of this page is conservative and would seem very straightforward to a regular comic book reader. But the assemblage of even a conventional page such as this is also typical of the structural arrangement often found confusing by nonfans. The action of this single page is itself rather simple: Hardware (who is in the midst of a battle with the Milestone universe's gang of rogue "bang babies," the Blood Syndicate) first ensnares one enemy in a type of electrical whip and then cybernetically draws his gun and fires on the other members of the Blood Syndicate while his thoughts silently narrate the events. Seems clear enough, right? Well, what is clear for fans is not always so for everyone else. Comic-book-illiterate people are generally confused by the nonlinear order of both the visual and the written elements presented in a page such as this one.

For example, visually the action flows from the large panel (1) in the top left corner to the smaller panel (2) in the top right corner, where Hardware begins to construct his "flow gun," then directly downward to the uniformly sized panels (3 and 4), where the gun is assembled and completed. In essence, a page such as this one follows the usual Western pattern of reading from left to right and top to bottom, but because panels overlap and are not in a strict sequential order like a newspaper comic strip, some readers become lost and move down to panel 5 immediately after the first panel and thus read the story

5.1   Hardware #29 (1995), page 18. Illustration courtesy of DC Comics and Milestone Media, Inc. Used with permission.

out of order. Although panel 5 directly overlaps panel 1 and is not *exactly* below panel 4, it is nevertheless the fifth lowest on the page and the farthest to the left on that level and thus its proper sequence is after all of the illustrations arranged above it. The shot fired in panel 5 is carried over to the left for panel 6, where we see most of the Blood Syndicate scatter, and then down to panel 7, where Fade continues to advance on Hardware. Besides the variation in panel sequencing, nonfans also tend to find the lack of visual agreement between the various action scenes unsettling. In other visual media, such as television or film, actions and effects are typically matched through conventional editing techniques. If Arnold Schwarzenegger fires his gun toward the right of the screen, the next scene matches the angle of the bullet as it hits the bad guys who are facing left. But then, cinematically, the shift from panel 5, where Hardware is shooting up and toward the left, appears disjointed with panel 6, where the bullets zing by to the right and the center of the frame. For those readers more familiar with the conventions of film than those of comic books, the flow of the action becomes awkward and contradictory, while for comics fans such linearly framed panel-to-panel transitions are unnecessary.

In conjunction with the visual sequence of events there are four separate written elements that the reader needs to comprehend on this page. The first is the writing in the shaded boxes (e.g., "Plasma Whip: Deployed"), which most fans recognize as a disembodied (because there is no directional point emanating from the dialogue box), computer-generated (because of the computerized font) voice. In this case it is the sound coming from Hardware's onboard computer system, referred to as Dobie, which controls the mechanical aspects of his armor. The second written element is the internal narrative of Hardware's thoughts, represented in the self-enclosed white boxes (e.g., "What the hell am I doing?"), which comments directly on the action occurring in the panels. This *internal* monologue is sometimes confused by non–comic book readers with the third written element of this page: the character's *spoken* dialogue. The depiction of Hardware's spoken words in panel 2—"Dobie? Initiate flow gun assembly."—is visually represented in a box which at first glance appears very similar to the box containing the character's internal thoughts; but it is distinguished by the convention of the box's frame, which has rounded edges and a jagged point that indicates the source of the voice. The last, but perhaps most stereotypically *comic-bookish*, written elements on this page are the onomatopoeic sound effects, "Pam, Pam," that represent the discharging of the gun in the final three panels. Even the action on a relatively simple page like this one can be quite confusing for new readers, and the problem is greatly compounded when the thoughts and voices of multiple characters are represented simultaneously.

For most fans, this form of literal reading of a comic page is just the most obvious and most directly text-bound step in forming an understanding of the book. But I do not mean to imply that comic book reading is easy and that those who cannot do it are slow learners. The perception that the comics are a childish medium and thus should be easy to understand has been the cause of many an adult's misinterpretations regarding the narrative intention of books, like Todd McFarlane's antiracism story in *Spawn*—not to mention their embarrassment at being out-read by eight year olds. Indeed, comic book reading is such a specialized skill that several academics have tried to deconstruct the symbolic conventions (Faust 1971; Abbott 1986; Schmitt 1992), while other scholars have attempted to explain the comic book's unique properties as akin to the language of film (Lacassin 1972; Fell 1975; Coleman 1985). Yet, to date, the most informative works for explaining the technical conventions of comic book language have come not from the critics but from the comics' creators themselves. Targeted toward fans and non–comic book readers alike, both Will Eisner's *Comics and Sequential Art* (1991) and Scott McCloud's *Understanding Comics: The Invisible Art* (1993b) are thoughtful, self-reflexive meditations on exactly how the comics page works to tell a story. Both Eisner and McCloud explain the conventions of the comic book style in great detail and with numerous graphic aids. McCloud's *Understanding Comics* is itself written entirely as a comic book with the author as an illustrated host who quite literally walks the reader through the world of comics language. They each outline such complexly stylized conventions as the numerous forms of panel-to-panel transitions, the various ways of representing emotion, sound, smell, movement, and time, and the multitude of techniques for effectively combining the written word with images in order to create a whole that is greater than either of its parts. More than just how-to instruction manuals for reading comics, Eisner's and McCloud's works demonstrate the complexity of skills that must be mastered before a consumer can feel comfortable with reading a comic book.

Beyond the fundamental technical skills required to read a comic book in the literal sense, comics are perhaps best understood as read by fans in the metaphorical sense as a unique genre of fiction closely tied to its medium of presentation. If we continue with "reading" as a loosely defined metaphor for what people do with popular texts, then we might consider the visual and structural components of the medium, in tandem with formalized genre conventions, as akin to de Saussure's concept of *langue,* the culturally shared knowledge of the grammatical rules that constitute a system of language, and the potentially unlimited utterances shaped by these rules, expressed in individual comic books and variably understood by readers as its *parole.* For adept comic book fans the unique structural qualities of the illustrated page have become an invisible foundation, just as film-editing techniques are overlooked by most viewers and grammatical rules are taken for granted by native speakers of a language. Instead, for fans, it is the understanding of the genre elements of comics' *langue* that is important.

Popular genres, regardless of the medium—be it literature, film, television, or comic books—essentially involve recognizable, often stereotypically one-dimensional characters acting out a relatively predictable formulaic story within a familiar setting. Individual texts are singular expressions of the overall genre and utilize standard narrative components (e.g., stock characters, plot devices, iconographic costumes) which have achieved an air of prior significance due to their accumulated use in other related works. In other words, the audience's relation to any specific genre text that employs recognizable conventions is dependent on their awareness of the genre as a whole. The audience negotiates a reading of a specific genre text premised on the preordained, value-laden narrative system utilized across the entire genre. For example, the solitary figure smoking a cigarette in a darkened bar was a conventional image in many

Hollywood films of the 1930s and 1940s. But the image and all of its elements, from the clothes, the lighting, and the music to the actor's face, take on an entire spectrum of associated meanings related to the larger identifiable genre of film noir. The generic whole becomes, in effect, greater than the sum of its parts in an individual text. The significance of the scene is based on the audience's familiarity with the tenets of the genre. As a particular instance of the film noir genre, this single scene acts like an encoded shorthand narrative device for viewers and suggests, at a glance, the desperate atmosphere of a doomed private investigator. Thomas Schatz, in his definitive work on cinematic genres, describes the emergence of recognizable genres as a combination of a repeatable form, style, and theme, a combination which is embraced by audiences: "It is not their mere repetition which endows generic elements with a prior significance, but their repetition within a conventionalized formal, narrative, and thematic context. If it is initially a popular success, a film story is reworked in later movies and repeated until it reaches its equilibrium profile—until it becomes a spatial, sequential, and thematic pattern of familiar actions and relationships. Such a repetition is generated by the interaction of the studios and the mass audience, and it will be sustained so long as it satisfies the needs and expectations of the audience and remains financially viable for the studios" (1981, 11).

Schatz's description is as applicable to comic books as it is to film. Comic book genres consist of elaborate, self-referential themes and conventions that produce a familiar story with a fundamental appeal for its audience. Even the smallest scene in a comic book is potentially rife with years of generic influence. For example, when Static is beeped by the police in issue #34 and shows up as a shadowy figure outside the window of a station house mumbling ominously, "You have summoned me, Commissioner?" most fans understand in an instant the tongue-in-cheek reference to the clandestine meetings of Batman and Commissioner Gordon and grasp the humorousness of Capt. Gil Summers disgruntled "Will you please cut that out . . . and get in here!"

As a mass medium the comic book, like the motion picture, has long incorporated a wide range of different genres including, but not limited to, science fiction, horror, Western, gangster, jungle, romance, and funny animals. And recently, particularly in Europe and in the expanding North American adult market, more mature-themed books have developed their own comic-influenced genres of social satire and criticism. But the genre most commonly aligned with comic books, and most crucial to an understanding of the entire medium, is the superhero genre. No other genre has been as closely associated with the medium as the superhero has been, with well over a thousand different costumed characters appearing within the industry's first fifty years. Just as

comic book readers need to develop their familiarity with the medium's technical conventions in order to understand the narrative, fans also define their
perception of the books according to their familiarity with the superhero genre.
This genre familiarity is a cumulative process. Only with repeated readings does
the genre's formulaic and thematic essence come into focus, and then the
readers' expectations begin to take shape. Like the novice readers who find
comic books difficult to read, many new comics enthusiasts struggle with the
often disjointed stories that are structured according to the peculiar logic and
narrative conventions of the superhero genre. Like all genres in all media, the
comic book superhero genre is a well-constructed world unto itself. In this
world men and women can fly, lift entire buildings with a single hand, run
faster than the speed of light, shoot electricity from their fingertips or plasma
rays from their eyes, all while parading around in colorful and revealing span-
dex tights. As absurd as these formulaic elements may seem, they are only the
most obvious cliches, and the easiest to comprehend for anyone with just a
minimum of exposure to the superhero genre. Beyond these surface conventions the superhero formula is also dependent on such generic elements as the
malleability of time (characters routinely travel to the future or the past or exist
in separate eras simultaneously), space (trips to the far end of the cosmos are
as common as going to the corner store), and even reality (dream realms and
different dimensions often merge with the characters' version of reality). In the
superhero genre anything can, and does, happen. But despite the seemingly
infinite possibilities, the world of the comic book superhero—like any genre—is
ordered according to certain rules of convention.

The narrative formula of the superhero story is essentially a modernized
version of the classical hero myth as described most notably by the likes of
psychoanalyst Otto Rank in *The Myth of the Birth of the Hero* (1909), folklor-
ist Lord Raglan in *The Hero* (1936), and mythologist Joseph Campbell in *The
Hero with a Thousand Faces* (1949). Despite their different backgrounds, each
of these scholars describes a similar heroic pattern or cycle whereby the hero,
who seems to be an ordinary man but is actually the progeny of exceptional
parents, must heed the call of adventure and set out on a quest to vanquish a
seemingly all-powerful evil force, thus protecting the community. Characteris-
tically, the hero acquires magical powers as a type of gift from the gods, as
well as an assortment of reliable helpers, and eventually he returns to his people with certain boons and a greater wisdom; he marries the princess and becomes the true king and leader that he was born to be. At their core,
contemporary comic book superheroes are not all that different from such legendary heroes as Hercules, Odysseus, King Arthur, Gilgamesh, or Robin Hood.
The only major difference between the adventures of comic book heroes and

those of their classical ancestors is one of marketing. Because the superhero must return every month for a new story, the hero's quest is never completely resolved via marriage and/or his reintegration into the community. Rather, the comic book adventure is a modification of the original heroic myth due to the cyclical nature of mass entertainments. The superhero is a perfect example of what Jewett and Lawrence (1977) have described as the American monomyth. Instead of a final resolution, the hero of contemporary commercial myths is required to repeatedly turn down the comforts of a normal life. The hero must ride off into the sunset ready to begin his quest all over again, with a new villain and a new batch of innocents to save from the ever-present forces of darkness.

In his essay "The Myth of Superman," in his book *The Role of the Reader* (1979), semiotician Umberto Eco takes this divergence between the hero of classical mythology and the superhero of modern narratives as a key to understanding the appeal of Superman tales as they relate to plotting and temporality. "There is, in fact," writes Eco, "a fundamental difference between the figure of Superman and the traditional heroic figure of classical or nordic mythology or the figures of Messianic religions" (108). This fundamental difference, Eco argues, is that the mythological character of the comic books must become an emblem, an easily identifiable archetype, but at the same time he must be marketed as a hero of a novelistic romance (i.e., he must be repackaged anew week after week). To this end, Eco continues, "Superman's scriptwriters have devised a solution which is much shrewder and undoubtedly more original. The stories develop in a sort of oneiric climate—of which the reader is not aware at all—where what has happened before and what has happened after appear extremely hazy. The narrator picks up the strand of the event again and again, as if he had forgotten to say something and wanted to add details to what had already been said" (1979, 114). For the most part, Eco is quite right about the hazy historical structure of these comic book narratives, particularly later on when he stresses the convergence of different stories all featuring Superman at various ages (e.g., as Superbaby, Superboy, and Superman). But I would take issue with his aside that "the reader is not aware at all" of these temporal distortions. Perhaps casual comic book readers are oblivious to this oneiric climate. But most comic book fans are very keenly aware of which stories have a canonical importance, thus making them more historically contingent than others. Serious fans are also clearly aware of where individual stories fit into the overall mythos and when the myths begin all over again. For example, in 1990 DC Comics cleaned house, as it were, and began the tale of Superman all over again, even renumbering all the subsequent comic books from #1 on again. In a sense, the superhero myth is both timeless—always renewing with little variation on the core formula—*and* temporally specific—allowing stories and genres to build on what has gone before.

The basic elements of the superhero genre have remained almost unchanged since the formula was established during the first wave of costumed heroes who followed in the footsteps of Superman in the late 1930s. Comics historian Mike Benton (1993) identifies the four main conventions established in those early years that are still employed today: (1) the hero must wear some form of distinguishable costume that sets him or her apart from ordinary people; (2) the protagonist must possess some form of superpower, be it of alien origin (e.g., Superman, the Martian Man-Hunter), granted by the gods (e.g., Wonder Woman, Captain Marvel), induced by science (e.g., Captain America, the Hulk), or developed through years of self-improvement (e.g., Batman, the Green Arrow); (3) the character hides behind the guise of a dual or secret identity; and (4) the superhero must be motivated by an altruistic, unwavering moral desire to fight against evil. These classic elements are woven around the typical adventure formula that sees the hero defending the lives of innocent people through his life-or-death struggle against a superpowered villain or an evil criminal mastermind. In the over fifty years that the superhero genre has existed numerous other conventions have been added into the mix. For example, such stock characters as the ultraviolent soldier of fortune, the mutant whose very powers exclude him from a normal life, the stern and diligent police chief contact, the nosy but beautiful reporter girlfriend, and the cheerful boy sidekick have all become part of the genre's narrative shorthand. For a fan familiar with the superhero genre, every appearance of a female reporter is instantly recognizable and measured in relation to the character's conformity or deviation from previous archetypes like Lois Lane (with Superman) and Vicki Vale (with Batman). Teenage characters who gain superpowers are understood in comparison to established expressions of the same convention, characters such as Captain Marvel or Spider-Man. Likewise, specific powers are assessed relative to other characters with the same skills. Each publisher's universe seems to have a superfast hero, a superstrong hero, an ocean-dwelling hero, and an expert archer. The common fan wisdom that in the world of comics there are "no new heroes, only new costumes" seems true enough. A few archetypal powers and personalities are merely shuffled around, mixed and matched, in the creation of new characters. Even Milestone's line of new heroes has to be measured in comparison to the established norms of comic book superherodom. The new heroes at Milestone, as we will see, are new in more than just their costume design.

The addition of new elements and the revamping of old ones is all part of a genre's natural evolution. Each new genre text must involve some degree of invention as well as convention in order to satisfy readers with a familiar narrative at the same time that it reinvents the story to keep it fresh and exciting. It is a curious bind faced by all producers of genre-aligned texts, whether they be popular genres such as Western, horror, or gangster fiction in comic books, film, or television or such classical genres as Gothic literature, cubism, chamber music, or even Roman architecture. Each creator must vary the format while simultaneously repeating the elements that made the genre popular in the first place. As each new genre text combines varying degrees of invention with certain requirements of convention, the genre itself evolves in both its formal style and in its relation to the audience. Indeed, it is the audience's ever-changing relation to the genre and its constantly shifting cultural position relative to the text's central themes that necessitates the reworking of any genre. The predictable evolutionary pattern of genres has been outlined in similar ways by critics working in different disciplines, from the broad classical humanities (Focillon 1942) to popular literature (Cawelti 1976) and popular film (Schatz 1981; Grant 1985). The comics' superhero genre has followed a pattern which closely corresponds to that of other genres in other media, going through the usual stages of experimentation, classicism, and refinement.

The initial experimental stage of a genre's development is the period where the narrative formula is established and the multitude of possible conventions are narrowed down to a few easily recognizable key ingredients. For the superhero genre this experimental phase is clearly marked by the emergence of Superman in 1938 as a culmination of heroic juvenile literature, pulp adventure serials, and the comic book medium's search for a defining story form. Through the early 1940s the superhero genre quickly formalized itself via a transparent and rather one-dimensional retelling of the basic Superman story and iconography under the guise of countless costumed heroes. By the time the United States joined World War II in 1941, the superhero genre was clearly defined and firmly ensconced in the collective consciousness of North American popular culture.

The 1940s and early 1950s are considered by many to be the classical era of superhero comics. During this period of wartime patriotism and postwar optimism the genre's formula and all its associated conventions were clearly established, and the comic book superhero sold more magazines every week than at any other point in the genre's over-fifty-year history. Schatz refers to this genre stage as one of *formal transparency*, when both "the narrative formula and the [film] medium work together to transmit and reinforce that genre's social message—its ideology or problem-solving strategy—as directly as possible to the audience" (1981, 38).

Following the proliferation of the classical period, a genre typically achieves an oversaturation of its basic message and the audience demands more sophisticated variations. Characteristic of the refinement stage, the genre's conventions that became so universally familiar during the classic era are reworked to the point of parody, subversion, and reinvention. For the superhero genre, and for the comic book medium as a whole, this stage of refinement was both facilitated and hindered by the moral panic and self-censorship of the industry brought on by the Wertham and Kefauver attacks. The superhero genre nearly collapsed in the late 1950s and early 1960s from the twin conditions of narrative exhaustion and censorious limitations. But during the later 1960s and early 1970s new life was breathed into the genre via the subversive superhero parodies circulated in the underground comics and, more importantly, through the onset of Marvel's flawed heroes, such as the Fantastic Four, the Hulk, and Spider-Man. By this stage the themes and conventions of a genre have become so ritualized that the genre often moves from formal transparency to opacity. The form itself becomes a focus of the message; the structure as well as the narrative constantly feed inward on themselves to reconfigure the staples of the genre to reflect a changing cultural environment.

Since the comic book medium is still considered a juvenile market, with a constantly shifting audience of new young readers and aging fans, the superhero genre is a unique combination of typical evolution and atypical non-evolution. What I mean is that the current crop of superhero comic book series ranges from those that might be considered classical in tone and style (formal transparency) to the majority of titles currently on the market, titles that carry on the classical formula but have updated it to meet the demands of young readers in the 1990s, and to those series that self-reflexively reconsider the entire genre and all its themes and conventions (opacity) at the same time that it perpetuates and celebrates the history and the future of superheroes. There are always new young readers who, at any given moment, are encountering superhero comics for the first time. For these readers new to the genre the industry supplies numerous titles in the classical mode with relatively simple stories and artwork, such as *The Adventures of Batman and Robin* series based on the syndicated Saturday morning program *Batman: The Animated Series*. The enormous popularity of a character like Batman makes him an ideal example of the concurrent variations of the genre. In addition to *The Adventures of Batman and Robin,* which is geared toward the youngest segment of the market, there are four other monthly Batman series, each addressing a nominally different level of genre familiarity (reflected, not incidentally, in the different cover prices). Both *Batman* and *Detective Comics,* with conventional, modernized superhero stories, are suited to the mid-range audience, while *Legends of the Dark Knight* and *Shadow of the Bat* appeal to older readers and those with a well-developed familiarity with the genre and the Batman mythos. But at the same time that the industry is able to retell the same "naive" or "childish" story over and over again to new audiences—the classical phase of the genre frozen in time—the fans who pride themselves on their intimate knowledge of the genre require works that adapt the superhero genre to their needs. Indeed, even the most archetypal of superhero characters are routinely reconstructed, literally reborn, in order to adapt their mythology for a different age. In the late 1980s, writer/artist John Byrne was alone responsible for reinventing such legendary characters as Superman, the Human Torch, the Sub-Mariner, and She-Hulk. Unlike film or other popular media where most genres are clearly geared toward adults, the circular and ever-renewing nature of a great portion of the comic book audience allows, in fact requires, the superhero genre to both develop and remain static.

This unique and apparently contradictory tension that arises from the comic book superhero genre striving to both evolve in order to satisfy the fans who are familiar with the established conventions and to retain the genre's traditional formula and style for new readers is occasionally combined in texts that simultaneously capture the genre's past, present, and future. Works such as the recent and extremely popular miniseries *Marvels* (1994–95), written by Kurt Busiek and illustrated by Alex Ross, exemplify the superhero genre's self-reflexive development, its ties to time-honored features, and the influence of subcultural knowledge on the fans' interpretation of the story. *Marvels* was a four-issue "Prestige Format" retelling of the entire history of the Marvel Publishing Company's fictional universe. Busiek's carefully woven script is structured as an autobiographical narration by Phil Sheldon, an average New York photojournalist, and is strikingly portrayed in Ross's painted panels with a sense of realism never before seen in comic books. In Marvels, Manhattan becomes a world filled with regular people who react in a myriad of different ways to the sudden presence of superpowered beings, or "Marvels" as they are dubbed. Through Phil's eyes we witness the birth of the superhero era in the late 1930s with the arrival of the Human Torch and the Sub-Mariner, the rise of the classical superheroes, and the fear and the prejudice surrounding the newer, less noble heroes such as Spider-Man and the X-Men. From adulation of these earthly gods—"Just to catch a glimpse of him [Captain America] always in motion, always moving forward, like a force of nature in chain mail. Never a hesitation or a backward glance . . . We were in awe of him. Of all of them."—to fear and loathing of these dangerous genetic anomalies—"Superpowered mutants. Freaks. They looked just like normal people, but you never could tell. Stinkin' Muties! In a way, the mutants were worse than the supervillains. Who would protect us from the mutants?"—the strength of *Marvels* is that it manages to explore the concept of superheroes from the point of view of average citizens, thus questioning and recontextualizing all of the fantastical features of the genre at the same time that it recounts every major event, and many of the minor events, in the Marvel universe's fifty-plus years of history.[3]

"The big things were obviously easy to spot," said Jordan, who at thirty-six years old is a longtime superhero fan as well as the owner of a small comic book and magazine store in London, Ontario. "The invasion of Galactacus, Spider-Man being blamed for Gwen Stacey's death, all that stuff I clearly remember from when I was a kid and what I've seen in reprints a million times since. But it was the great little details that made *Marvels* so interesting. You know, seeing all those classic events again but through the eyes of real people really made me rethink what's going on in superhero books." Many of the younger readers ignored *Marvels* altogether or found it an interesting yet somewhat confusing and depressing book. But for fans with a detailed sense of the genre's history, particularly older fans who fondly remember the classic comics from their childhood, *Marvels'* unique twist on the genre's core formula layered an additional level of elegiac meaning onto the historical narrative at the same time that it retained all of the formal conventions. The breadth of the story manages to question both the formal transparency of the genre's classical era and the initial opacity of its modern period. By working so clearly within the genre but shifting the narrative focus onto the more realistic effects that superpowered heroes would have on the world around them, *Marvels* develops the potential dark side of the genre for readers who are already well aware of the historical and formulaic significance of key events. Indeed, *Marvels'* attention to retelling and recontextualizing even the smallest of details in a new, less one-dimensionally "cartoony" light was so pervasive and accurate that the subsequent graphic-novel version of the story included a page-by-page index of original sources in its postscript. Likewise, many of the fans pointed to Alex Ross's incredibly realistic depictions of familiar and legendary scenes as allowing them to rethink just what it would be like if superheroes really did exist, right down to the wrinkles in their costumes.

Marvels is not the only example of a mature, self-reflexive reworking of the traditional comic book superhero genre. It is merely one of the most recent and most critically acclaimed series to evolve beyond the traditional formulaic narrative. As the subculture of comics fans with a thorough and sophisticated understanding of the genre has come to represent a central core audience, other creators and the publishers have also successfully satisfied the innovation desired by this constituency at the same time that they continue to offer the same classic narrative to new and/or younger readers. As I mentioned earlier in this chapter, Frank Miller's now legendary depiction of the caped crusader in the 1985 *Batman: The Dark Knight Returns* set the standard for reinventing and elevating the genre. "He [Miller] has taken a character whose every trivial and incidental detail is graven in stone on the hearts and minds of the comics fans that make up his audience and managed to dramatically redefine that character without contradicting one jot of the character's mythology," writes Alan Moore in the introduction to the graphic-novel version of *Dark Knight.* "Yes," Moore continues, "Batman is still Bruce Wayne, Alfred is still his butler and Commissioner Gordon is still chief of police, albeit just barely. There is still a young sidekick named Robin, along with a batmobile, a batcave and a utility belt. The Joker, Two-Face, and the Catwoman are still in evidence amongst the roster of villains. Everything is exactly the same, except for the fact that it's all totally different" (1986, 3). At the same time, Moore's own miniseries *Watchmen* (1986), illustrated by Dave Gibbons, reconsidered the entire history of superhero adventures through a complex story of global conspiracy with a cast of original costumed characters representing conventional heroic types (e.g., a Superman type, a Captain America type, a Punisher type, etc.) from both the classic and modern era of the genre. By using recognizable superhero types grounded in the most conventional of cliches Moore was able to critique the shortcomings of the genre while simultaneously raising it to new heights of clarity. This self-reflexive, parodying technique has grown very popular in such recent series as *Golden Age* (1994–95) and again in Kurt Busiek's comic book *Astro City* (1995).

It is within this self-reflexive vein that the Milestone comic books are read by many of the fans. Although, at first glance, the Milestone titles may not seem as consistently concerned with questioning the superhero genre—at least not as explicitly as such miniseries imbued with as heavy a sense of historical gravitas as the *Marvels, Dark Knight,* or *Watchmen* sagas—the Milestone books are still understood as they relate to the genre as a whole. In other words, many readers interpret the Milestone books as a natural development that brings into question the traditional racial bias of the genre; and for fans familiar with the medium's established representation of black characters, these new heroes are understood as a redressing of the one-dimensional blaxploitation comics of the 1970s.

Unlike many of the other minority-oriented comic books on the market today, all of the Milestone titles are firmly grounded in the traditions of the superhero genre. Numerous other African American series (some of which are discussed in more detail in other chapters) are using the comic book medium as a means to express alternative stories ranging from a cartoonishly illustrated depiction of urban black teenage life in Rex Perry's *Hip Hop Heaven* to the starkly realistic historical biography of Martin Luther King Jr. in Ho Che Anderson's *King*. But the editors at Milestone have very consciously chosen to work from within the industry's most dominant genre. As Milestone writer Matt Wayne explained in the first editorial page of the company's superteam miniseries simply entitled *Heroes*, "The idea of a bunch of world-famous superheroes having tremendous battles and hair-raising adventures may seem generic, but that's what we get for working in a genre." Like every costumed hero that has emerged in the last sixty years, the Milestone characters are relatively simple variations of the core model of the comic book superhero. In fact, comic book historians argue that "almost all of the original superhero concepts were developed between 1938 and 1943 (with the exception of the early '60s Marvel characters like the Hulk, Spider-Man and the Fantastic Four, whose super powers resulted from radiation exposure). Of the seven most significant comic book superheroes [Superman, Batman, Wonder Woman, Spider-Man, Captain America, Captain Marvel, and Plastic Man], only one was created after 1943" (Benton 1993, 176). All subsequent comic book heroes have been mere variations of these basic types.

The resemblance of key Milestone heroes to stock characters of the superhero genre is obvious. Much has been made of Icon's uncanny similarity, in both powers and personality, to the Man of Steel himself, Superman. But the resemblance of the other Milestone heroes to conventional superheroic types has not gone unnoticed by the fans. Icon's teenage partner, Rocket, fits the classic mold of "sidekick" first established with the inclusion of Robin in the Batman titles and later repeated almost endlessly with such youthful characters as the Green Arrow's Speedy, Captain America's Bucky, the Human Torch's Toro, and Aquaman's Aqualad, to name just a few. Other Milestone characters are an amalgam of previous heroic types and conventions. Static is a wisecracking, nerdy teenage superhero comparable to the original portrayal of Spider-Man, and he wields electrical powers much like those of DC Comics' off-again-on-again character Black Lightning. Likewise, Hardware seems to embody the grim outlook, intelligence, and determination of a Batman and the weapons-filled superarmor of an Iron Man. And of course, the team format of the Milestone series' *Blood Syndicate, Shadow Cabinet,* and *Heroes* is informed by such prototypical superteam titles as DC Comic's legendary *Justice League of America* and Marvel's extremely popular *The Avengers* or *The X-Men*.

The self-referentiality inherent in a genre as tightly and consistently defined as the comic book superhero genre is, on occasion, made very explicit. For example, for the month of November 1995 all of the Milestone titles featured nostalgic covers designed to pay tribute to favorite Golden Age artists and illustrated by guest creator Howard Chaykin, himself an almost legendary fan favorite among comic book artists and writers. Each of the covers depicted their respective Milestone heroes in a scene and style imitative of classic covers from the dawn of the superhero genre. Compare the cover from *Icon* #31 (fig. 5.2) with the famous 1940 cover of *Batman* #1 by Bob Kane (fig. 5.3). The other Milestone titles in the nostalgia series were similarly self-reflexive. *Hardware* #33 was modeled after *Hit Comics* #10 by Lou Fine; *Static* #29 was modeled after *Captain Marvel Jr.* #7 by Mac Raboy; *Blood Syndicate* #32, after *All-Winners Comics* #1 by Bill Everett; and *Xombi* #18, after *Adventure Comics* #73 by Joe Simon and Jack Kirby. "I felt," Chaykin claimed of his inspiration, "that it would be in keeping with the boyishness at the heart of comics to pay tribute [to the Golden Age creators] in bright color and heroic imagery." But by literally inserting the ethnically diverse Milestone heroes into these classic scenes originally dominated by white-only superheroes, these nostalgic covers emphasize more than just typical genre homage. This series of images also stresses the cultural and racial bias that has long dominated the

5.2   Icon #31 (1995). Illustration courtesy of DC Comics and Milestone Media, Inc. Used with permission.

5.3   Batman #1 (1941). Illustration courtesy of DC Comics. Used with permission.

mainstream comics industry and the fact that the Milestone characters represent a fundamental reworking of even the most basic and time-honored conventions of the genre.

Initially, many fans I spoke with referred to the Milestone characters in
much the same terms that the Ania group and other Afrocentric publishers
used, referring to Icon as a black Superman and to Hardware as a black Iron
Man. But where the Ania members and their like meant the descriptions as a
harsh defamation of Milestone's characters as culturally invalid, the readers'
use of these terms did not necessarily denote criticism. While it is true that
some readers were concerned that a character like Icon was so obviously similar
to Superman that he could not possibly be more than the Man of Steel in
blackface, most Milestone fans immediately welcomed the character as a long
overdue variation on the Superman type.

I met Michael and Eric, two fourteen-year-old Jamaican Canadians, at The
Comics Cavalcade, a small specialty store in a lower-income area of North York,
just beyond the edges of York University campus. Despite being best friends
and having long shared an almost identical comics-buying list, Michael and Eric

are keenly divided over the issue of Icon as a black Superman. "I don't buy it, man," declared Michael as he tilted his head to indicate the back issues of Icon displayed in the store's carefully haphazard front window. "I mean, a lot of people I know buy that book but it hasn't really caught me yet. I can go for Hardware and Static—yeah, Static's cool. But if I want a Superman book—which I don't—I'd go to the original." "Don't believe him," Eric told me, as he leaned back against the faded "No Loitering" sign. "He's just dissing Icon 'cause the rest of us all like the book and he wants to be different. Besides, I'm worn out from all this 'Super-Oreo' crap about Ike. You can tell the man is black. Just look at him! And don't be telling me he don't act black. I mean, how's black supposed to act? Hmm?" Eric checked his rising voice as he and Michael both glanced at a group of teenage girls passing into the convenience mart next door. While Michael brushed imaginary dirt from the sleeves of his Toronto Raptors starter jacket, Eric adjusted his oversized, low-rider jeans, pulled up the tongue on his untied Air Jordans, and resumed, "And I don't really care if he is a black Superman. Is that supposed to mean that a black man can't be Superman? I don't think so. So what if he's a little uptight sometimes. Black can be uptight. I like Icon being black; it's cool, but really skin color don't have to mean all that much in comics." "That's true," Michael chimed in. "You've already got guys who are green, blue, purple, red, and all kinds of other weird colors." "Really," Eric continued, with a look of revelation on his face, "Icon isn't even black; he's really this kinda blue-silverish-looking alien who has only taken on a black identity as a disguise while he's on Earth."

In fact, Eric's defensive observations about Icon hit on a couple of key concerns associated with the Milestone characters, concerns that fans often repeat in various ways. The first concern—"How's black supposed to act?—which was discussed in some detail in the chapter related to the development of Milestone and the editorial dispute with other Afrocentric publishers, is that to deny Icon (or any of the other Milestone characters) as a legitimately black character because he is a successful lawyer and a straight-arrow Republican is to deny anything but the most monolithic perception of black culture. The Milestone books are far from representing the black experience in the United States as a darkened reflection of white culture; instead, they show a diversity of possible and existing social and political situations. Even at an economic level, Icon, whom the Milestone founders fully admit owes much historically to the image of Superman, has the implications of the Superman relation tempered by the inclusion of Rocket, an unwed teenage mother from the projects, as the team's driving force.

The second often repeated observation—"black identity as a disguise"—links the development of mainstream-published black superheroes not explicitly with a social and political need to provide positive images but rather with the larger genre traditions that necessitate variations on the basic model of the comic book hero. Because all of the Milestone characters are so identifiably situated within the superhero tradition, their visible ethnicity is read by some fans as just another logical variation of established types. In effect, ethnicity is read almost like another layer of the colorful costume, with skin pigment operating metaphorically in tandem with the actual mask traditionally worn by comic book heroes. Moreover, at the time of Milestone's inception early in 1993 some of the fans I spoke with, both black and white, accepted the parallels between Icon and Superman as a natural evolutionary step to be taken by a company linked with industry giant, and Superman publisher, DC Comics. In a self-perpetuating industry where no good character goes without spin-offs, an archetypal figure like Superman can beget such diverse variations as Supergirl, Superboy, Bizarro Superman, and even Superdog, Supercat, and Supermonkey. So why not a black Superman? Indeed, the launch of Icon was doubly suspect for some fans not just as an imitation of Superman but as a possible replacement.

Just months before the first Milestone books were released, the Superman character, the most recognizable figure in comic books, was killed off in a much publicized battle with an alien villain named Doomsday. DC Comics spent nearly a year flogging possible Superman reincarnations, including a new Superboy, a cyborg Superman, a dark vigilante-style Superman, and, perhaps most significantly, a black Superman. The character, dubbed Steel, was a mysterious mallet-wielding African American steelworker (John Henry Irons, an obvious nod to the African American folk hero John Henry) and was clad in an armored Superman-like costume. While the cyborg and the vigilante Superman were eventually run off, Irons' character was granted its own series, *Steel*, after the original Superman finally returned. With the reinstatement of the archetypal Superman at the pinnacle of the Superman family of characters, the true origin of Steel was finally revealed, thus situating him clearly within the realm of Superman variations. In the story "In the Beginning!" which appeared in *Steel* #0 (1994), written by Louise Simonson and pencilled by Chris Batista, we find out that John Henry Irons is indeed named after the folk hero who died proving he could pound railway steel faster than a steam-driven machine could. "That's why your pa named you after him," John's grandfather explains to him in a flashback sequence. "John Henry used his muscles to beat one machine, an' your pa hopes you'll use your brains . . . and become the machine's master." Indeed, the theme expressed so succinctly in this origin tale, the theme of heroic black men shifting from purely muscular achievements to more cerebral triumphs, is a central concern of some Milestone readers, and I will be returning to it in much greater detail in the next chapter. The story goes on to explain that the young John Henry Irons is orphaned when his parents are senselessly killed because they attended a freedom march (shades of countless other orphaned heroes), and he is raised by his paternal grandparents. Irons attends Yale on a baseball scholarship and excells at the science of ballistics. From there he goes on to be a top research scientist for Amertek, until he witnesses firsthand the mass destruction caused by one of the weapons that he designed for the military. Irons deletes his other designs, fakes his own death, and becomes a skyscraper steelworker in Metropolis, where Superman saves his life one day after a support cable snaps. Thus, when Superman dies in his battle with Doomsday, Irons takes it upon himself to be the new Superman. "Still owed him my life," Irons recounts, "so I decided I'd try to take his place, do what he would have wanted." So now the official Superman family really does include a black Superman.

Though some fans incorporate the visible ethnicity of the Milestone heroes into an understanding of a genre system constantly struggling to reinvent its core character types, that does not mean that they discount some of the deeper changes implied by the development of a hero like Icon just because he is Superman-like. Whereas Steel's position as the designated black hero in the official Superman family of comics is sometimes commented on because of his direct relationship to the original Superman (as a temporary replacement and because they are, after all, acquaintances who both originally worked in Metropolis), the fans' general awareness of Milestone as a black–owned and controlled publishing company tempers most of the suspicions of tokenism. In other words, though the Milestone heroes' generic lineages are clearly associated with several key white characters, that does not negate their symbolic significance as some of the most truly innovative comic book characters to appear in decades due to their emphasis on ethnic variety, including East and West Asian, Hispanic, and Native American characters as well as their leading African American heroes.

While at the Chicago Comicon I struck up a conversation with a seven-year-old-boy dressed head to toe in matching Tommy Hilfiger clothes. He was glad to list all of his favorite Milestone fight scenes for me as I scrambled to write them all down. As I listened to his sound-effects-filled lecture on why Static could probably kick Spider-Man's ass and why the Blood Syndicate had it all over the X-Men, I noticed a concerned-looking man in well-pressed jeans and a black Nike pullover approaching us. The man, who appeared to be in his early thirties, turned out to be the boy's father and quite diplomatically but firmly asked, "What are you talking to my son about?" When I explained that

I was doing some research on Milestone comics he smiled, introduced himself as Matt, and sent his son to wait in an autograph line with his friends. "I'm a Milestone fan, too," said Matt as he tapped a small black and gray pin on his chest that was decorated with the company's trademark M. "Just picked up a handful of these over at the DC booth." I asked who had been the Milestone fan first, he or his son. What I got in reply was a thoughtful comment on the relationship between the different generations of black superheroes and comic book fans.

"Well," Matt replied as we sat down in wobbly chairs around a dirty plastic table next to the overpriced pizza and hot-dog concession stand, "I have to admit that Tim introduced me to some of the Milestone titles even though I was the one who got him started on comics just a year or so ago. I used to collect comics as a kid, mostly Marvel stuff, but I had gotten out of it as an adult. Then Tim's teacher told us that his reading skills were coming along too slowly, so I began picking up some basic books like Supermans and Batmans to read with him. Now he's an avid reader. Of course, I would have liked him to be reading about heroes that were black rather than always having white role models, but I didn't think there was much out there that was appropriate for someone as young as Tim. I read Luke Cage and the Black Panther as a kid and loved them. Oh, yeah, and I vaguely remember seeing what's his name— The Black Hornet? No. The Brown Hornet! That's it—on *The Fat Albert Show* and even thinking that he was cool, though he was just a weird little cartoon superhero. Anyway, they may all have been pretty silly but I thought they were great at the time; they let me see someone like me doing good things, saving people, beating up drug dealers, and not being just a bad guy or a sidekick. But those guys, as out of date as they were, are long gone. Then Tim borrowed a copy of *Hardware* from a friend of his and we read it together. It blew my mind. Here was a brother of today doing it all. From that point on I've encouraged Tim to include all the Milestone titles with his weekly buys. I even give him extra allowance to make up the difference, and we both read them. These characters are maybe better, more realistic than guys like Cage. They're not spending all their time trying to be really black, but they're doing the same thing that the books I used to read were doing. They may be new versions of the old guys, but they let my kid dream about saving the world."

As Matt's comments about his old reading experiences and his new ones with his son imply, reading the Milestone comics in relation to the superhero genre as a whole is only one of the most basic points of comparison, one that shapes the fans' understanding of the books. More specifically, many comics fans I spoke with, and every one of them who, like Matt, was old enough to remember or have read reprints of books from the 1970s, mentioned that they enjoyed the Milestone stories as a reworking of the famous blaxploitation comics from a generation ago. Though the politically contentious blaxploitation comics of the 1970s served, for a while, the needs of young black fans who felt alienated from most mainstream comic book products, none of these tough, streetwise characters stood the test of time. The original Black Panther lasted only fifteen issues after moving from Jungle Action to his own title in 1977. Black Lightning only appeared in eleven issues of his own series before being relegated to the occasional backup story in the books of more popular DC heroes. And even the best known "superspade" from the era, Luke Cage, Hero for Hire, who began his adventures in 1972, was finished by 1986 and could not survive a short-lived revival in 1992. Much like the blaxploitation films that preceded them, these jive-talking heroes are remembered, albeit fondly, as an embarrassing period in comics' history. Yet, for better or worse, these macho men of blaxploitation remained the only significant representation of black heroes until Milestone appeared on the scene a few short years ago. In a medium that revolves around creators and fans who are perhaps more self-consciously aware of the historical developments of the superhero genre than the participants in any other popular genre of entertainment are, it was only natural that Milestone would explicitly address the blaxploitation period.

When I first met with the principal founders of Milestone they had just published a few weeks earlier a tale in *Icon* #13 (fig. 5.4), written by Dwayne McDuffie and pencilled by M. D. Bright, a tale that a great majority of the fans would subsequently point to as a particularly important and enjoyably self-referentially loaded narrative (every single fan of the Milestone books chose this issue of Icon as one of their five favorite stories). The story marks the debut of Buck Wild, Mercenary Man, an obvious tongue-in-cheek parody of Luke Cage, Hero for Hire. It is a slice of pure 1970s blaxploitation, right down to the disco-era superhero costumes, funky headband, and Buck's humorously inappropriate catchphrase exclamation, "Sweet Easter!"[4] The story dives right into Buck Wild's raid on a criminal hideout, where he overpowers several armed thugs. Unfortunately, Buck is captured and entranced by the "P-Whip" of his archenemy, Lysistra Jones.[5] She is a hip-hugger-wearing parody of the Tamara Dobson and Pam Grier type of roles from such blaxploitation films as *Cleopatra Jones* (1973) and *Foxy Brown* (1974). Still under the magical sway of the P-Whip, Buck is sent to fight Icon and Rocket, who are trying to close down a crack house which, as Buck puts it, "is sho 'nuff property of my main mistress, Lysistra Jones." After a brief battle—"Aunt Jemmima's Do-Rag!" declares Buck after Icon recovers from one of his patented "belief defying" strong punches, "you's about one tough son of a biscuit"—Icon and Rocket are able to subdue the out-of-place hero.

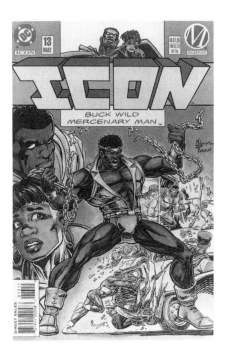

5.4   Icon #13 (1994). Illustration courtesy of DC Comics and Milestone Media, Inc.
Used with permission.

   To Icon and Rocket's surprise, Buck is defended by a crowd of onlookers
until the pain of Icon's grip helps Buck remember who he is. "I do remember,"
Buck mutters through clenched teeth as he proceeds to narrate a sequence of
flashbacks that more than subtly mirrors the origin story of Luke Cage (see
chapter 2). "It all started when I was convicted for a crime I didn't commit . . .
the joint wuz rough, but I wuz gonna do my time real quiet-like and go
straight. But one of the racist pig prison guards had other ideas . . . You call me
mister Charlie, boy!—mebbe it wuz cause I useta date his sister, I dunno. I
knowed right then that there was no way I'd survive my sentence. That's when
I volunteered fo' the experiment. They was experimenting with freezing people, and unthawin' em years later. Like frozen food. The deal was, if I survived
the experiment, they'd knock some time offa my sentence. But it didn't work."
Whoom! The lab where Buck was being frozen in a cryogenic tube exploded.
"Before the explosion," Buck continues, "nuthin' had frozen yet but my brain.
But somehow the accident gave me Tungsten-hard skin and belief-defyin'
strength." Thus Buck explains how his brain was frozen in 1972 and hasn't
thawed out yet, and Icon and Rocket decide to help Buck defeat Lysistra Jones.

After a quick arrest, Rocket sums up this story's nod to history when she tells Buck in the final panel "You are what you is. And 1972 was a long time ago. Maybe it's just time to move on."

When I asked writer and Milestone editor in chief Dwayne McDuffie, who was jokingly billed as "Trouble Man" in the credits to this particular issue, about Buck Wild, he was reluctant to admit that the character was meant as anything more than good fun for a bunch of fans turned creators. "Nothing more?" I pressed. "You mean, like a scathingly accurate social satire?" Denys "Black Caesar" Cowan, Milestone's creative director, joked from the corner of McDuffie's cramped office, which was packed with art samples for upcoming issues. "Nah . . . we were just having some fun with the old stuff." In this specific case, as with their entire line generally, it was clear that the folks at Milestone were wary of positioning their stories as anything more than good clean hero fun—in fear of being perceived as political rather than entertaining. But it is also clear that characters like Buck Wild and Lysistra Jones operate as both a nod to the troubled history of black superheroes and as a point of reference against which the Milestone characters can be read as a reinvention of the heretofore dominant black superheroic type. This is certainly how many of the fans read Buck Wild, and by extension the entire line of "new" heroes published by Milestone. While the Milestone characters are undeniably fresh variations of the overall superhero type, part of the pleasure that fans derive from their close readings of the books, made possible by their subcultural knowledge, relates to their perception of the Milestone characters as emerging from a specific, albeit short-lived, historical context.

While the heavy-handed comics from the blaxploitation era, like the motion pictures that inspired them, may in hindsight be characterized as having failed "in certain ways to represent the aesthetic values of black culture properly" (Lott 1991, 42), their influence is not forgotten by the Milestone creators or their fans. They may not have been perfect, but they still facilitated a sense of identification with the heroic for many young readers. By today's standards a character like Buck Wild is obviously a playful spoof of one of the genre's most awkward periods in time, but he is also a validation of the positive aspects of those past heroes. Working on at least two levels, Buck Wild is both history lesson and camp. Fans loved the character as either parody or homage. Many wrote in asking for Buck's return or maybe his own series. His trading card was, according to several young fans, the most sought after in the Milestone series of over fifty cards, and at least one fan took to painting him on the sleeve of his jacket. Recognizing his popular appeal, Milestone brought Buck back for several issues, even having him stand in for the original Icon when he was off in space contemplating a return to his own planet. Yet, finally, in perhaps one of comics most self-reflexive and metaphorical moments, Buck was killed off; and in *Icon* #30—"Because you demanded it!"—his funeral laid to rest not just Buck Wild but all the blaxploitation characters that he represented.

This hilarious thirtieth issue of *Icon* is full of so many allusions to historical characters that only a real genre fan would be able to catch them all. In this story Milestone manages to pay tribute and mark the end of an era that has haunted black comics for decades. In the story, which is told mostly in flash-back sequences, Icon's eulogy is repeatedly interrupted by various villains who had each previously fought Buck while he personified different blaxploitation heroes. First, Lysistra Jones—"in the fine, foxy flesh, baby!"—describes her first battle with Buck when, on the edge of defeat, he swallowed an "experi-mental growth serum created by a White guy much smarter than [him]" to become the giant Buck Goliath (a nod to Marvel's Black Goliath). Next, the pink-suit-wearing pimp Sweet Stick Max describes his battle with Buck when "he was working as a sidekick to that World War II hero, you know, The Pa-triot." After Max's "Ho Hordes" subdued the Patriot, it was Buck in a crazy flying suit that saved the day as Jim Crow (a parody of Captain America's black sidekick, the Falcon). The Cockroach Andy, who mutated into a giant cock-roach when his ghetto tenement was used as a dumping ground for nuclear waste, tells of how Buck Lightning (i.e., DC's Black Lightning) destroyed his plans to set off a roach bomb that would have mutated everyone in the city of Dakota. And finally, in a tribute to the Black Panther and all the other forgotten black characters that were associated with African royalty and dark magic, the Kingfish temporarily reanimates him as Buck Voodoo for one last battle before Darnice, Buck's partner while he was the substitute Icon, tells him, "I love you, Buck, but your time has passed."

In a eulogy for a comics era, thinly disguised as a eulogy for a specific char-acter, Icon's speech sums up the attitudes of both the Milestone creators and many of their fans. "I am considered by many to be a hero, an example of possibility and achievement. And recently, Buck has patterned himself after me," the character of Icon declares in a speech dripping with extratextual self-awareness. "But years before I arrived, Buck Wild was already there, fighting the good fight. Although we may, from our current perspective, have found him crude and ill-informed, we cannot deny his importance. Intentions count as much as actions. And Buck was nothing if not well-intentioned. He spent his life fighting for what is right, all the while struggling with questions of identity and public perception that we still do not have answers for. He reinvented himself time and again, searching for a comfortable way to present himself to the world. And while we winced on occasion at his embarrassing speech and demeaning behavior, more often we cheered him on . . . Because whatever else he was, he was always a hero. A hero for those of us who had no heroes. Were it not for him, we wouldn't be here today . . . And for all his failures, he died as he lived, trying to do what was right. Let us hope that when our day is done, history remembers us as kindly as it remembers him.''

Ironically, despite the criticism made of Milestone by Ania and other independent African American comic book publishers (see chapter 2), criticism that their characters could not possibly be authentic because they were tied through distribution with industry giant DC Comics, a number of the comics fans I talked to regard the Ania-type books as stuck in the blaxploitation era. By adamantly and very self-consciously creating comic books that emphasis a Black Aesthetic whereby all Afrocentric art must be separate from, and in opposition to, the dominant white cultural industries, some independent publishers are actually perceived as less progressive by the core audience of fans. For example, when I asked Matt, at the Chicago comicon, if either he or his son, Tim, had come across any other black comics that they enjoyed as much as the Milestone titles, with only a moment's hesitation he said they had not. ''There is some good stuff out there with Marvel and DC, like Storm and Bishop and Steel, but I'm kinda turned off the big companies right now, anyway. I have been looking at some of the small-scale stuff that gets hocked around here and at some of the shops back home. Some of it's pretty cool, but a lot of the superhero stuff is way too sexual in a juvenile let's-draw-dirty-pictures kind of way, and lots of it is trying so hard to bring in black solidarity and weirdly screwed up politics that they're a little embarrassing, and definitely not for my kid yet. I mean, running around in a leopard-skin G-string for back-to-Africa-ness? Come on! Haven't things changed since the Black Panther? Time to move on.'' It would seem that by focusing on the politics of cultural nationalism the Ania form of comic books are seen by some as ridiculously out of place.

It is a problem faced by the entire medium. Perceived as eternally childish by nonfans and restricted by the genre-based tastes of the bulk of comic book buyers, it is difficult for superhero comics to address serious issues. Certainly it has been done on occasion in even the most mainstream of books with great maturity and shocking effects. In recent years The Hulk has carried a story line in which a major character died of AIDS; in *Captain America* Steve Rogers was diagnosed with a rare cancer caused by the very growth serum that gives him his tremendous powers, and in *Night Cries* Batman was confronted with the effects of child abuse. But other examples illustrate the limitations that hinder social awareness in comics. In 1991 Marvel published a miniseries featuring a minor character, North Star, from the Canadian superhero team Alpha Flight. The story centered on North Star's coming out of the closet, and it garnered a lot of media attention. Even though the character was a practically unknown commodity, the fact that a superhero in comic books for children was gay seemed outrageous to a good deal of the public. For Ania and other Afrocentric publishers, the risk is that by presenting their political views in the form of a comic book, those views become lessened to the point of self-parody. A loin-cloth-wearing, spear-carrying hero may seem to be the perfect embodiment for radical black politics, but in the pages of a comic book it also resembles some of the most embarrassing stereotypes of black characters.

Milestone, on the other hand, by recognizing its development within the context of the superheroic genre and in relation to blaxploitation characters in particular, seems to have produced books that satisfy the fans' desire for traditional adventure narratives first and weave the racial/political dimension in as a result, rather than as a cause, of the comics. Rather than producing ethnically informed and explicitly counter-hegemonic books from the fringes of the industry, Milestone has managed to construct racially informed comics that are more subtly counter-hegemonic and work from within the mainstream of the superhero genre. By situating themselves so firmly within the most basic of comic book traditions, while reworking and critiquing those very same traditions, Milestone's presentation of black superheroes has managed to push the envelope. One of the most startling confessions I heard while interviewing comic book fans was from a thirteen-year-old boy in Toronto's grand mecca of comics stores, The Silver Snail. "I think I used to be pretty racist," he told me under his breath after looking around to see that nobody else was in listening distance. "I didn't like any of the black kids at school, or nothing. They always seemed kinda stupid hanging around acting tough in their baggy jeans and big jackets, and all. I don't even like rap or anything like that. But I've always been a big Spider-Man fan. I pick up everything with Spidey in it. So anyways, one day I'm talking to the guy behind the counter here who usually pulls my books for me and he says that if I like Spider-Man I should give Static a try. At first I thought, "Yeah, right!" But then I picked up a couple of issues one day when I had some spare bucks, and I really liked them. Static's pretty cool. So I don't know; maybe I've just grown up or something, but I do know that I look at black people differently now. Or really, I should say I don't look at them differently anymore." Quite a feat for a comic book.

6

Reading Comic Book Masculinity

Following in the footsteps of feminist scholarship, there have been, in recent years, a number of studies which have begun to consider masculinity, particularly heterosexual masculinity, as a social construction. Masculinity, always regarded as a natural, stable gender identity, is in the process of being deconstructed on a variety of levels from social politics to pop psychology. Moreover the masculinity of our media-generated heroes is increasingly recognized in much the same way that femininity has been understood, not as a real and unified subject position, but as a carefully orchestrated performance, or in other words as a masquerade. But if the heterosexual male is the site of gender and sexual privilege in North American culture, as it is perceived to be, then we might ask just what the masculine masquerade disguises? And how might black masculinity fit into the equation?

It is feasible that a clue to these questions lies in the very notion of the masquerade and the implication of an underlying, unstable level of gender identity. Indeed, the split personality implied by the concept of a masquerade seems to be one of the most archetypal metaphors for the masculine condition in Western culture. Whether in Jungian psychology or low-budget horror films, great literary works or modern comic books, masculinity has often explored its own duality. The male identity in the twentieth century is perceived in extremes: man or mouse, he-man or ninety-eight-pound weakling. At the one end is the hypermasculine ideal with muscles, sex appeal, and social competence, at the other end is the skinny and socially inept failure. But these two male extremes are not as far removed as they might seem. Warrior and wimp exist side by side, each defining the other in mutual opposition. In this chapter I want to explore the concept of duality in masculinity—and more specifically *black* masculinity—as it is currently presented in the superhero comic book. At its most obvious and symbolic level comic book masculinity characterizes for young readers a model of gender behavior that has traditionally struggled to incorporate both sides of the masquerade, yet has recently slipped into the domain of the almost exclusively hypermasculine.

The audience for comics is a truly multicultural one, in fact it is more ethnically diverse than are the heroes they read about. Thus, I want to reemphasize that my argument is not based only on young black readers of Milestone but on fans from a diversity of cultural backgrounds. Given the diversity of the comics-reading audience, it is important to understand what fans think of the books across racial lines rather than just how they speak directly to black members of the audience. Time and again, when asked about the appeal of the Milestone titles, many of the comic book readers I interviewed would return to the way the characters acted as heroes and as men. "For me it really isn't an issue of whether they're black or white," a twelve-year-old fan told me when I began research. "I like Icon and Static and Hardware because they're tough guys, but not *too* tough, if you know what I mean." At the time I did not know what he meant ("tough guys, but not *too* tough"!?), but as I spoke with more comic book readers it became increasingly apparent that masculinity in contemporary comic books is understood according to the medium's quintessential depiction of masculine duality. Superhero comics have always relied on the notion that a superman exists inside every man; and while the readers are well aware of this most fundamental convention, they are also aware that several new and incredibly popular comics are erasing the ordinary man underneath in favor of an even more excessively powerful and one-dimensional masculine ideal. Those young fans who count the Milestone books among their favorites do so because they offer an alternative to the extreme of hypermasculinity, or, as one reader put it, "With Milestone it isn't always the guy with the biggest arms that wins . . . it's the guy with the biggest brain."

Before turning specifically to the reading of Milestone comic books, it is important to understand the traditional gender framework against which these new black superheroes are read. Classical comic book depictions of masculinity are perhaps the quintessential expression of our cultural beliefs about what it means to be a man. In general, masculinity is defined by what it is not, namely "feminine," and by all its associated traits—hard *not* soft, strong *not* weak, reserved *not* emotional, active *not* passive. One of the most obvious and central focal points for characterizing masculinity has been the male body. As an external signifier of masculinity, the body has come to represent all the conventions traditionally linked to assumptions of male superiority. "Of course," Susan Bordo has observed in her discussion of contemporary body images, "muscles have chiefly symbolized and continue to symbolize masculine power as physical strength, frequently operating as a means of coding the 'naturalness' of sexual difference" (1993b, 193). The muscular body is a heavily inscribed sign; nothing else so clearly marks an individual as a bearer of masculine power (I will be returning to the symbolic significance of muscles in relation to both black and comic book masculinity later). In fact, muscles are so adamantly read as a sign of masculinity that women who develop noticeable muscularity (e.g., professional bodybuilders) are often accused of gender transgression, of being butch or too "manly," in much the same way that underdeveloped men are open to the criticism of being too feminine.

The status and the power of the hard male body are only achieved in contrast to those cultural identities represented as soft and vulnerable. This myth of idealized masculinity, which is still incredibly pervasive, remains dependent upon the symbolic split between masculinity and femininity, between the *hard* male and the *soft* other. And in the misogynistic, homophobic, and racist view of this ideology, the despised other that masculinity defines itself against conventionally includes not only women but also feminized men. It is, I think, important to note that this standard of masculinity so vigorously reinforced in Western culture is largely focused on white masculinity and is at root a fascist ideology. In his exploration of masculinity and fascist ideology, *Male Fantasies* (1977), Klaus Theweleit outlines the existence of two mutually exclusive body types observed by German fascists. The first was the upstanding, steel-hard, organized, machine-like body of the German master, and the second was the flaccid, soft, fluid body of the perennial other. According to Theweleit, the hard masculine ideal was the armored body, armored by muscles and by emotional rigidity marked by a vehement desire to eradicate the softness, the emotional liquidity of the feminine other. But the emasculating (i.e., castrating) criticism of effeminacy was also routinely projected by the dominant onto those marked as other primarily by their cultural or religious backgrounds. Although the feared body of the other was most directly modeled on the feminine, it was, as we know from Nazi practices of extermination, also projected onto the homosexual, the Jew, and a long list of non-Aryan others. While Nazi Germany may be an extreme example, the underlying rhetoric is far from alien to modern Western culture. Even today, for example, gay men are labeled as excessively feminine, Jewish men are characterized as meek, frail, and hen-pecked, and Asian men are derided in stereotype as skinny, weak, small, and humorously nearsighted. We must keep in mind that the standard phallic version of the masculine ideal is deeply grounded in not just misogynistic and homopho-bic ideology but also in thinly veiled racist terms.

But not all others have been constructed as equal by the dominant masculi-nist ideology. While the gay man, the Jewish man, the Asian man (and many other "others") have been burdened by the projection of castrated softness, the black man has been subjected to the burden of racial stereotypes that place him in the symbolic space of being *too* hard, *too* physical, *too* bodily. Ironically, much of the tension regarding the hypermasculine stereotype of black men is a logical cultural development for a group systematically denied full access to the socially constructed ideals of masculinity. In his discussion of the sexual politics of race, Kobena Mercer argues that black masculinity must be under-stood as a paradoxical position in relation to dominant gender ideals. Mercer puts it thus:

Whereas prevailing definitions of masculinity imply power, control and authority, these attributes have been historically denied to black men since slavery. The centrally domi-nant role of the white male slave master in eighteenth- and nineteenth-century planta-tion societies debarred black males from patriarchal privileges ascribed to the masculine role. For example, a slave could not fully assume the role of "father," as his children were legal property of the slave owner. In racial terms, black men and women alike were subordinated to the power of the white master in the hierarchical social relations of slavery, and for black men, as objects of oppression, this also canceled out their access to positions of power and prestige which in gender terms are regarded as the essence of masculinity in patriarchy. Shaped by this history, black masculinity is a highly contradic-tory formation of identity, as it is a subordinated masculinity. (1994, 142)

In 1990s North America the situation has not changed all that dramatically for a large majority of black men. Legally sanctioned institutions of slavery may no longer exist, but persistent racist fears and ideologies continue to economi-cally, politically, and socially oppress black men. According to recent statistics (Goar 1995, A-1), the unequal discrepancies between black and white America are as clear as ever. One-third of the 29 million black citizens in the United States live in poverty; the average black American earns $6,700 less per year than the average white worker and is twice as likely to be unemployed. One in every three black children is currently growing up without a father in the home; and perhaps most shocking, although black Americans constitute only 12 per-cent of the nation's population they represent 51 percent of the country's prison population. Yet, society at large still presents a cultural ideal of masculin-ity that black men are expected to measure up to, at the same time that it denies a great many blacks access to legitimate means for achieving that ideal.

The history of the black male paradox—emasculated, but at the same time feared—is grounded in a long tradition of subjugation and resistance. The

black man's cultivation and embrace of a hypermasculine image has been described by bell hooks as a logical response to antebellum and post-antebellum
views held by white supremacists, views that characterized black men as feminine, a rhetoric that "insisted on depicting the black male as symbolically castrated, a female eunuch" (1994, 131). The clearest, and most often cited,
examples from the first half of this century are the boxing phenomenons Jack
Johnson and Joe Louis, both of whom personified black hypermasculinity as a
means to resist the emasculation of racism; their prowess in the ring was reinforced by widely circulated images of the two men shirtless and intimidatingly
muscular. By the time of the Civil Rights era, the more overtly political and
rebellious Black Panther movement articulated what Hunter and Davis refer to
as "a radicalized Black manhood, throwing off the imagery of the emasculated
and shuffling Black male dictated by racial caste" (1994, 23). Even in contemporary Western culture, the most pervasive and influential images of black men
are tied up in hypermasculine symbols. The two primary means to legitimate
success for black males in popular culture, sports and music, ensure the replica-
tion of such ideals from the world of sports as Michael Jordan, Mike Tyson, Bo
Jackson, and Shaquille O'Neil and such overtly masculine examples from music
as L. L. Cool J., Snoop Doggy Dog, and Tupac Shakur—images that consistently
associate black men with extremes of physicality and masculine posturing.
Over the years, in a diversity of ways, black men have responded to their
shared experience of cultural alienation by adopting "certain patriarchal values
such as physical strength, sexual prowess and being in control as a means of
survival against the repressive and violent system of subordination to which
they were subjected" (Mercer 1994, 137).

Recently, Richard G. Majors' concept of "cool pose" has proven an insightful term for understanding the dynamics of black masculinity as it has developed in response to unequal conditions in the modern urban environment. In
a series of closely related works (see Majors 1986, 1990; Majors and Billson
1992; Majors et al 1994) Majors argues that black males have accepted the
traditional values of masculinity but are so restricted by social and political
factors that many of them have been deeply frustrated by their inability to
enact these traditional masculine roles. "In brief," Majors explains, "cool pose
originated as a coping mechanism for the 'invisibility,' frustration, discrimination, and educational and employment inequities faced by Black males. In response to these obstacles, many of these individuals have channeled their
creative talents and energies into the construction of masculine symbols and
into the use of conspicuous nonverbal behaviors (e.g., demeanors, gestures,
clothing, hairstyles, walks, stances and handshakes)" (Majors et al 1994, 246).
Majors includes in his examples of the cool pose such diverse behaviors as the

use of humor, feigned emotional detachment, and specific stylistic expressions like the black athletes' inventive basketball dunking, football spiking and end-zone dancing, as well as black musical performers' aggressive posing and graceful yet strenuous dancing styles. A prime ingredient of the cool pose as a compensatory form of masculinity is an exaggerated style of toughness. "Symbolic displays of toughness defend his identity and gain him respect; they can also promote camaraderie and solidarity among black males" (Majors and Billson 1992, 30). Unfortunately, as Majors is always careful to point out, the ritualized hypermasculinity performed by many black men as a cool pose, particularly the preoccupation with enacting a tough persona, is rife with the negative potential to promote dangerous lifestyles (e.g., gang bangers, tough guys, drug dealers, street hustlers, or pimps) and to reinforce harmful stereotypes.

The cool pose that is so important to the understanding of black masculinity in contemporary Western culture is, in essence, another metaphorical mask. "For some black males," Majors and Billson write, "cool pose represents a fundamental structuring of the psyche—the cool mask belies the rage held in check beneath the surface . . . black males have learned to use posing and posturing to communicate power, toughness, detachment, and style" (1992, 8). Of course, the concept of black culture's employment of a mask is not a new one. James Baldwin's novels were about the complexity and effectiveness of masking as a defensive strategy; and psychoanalytic accounts of the black position, such as Frantz Fanon's much cited *Black Skin, White Masks* (1970), have formalized the concept. What is interesting, though, about the cool pose as a mask of masculinity is that by its very definition—a mask of a mask—it becomes a location of exaggerated masculine signifiers. Hence, both by projection of the dominant white society's fears and the black male's embrace and overcompensating performance of extreme masculine values, many black males (consciously or unconsciously) are perceived as relatively *too* masculine. While the cool pose can, and often does, embody attitudes beyond those of toughness and fearlessness, attitudes that suggest alternative forms of masculinity that might exercise a genuine control over traditional masculine features of symbolic physicality as power, it is the trope of toughness and bodily presence—as reductionist and potentially harmful a stereotype as this is—that is most commonly associated with popular images of black masculinity in the modern world.

Throughout history, white society's fear of the black man has been grounded in notions of masculine physicality and sexuality. While muscles act as a visible signifier of masculine power as physical strength, Bordo points out, "they have often been suffused with racial meanings as well (as in numerous film representations of sweating, glistening bodies belonging to black slaves and prizefighters)" (1993b, 195). Under the racial and class biases of our culture and compounded by the hypermasculinization of the cool pose, muscles, as a signifier of "natural" power, have been strongly linked with the black male body. So strong is the association, Kobena Mercer argues, that classical racism "involved a logic of dehumanization, in which African peoples were defined as having *bodies but not minds*" (1994, 138). The dehumanizing aspect of this myth, a myth that Mercer claims many black men do not want demystified because it in some ways (e.g., strength, sexual prowess) raises them above the status of white men, is that while an emphasis on the body as brute force is a marker of the difference between male and female, it is also a key symbol in the division between nature and culture. As much as the body has been related with the "virtues" of masculinity, it has also been associated via racial and class prejudices with the insensitive, the unintelligent, and the animalistic. Moreover, the more one's identity is linked to a hypermasculine persona based on the body, the more uncultured and uncivilized, the more bestial, one is considered to be. Following the binary logic of the male/female, nature/culture, uncivilized/civilized, body/mind dynamic, blacks have historically and symbolically been represented as pure body and little mind.

Because of this racist ideological paradox, blacks in Western culture have been forced to shoulder the burdens of the body itself. In contemporary culture black men are often seen more as beasts, rapists, gangster, crack heads, and muggers—literally as bodies out of control—than as fathers, scholars, statesmen, and leaders. It is perhaps this split between the mind and the body that marks one of the greatest threats of (self-)destruction facing blacks today. Like Majors' concern for the negative consequences of the cool pose as a lifestyle choice in an urban environment of unequal opportunity, bell hooks also heartfeltly writes, "I continue to think about the meaning of healing the split between mind and body in relationship to black identity, living in a culture where *racist colonization has deemed black folks more body than mind.* Such thinking lies at the core of all the stereotypes of blackness (many of which are embraced by black people) which suggests we are 'naturally, inherently' more in touch with our bodies, less alienated than other groups in this society" (1994, 129). Recognizing the ruinous consequences of this perceived split between black men's bodies and minds, Mercer, Majors, hooks, and numerous other black scholars and cultural critics see the need for new models of black masculinity to develop, models that counter the dominant stereotypes not by reforming the hypermasculine image of the black male into an image of refinement, restraint, and desexualization but by incorporating the associated properties of the mind (e.g., intelligence, control, wisdom) into the popular presentation of black male identity. It is here that the Milestone comic books seem to work for many readers as a promising alternative form of black masculinity, specifically, and Western masculinity, in general, particularly when read against the most pervasive form of comic book masculinity on offer from other comic book publishers.

With its reliance on duality and performative masquerade the popular image of black masculinity seems to parallel comic book conventions of masculinity. Certainly, superhero comics are one of our culture's clearest illustrations of hypermasculinity and male duality premised on the fear of the unmasculine other. Since the genre's inception with the launch of Superman in 1938 the main ingredient of the formula has been the dual identity of the hero. While the superhero body represents in vividly graphic detail the muscularity, the confidence, the power that personifies the ideal of phallic masculinity, the alter ego—the identity that must be kept a secret—depicts the softness, the powerlessness, the insecurity associated with the feminized man. As his very name makes clear, Superman is the ultimate masculine ideal of the twentieth century. He can fly faster than the speed of light, cause tidal waves with a puff of breath, see through walls, hear the merest whisper from hundreds of miles away, and squeeze a lump of coal in his bare hands with enough pressure to create a diamond. He is intelligent, kind, handsome, and an ever vigilant defender of truth, justice, and the American way. Superman, however, has never been complete with out Clark Kent, his other self. Emphasizing just how exceptional a masculine ideal Superman is, Clark Kent represents an exaggeratedly ordinary man. He is shy, clumsy, insecure, cowardly, and easily bullied by others. In short, where Superman is associated with all of the social attributes prized in men, Clark Kent represents those attributes traditionally associated with femininity and thus feared as unmasculine. In his study of the masculine myth in popular culture, Antony Easthope claims that "stories like Superman force a boy to choose between a better self that is masculine and only masculine and another everyday self that seems feminine" (1990, 28).

Yet, despite the derisively castrated portrayal of Clark Kent, it is this failure-prone side of the character that facilitates reader identification with the fantasy of Superman. This archetype of the Clark Kent, who can transform in a moment of crisis into a virtual superman, is a fantasy played out over and over again in superhero comic books. "Though the world may mock Peter Parker, the timid teenager," declares the cover of *Amazing Fantasy* #15 (1963), ". . . it will soon marvel at the awesome might of Spider-man!" Spoiled playboy Bruce Wayne becomes Batman. Shy scientist David Banner transforms into the monstrous Hulk when he gets angry. Young Billy Batson becomes the world's mightiest mortal, Captain Marvel, merely by uttering the acronym "Shazam."

Scrawny Steve Rogers becomes the invincible Captain America after drinking an experimental growth serum. The list is endless; for nearly every comic book hero there is a variation on the wimp/warrior theme of duality. The story of superheroes has always been a wish-fulfilling fantasy for young men. Even comic book advertisements, such as the legendary Charles Atlas "98-pound weakling" ad, often revolve around the male daydream that if we could just find the right word, the right experimental drug, the right radioactive waste, then we, too, might instantly become paragons of masculinity. For young comic book fans the superhero offers an immediate and highly visible example of the hypermasculine ideal. The polarized attributes coded as desirable/undesirable, masculine/feminine are simplified in the four-color world of the comics page to the external trappings of idealized masculinity. Even more than the flashy, colorful, and always skintight costumes that distinguish comic book heroes, their ever-present muscles immediately mark the characters not just as heroes but as *real* men.

This link between masculinity and muscles is an important association for comic book heroes (and in a parallel form an important association within the stereotyping of black men). Yet, by focusing on the external trappings of masculinity characterized by the musculature of the superhero's body, young readers may run the risk of overinternalizing these rather one-dimensional gender symbols. In his insightful ethnography of a southern California gym, Alan Klein (1993) discusses bodybuilders as men who have overidentified with what he calls comic book masculinity. "Comic book depictions of masculinity are so obviously exaggerated," Klein claims, "that they represent fiction twice over, as genre and as gender representation" (267). "Moreover," Klein continues "the reader is set up to be simultaneously impressed by the superhero and dismissive of the alter ego, a situation that underscores the overvalued place of hypermasculinity for readers of this genre of comic books" (268). Klein argues that for many bodybuilders the obsessive quest for ever larger, more imposing, more powerful-looking physiques is very similar to the comic book readers' fantasy of negating the soft, fearful, feminine side that they so despise in themselves. Superhero comics clearly split masculinity into two distinct camps, stressing the superhero side as the ideal to be aspired to; but unlike the fascist ideology of phallic masculinity as mutually exclusive of the softer, feminized other, comic book masculinity is ultimately premised on the *inclusion* of the devalued side. Even if Clark Kent and Peter Parker exist primarily to reinforce the reader's fantasy of self-transformation and to emphasize the masculine ideal of Superman and Spider-Man, they are still portrayed as a part of the character that is essential to their identities as a whole.

Rather than an outright condemning of comic book depictions of masculinity, Klein reserves his criticism for societal constructions that lead readers to value and identify with the hypermasculine rather than other potentially radical, liberating, or transgressive gender traits. In fact, Klein recognizes that "insofar as these comic book constructs are part of childhood socialization, their dualism could be functional, even therapeutic, were one to acknowledge the positive attributes of the superhero's alter ego and the dialectical relationship between wimp and warrior," after all, "both male and female co-exist within the Superman/Clark Kent figure" (1993, 267–68). Unfortunately, the potential that Klein sees as possible in the superhero's codependent male/female identified personas, were it not for our overvaluation of the purely masculine side, is presently even more disparaged in the extremely popular line of Image comics. Since Image's inception in the early 1990s it has become the fastest growing comics publisher in the history of the medium and is currently second only to the industry giant Marvel in monthly sales. As might be predicted of a company formed by popular artists rather than writers, Image's success can be credited to their flashy artwork depicting excesses of costumed heroism and constant large-scale battles. The Image books are identifiable by a distinctive in-house style of portraying the heroic body. As eager participants in the Bad Girl trend, Image women are uniformly illustrated as impossibly sexy, silicone injected, and scantily clad babes wielding phallically obvious swords. Even more pronounced than the unrealizable physical extremes of the Image women are the incredibly exaggerated representations of the male hero's body as a mass of veiny muscles. The Image trademarks of buxom cheesecake women and massive beefcake men are well illustrated in a typical cover for one of the company's crossover specials featuring Prophet and Avengelyne (fig. 6.1). The male's hulking form dwarfs the dominatrix-like superheroine; indeed, his bulging arms alone are bigger than her entire body. And these two characters are among Image's most modest.

With the Image books, the already reductive aspects of comic book masculinity are reduced even further into the realm of the purely symbolic. Image's very name suggests the extremes that their stylized portrayals of masculinity have taken as pure form, as pure *image*. Image provides hypermasculine ideals that are more excessively muscular than Superman or Batman ever dreamed of being. The Image heroes set a new standard of hypermasculinity. In fact, Image has frequently done away with the superhero's mild-mannered alter ego all together. Where the classic superhero comic book may have asked "boys to identify with Superman as a super-masculine ideal by rejecting the Clark Kent side of themselves" (Easthope 1990, 29), the Image books have made that rejection unnecessary. Clark Kent, it seems, no longer exists. By downplaying, or completely erasing, the hero's secret identity the Image books mark an ex-

6.1   Avengelyne and Prophet #1 (1996). Used with permission.

treme shift to the side of hypermasculinity as an ideal not even tokenly tempered by a softer, more humane side. Scott Bukatman has likened the Image
hero to Klein's bodybuilders, who value the hypermuscular body for its ability
to communicate masculinity without an act—via the obvious overpresence of
masculine signifiers—the body's presence becoming, in effect, its own text.
Bukatman insightfully notes, "In these postmodern times of emphatic surfaces
and lost historicities, origin tales are no longer stressed: the hyperbolically muscular heroes of Image Comics are nothing more or less than what they look
like; the marked body has become an undetermined sign as issues of identity
recede into the background. Most of these heroes seem to have no secret
identities at all, which is just as well [since] some have purple skin and are the
size of small neighborhoods" (1994, 101). The feminine side of the equation
has been so successfully sublimated that it ceases to exist at all. Even the limited
two-dimensional depiction of masculinity that superhero comics have represented ever since Superman emerged in 1938 has now begun to skew toward
a more macho, more one-dimensional depiction. If the hypermasculine identity
of the masked superhero has traditionally stood as a utilizable, imaginative

fantasy masquerade of idealized masculinity, then with the Image style of hero the masquerade has come to be all there is, an entity unto itself. The external trappings of masculinity, the message seems to be, are all one really needs to be a man.

It is in relation to this hypermasculine style of superhero books, either Image's own titles or the many imitations they have inspired, that many readers interpret the Milestone books. Compared to Image, the Milestone comic books offer readers an alternative model of masculinity, a model that is all the more progressive because it is incorporated within the dynamics of contemporary black masculinity.

If comic book superheroes represent an acceptable, albeit obviously extreme, model of hypermasculinity, and if the black male body is already culturally ascribed as a site of hypermasculinity, then the combination of the two—a black male superhero—runs the risk of being read as an overabundance, a potentially threatening cluster of masculine signifiers. In fact, prior to the emergence of Milestone, the dominating image of black superheroism was the often embarrassing image of characters inspired by the brief popularity of blaxploitation films in the mid 1970s. Such comic book heroes as Luke Cage, Black Panther, Black Lightning, and Black Goliath, who emerged during the blaxploitation era, were often characterized in their origins, costumes, street language, and antiestablishment attitudes as more overtly macho than their white-bread counterparts. In many ways the Milestone characters have functioned for fans as a redressing of these earlier stereotypes, providing a much needed alternative to the jive-talking heroes of yesterday, as well as on occasion spoofing the blaxploitation heritage and placing it in an acceptable historical context.

Yet, even today, black superheroes seem to oversignify masculinity to the point of being repositioned for the general public as humorous characters. Recently, white comic book superheroes have been seriously and faithfully adapted for such successful feature films as the *Batman* series (1989, 1992, and 1995), *The Mask* (1994), and *The Crow* (1994). Unfortunately, the same cannot be said for black superheroes. Instead of the grim, serious neo-noir success of other comic books turned into films, the only black entries in this ever-expanding movie genre have been the comedies *Meteor Man* (1993) and *Blank Man* (1994). Rather than legitimate superpowered heroes, Meteor Man and Blank Man, as enacted by Robert Townsend and Damon Wayans, respectively, are bumbling spoofs. Although well-intentioned films, with ultimate true heroism from the comedic protagonists, they are overwritten by the image of the black-costumed hero as a failure, as a buffoon incapable of exercising real power. Even the short-lived television series *Mantis* (1994), starring Carl Lumbly as a crippled black scientist who fights crime with the aid of his exoskele-ton-reinforced Mantis costume, was so done on such a low budget that it was considered a comedy by most comic book readers when in fact it was meant as serious science fiction drama.

Many of Milestone's most popular characters face the difficult task of play-ing it straight as black superheroes at the same time that they emphasize their intelligence as one of their most significant attributes, all without diminishing the masculine power fantasy so important to fans of the genre. In direct com-parison to the typical Image hero, Milestone heroes are much more realistically depicted, both narratively and in portrayal of the muscular male body—compare the overinflated body on the cover of Image's *Union* (fig. 6.2) with the portrait of a relatively skinny Static, Milestone's electricity-wielding teen-age superhero, on the cover of *Static* #1 (fig. 2.7). "I really like the Milestone titles for what they're not, namely, Image books," a thirteen-year-old African American comics fan claimed while organizing his purchases just outside the dealers' hall of a local comic book convention. "Static and Hardware and even Icon are a lot more realistic, not so cartoony. I mean . . . I know they're comic

6.2   Union #2 *(1994). Used with permission.*

books but come on, look at those guys [in the Image books]; they're fucking *huge!* At least the characters at Milestone look like they could fit through a doorway." I should point out that some of the readers I have studied related to the Milestone books primarily as an alternative or a variation on the theme of black superheroes as presented in the earlier blaxploitation-style comics of the 1970s and/or the contemporary Afrocentrist and more politically extreme books personified by the Ania publications. But the reading formation I am primarily concerned with here is the way in which many fans, both black and white, understand the Milestone line as it stands in relation to the dominant Image-style emphasis on hypermasculine/hypermuscular bodies and underdeveloped narratives featuring what one comics dealer called "brainless brawl after brainless brawl."

What Milestone comic books do is put the mind back in the body, the Clark Kent back in the Superman. Milestone does this so often with black superheroes that this allows them to develop the image of powerful black men as much more than mere hypermasculine brutes—"tough, but not *too* tough." When the conclusion to Milestone's third crossover event, "The Long Hot Summer," was published, many of the readers I had spoken with were eager to point out that the surprisingly peaceful resolution to an amusement park riot was indicative of the company's approach to brains-over-brawn. "Man, just when you thought everything was going to get really, *really* bloody," a fan in his early twenties explained, "Wise Son [leader of the Blood Syndicate, Milestone's multicultural supergang] gets to the park's communication systems and simply talks people out of hurting each other . . . basically shames them into being responsible for their actions." Likewise, one fan who was a senior university student was able to recall, almost word for word, his favorite bit of dialogue from *Hardware* #9, a series featuring a black scientific genius who dons his self-constructed superarmor to fight crime. "Hardware is fighting this Alva Technologies–created female version of himself called Technique," the student recalled, "when he loses his jet pack and is falling from thousands of feet up. He grabs his pack and tries to fix it while he's falling, thinking, 'So here's where I find out if I'm the genius that my IQ tells me I am.' When the pack works again, moments before becoming street pizza, he says, and this is a great line, 'Worked like a charm! Who says those tests are culturally biased?' " One especially enthusiastic and thoughtful black fan in his late teens remarked, "It's nice to see cool brothers in the comics who can *think* their way out of a rough spot. You know, Icon's a lawyer, Hardware's an all-purpose science supergenius, and Static, well, he's just a high school kid but he's the coolest, and I think the smartest, of all them. Yeah, I'd stack Static up against any other superhero any day. He's the man." Other readers seemed to agree: "Oh yeah, Static, he's got the best sense of humor and the thing is everybody thinks he's just this kid with wimpy lightning powers, but he's the smart one, always putting down guys bigger than him by being smarter." As an example of the preferred Milestone brains-over-brawn style, several fans chose one of Static's earliest adventures as among their favorites.

The story entitled "Pounding the Pavement," written by Robert L. Washington and Dwayne McDuffie, appeared in the August 1993 issue *Static #3.* The tale features the first appearance of a powerful new villain, Tarmack, in Milestone's fictional setting of Dakota City. As the characters in the book point out, Tarmack looks and acts like a black version of the evil, liquid metal T2000 from the popular movie *Terminator 2: Judgment Day* (1992). Essentially, he is a shape-shifting mass of, *well,* tarmac. Usually configured in the shape of a large and muscular black male body, Tarmack can transform himself into a liquefied state or change his appendages into whatever weapon he desires, including knives, hammers, and anvils. One of Virgil (Static) Hawkins' friends describes Tarmack as "a six-foot blob of silly putty that turns into Riddock Bowe whenever it wants to." The problem is that Tarmac has his sights set on making a name for himself as the guy who takes down Static. He first tries to challenge Static to a fight by destroying a local high school hangout. Unfortunately, Static, who was tied up washing dishes at his part-time job in a nearby burger franchise, arrives too late to fight but in time to rescue bystanders trapped in the building's rubble.

At school the next day, while Virgil is asking his friends to describe Tarmack, word comes that "the guy who trashed Akkad's is at the playground calling Static out!" Tarmack taunts Static's masculinity, calling him a coward unless he shows up to fight. "Static! Are you deaf, or just afraid?" Tarmack bellows while tearing up all the rides at the playground. "Hidin' behind yo' ugly *momma* won't help boy!" Making up an excuse about having asthma and the excitement being too much for him, Virgil sneaks off to change into his Static costume and returns to confront Tarmac with his usual wit. "Hey, Hatrack," Static calls, "let's work this out over coffee, some cappuccino for *me* . . . a nice cup of silt for *you.*" They proceed to battle for a while with neither gaining the upper hand, then, when Static proves more concerned about the safety of innocent bystanders than with the contest, Tarmac dares Static to show up at a deserted parking lot at midnight in order to decide who's the toughest.

While riding the subway home after school, Virgil and his friends debate what will happen in the final showdown between Static and Tarmac. "I think the high n' mighty Static is gonna get his ass handed to him," argues Larry. "Tarmack has all the *Terminator 2* moves! Hammerhands, spike hands whatever! He can melt whatever he touches!" "Well, I think Static's gonna kick butt!'' Virgil argues back, a little defensive, a little nervous. ''I think you're both wrong,'' interrupts Frieda, the only one of Virgil's friends who knows his secret identity. ''Static's too smart to fall for such an obvious trap.''

''That guy's too dumb to set such an obvious trap, or any trap. Static'll fade 'im,'' Virgil counters good naturedly. ''You think ol' stinky goo head is out of Static's league?'' ''He's older! And Bigger! Static should leave him to Icon!'' Frieda warns. ''Listen,'' Virgil confides to Frieda under his breath. ''I know it's dangerous. I'm not buying into this anymore than you. But I've got two things he doesn't. A brain . . . and a plan.''

Later that night, in the Avalon Mall parking lot, a lone and angry Tarmac bellows, ''Static! It's ten after midnight! If you're hidin', you best come out *now*!'' Tarmac spins around just in time to see a trench-coat-clad figure surf to the ground on electrical currents. ''That's better! Turn around! I want to see your face when you die!'' Tarmac screams as he winds up a massive hammer-hand punch. ''Have it your way toyboy . . . wha!?'' As Tarmac delivers his blow the body bursts in a spray of water. Tarmac is left soaked and clutching a deflated plastic clown. ''What the @#&* is this?''

''Kawarim!!!,'' the real Static replies from the shadows as he shoots a powerful charge of electricity through Tarmac. ''Ancient Ninja art of misdirection. All you need is something some idiot could mistake for you and . . . some idiot. Guess which one you are.'' Angrier than ever, Tarmac chases Static across the parking lot. Suddenly, Static turns and uses his electromagnetic powers to wrap a wire fence around Tarmac. ''How do I do it, you may ask. How do I stay one jump ahead of you?'' Static taunts. ''How you want to *die*, is all I'm askin'!'' Tarmac yells, as his body begins to liquefy and escape through the links in the fence. ''It's easy. You're a moron.'' Static continues in a fake British accent. ''Also, I was here early. Several hours, in fact. Been shoppin.' ''

''What're you dumpin' into meeee!?'' screams Tarmac as Static throws several canisters into the now completely liquid villain. ''Old aerosol cans,'' Static explains, ''Got 'em on sale. Freon, don't you know. Amazing what you can find in a bargain bin, huh. Wanna see what else I got?'' All Tarmac can do is howl in pain and frustration as Static hurls flashbulbs and dry ice onto the quickly solidifying form lying on the ground. ''Sheesh! I gotta get a better class of supervillain,'' Static scoffs as he spells out his plan for Tarmac. ''See, I figured your liquid body and all that heat went hand in hand. So if you went through some changes, you'd burn up.''

''SSllowwinn' downnn . . . brrr,'' Tarmac gasps. ''Brrr? You actually say brrr? I don't be-*lie*-ve it!'' Static jokes as he pours a canister of freezing liquid oxygen over the now-defeated Tarmac. And as a final insult, Static climbs aboard a steamroller from a nearby construction sight and proceeds to literally flatten

Tarmac. "You are sorely in need of a name change, dude. That 'Mack' thing is so '70s . . . I know what . . . how about I paint a stripe down your middle and . . . Presto! Ta-da! 'I-75, the Living Interstate!' "

Static #3 ends with the humiliating defeat of Tarmac and the arrival of Holocaust, a bigger and badder villain for Static to deal with in the next issue. On one level it is tempting to develop the case that this issue of Static critiques an outdated model of black masculinity. After all, apparently inspired by Tarmac's one-dimensional macho posturing, Static even goes so far as to declare, "That 'Mack' thing is so '70s." But for the Milestone fans who pointed to this specific book as a favorite, it is the story's difference from the current hypermasculine and "brainless" Image comics that makes it important. The message of "Pounding the Pavement" is clear: brains win out over brawn. Nor is this message an isolated incident. *Static* story lines have repeatedly portrayed the teenage hero as victorious because of his quick thinking. Numerous bragging and swaggering supervillains have faced Static, most of whom are clearly more powerful than him and boastfully macho about their intentions to beat him up. Yet time and again Static outthinks the baddies. Other examples cited by readers include Static's capture of a superpowered car thief, Joyride, by pretending to lose a drag race, thus playing on the villain's ego and tricking him into stepping out of his car, whereby he loses all his powers; or Static's continual outsmarting of the recurring villain Hotstreak, who is too stupid to realize that the new hammer he wields so proudly is made of metal and thus can be controlled by Static's electrical currents. Static's form of intelligent victories is clearly read by some Milestone readers as a positive alternative to the standard formula found in the market-dominating Image-type books. "You'd never really see an Image hero winning a fight by being funny and smart enough to know dry ice and aerosol cans could knock out a serious bad guy," a thirteen-year-old *Static* fan explained. "In other comic books they're much more likely to just keep on pounding each other until the good guy rips the villain's head off, or something crazy like that."

By emphasizing brains-over-brawn as a fundamental problem-solving technique in many of their stories, Milestone comic books suggest acceptable variations of the masculine ideal for their readers. Rather than espousing the reductionist hypermasculine might-makes-right norm of the Image books, Milestone's series continually depict heroism as a matter of intelligence first and power second, showing that, in fact, intelligence *is* the greatest power of them all. For black readers, and for nonblack readers sensitive to minority concerns, the alternative depiction of *black* masculinity bearing the attributes of both mind and body is, as one fan declared, "progressive, realistic, radical, and a much needed reworking of the African American image in the media."

Although it is clear how the Static tale recounted here stresses the reincorpora-tion of "a brain . . . and a plan" as more significant than muscles and brute force, its typical comic book superhero*ish* narrative might seem to undercut any claims made about it representing new forms of masculine ideals. It is, after all, still a relatively straightforward comic book story about two superpowered, costumed characters fighting it out. But when carried to its furthest extreme, Milestone's narrative style, which is interpreted by many readers as antithetical to the dominant hypermasculine Image style, offers alternative models.

The most apparent revisionist models are usually presented within the pages of Milestone's flagship title *Icon*. Unfairly derided by several other African American publishers as nothing more than a chocolate-dip Superman, this pop-ular series follows the adventures of Icon (aka Augustus Freeman IV), an alien with enormous powers (yes, much like Superman's) who has lived in the form of a black man since crashing on a slave plantation over 150 years ago, and his teenage sidekick, Rocket (aka Raquel Irvin), who can fly and redirect vast amounts of energy thanks to the alien technology of her power belt. With Icon's enormous powers and incredibly straight-arrow persona and Rocket's passion and social conscience, the series is Milestone's most emblematic affir-mation of black heroism. "They can be a little preachy sometimes," a fourteen year old told me when I noticed him reading an issue of *Icon* in a shopping mall's food court, "but it's really my favorite book right now. The characters are well done, and the art is usually first rate. And," he looked around a little sheepishly, "I like the stories where they show how Icon has affected normal people in Dakota, you know, inspired them." In his hands was a particularly clear example of Icon's inspiration as a promotion of how readers might pursue masculine ideals built on well-rounded self-improvement rather than the one-dimensional pursuit of hypermasculine power fantasies. *Icon* #32, "Learning to Fly," written by Greg Middleton and illustrated by Elim Mak, is really the story of Lenny, a black youth from the same projects as Icon's partner, Raquel (Rocket) Ervin. Lenny was with Raquel and the others on the night they tried to rob the house of Augustus Freeman, who, under pressure from Raquel, would later become Icon. Years after that first incident, Raquel arranges for Icon to meet and counsel Lenny, who has had trouble staying on the "straight and narrow" since that fateful night.

"I told you, you changed my *outlook*," Lenny tells Icon as they stroll along the city's waterfront. "But now the funds ain't what they used to be, so me and my girl Susan been fighting. I found out she's seeing Caesar, down the block. He's *not* 'on-the-straight-and-narrow.' Of course we broke up, but . . . I don't know, man. The so-called *right thing* ain't so easy."

Icon tells Lenny a little about his own past experiences—opportunities lost, loves lost. "Uh-huh. What's your point?" Lenny asks. "Life on Earth is too brief to let us lick our wounds," Icon explains. "Only by confronting this sort of problem will you overcome it." "Ha! You can say that . . . you got *every-thing* going for you. I'll bet life never sneaks up on *you*. You told us to have faith in our abilities, but one rich man who can fly don't mean I can fly too," replies Lenny. "You know better than that," Icon responds. "There are enough hardships for each of us. I've had first hand experience. But we were discussing *your* abilities, and what *you* make of them. I can only encourage you to live up to your own potential." "Hey, I'm not going back to my old habits, if that's what you mean," a dejected Lenny says. "It's just . . . not easy . . . ya know."

A couple of pages later we see Lenny trying to live up to his own potential. A collage superimposed over Icon's masked face shows Lenny being all he can be (fig. 6.3)—a virtual one-page self-help manual for readers. We see Lenny resisting the lures of gang life, excelling in school, caring for younger children, developing his body in the gym, playing wholesome sports, and even helping a little old lady with her groceries. "It ain't easy," Lenny narrates over the following pages. "Here I am, an upstanding, Icon inspired, strong black man

6.3   Icon #32 (1995). Illustration courtesy of DC Comics and Milestone Media, Inc. Used with permission.

. . . but staying on the right track helps keep my mind off my problems." Eventually, Lenny is applauded as a hero when he helps Icon and Rocket save a little girl trapped in a burning building.

Back along the waterfront, Icon tells Lenny, "I'm proud of the way you've been handling yourself. Your community is looking up to you . . . for all the right reasons. I wouldn't hesitate to say that you are something of an 'Icon' yourself." "Listen, I got a date with a new lady," Lenny says. "So all I wanted to say was . . . thanks for being there." "You deserve all the credit," Icon smiles as he shakes Lenny's hand. Lenny smiles proudly. "Be good brother."

Despite the Milestone founders discussed preference for avoiding the *ABC Wednesday after School Special* type of preachiness in their comic books, Icon stories such as the one recounted above veer dangerously close to this pattern. Other issues of *Icon* have dealt just as directly with issues of social responsibility, from a child's hero worship to teenage pregnancy. That these stories can be fully recognized by many fans as "a little preachy sometimes" but still enjoyed is the strength of the Milestone books. I do not want to suggest here that the Milestone message is incredibly well-concealed propaganda that serves a specific agenda, rather I believe that it forthrightly admits—and is recurringly interpreted as—an alternative to the traditional patriarchal masculine norm that has recently, in other comics and other media, become increasingly skewed toward absurd heights of hypermasculinity. That these books also so consciously use black heroes as simultaneously masculine and thoughtful characters further emphasizes the novel reconstruction of masculinity and ethnic identity based on less traditional notions of gender roles and limiting racist stereotypes.

Although the Milestone line of comic books are read by many fans as an alternative depiction of masculinity in comparison to the Image books and by others (particularly those from minority backgrounds) as "a thinking black man's heroes," they are by no means the sole voices of change present in contemporary culture. Outside the superhero genre, several other comic book series, including *The Sandman, The Books of Magic, American Splendor,* and *Maus,* have offered much less hyperbolic models of masculinity. Unfortunately, unlike the Milestone books, most of the other revisionist types of comic books are classified as "Mature Reader" titles and are clearly not geared toward the traditional preadolescent consumer. Likewise, less hypermasculine, less "cool pose"–informed images of black men occasionally emerge through the cracks of popular culture. As bell hooks concludes in her chapter on reconstructing black masculinity, "Changing representations of black men must be a collective task" (1992, 113). For true change to take place, for stereotypes (both imposed and internalized) to be broken, alternative representations of blackness in relation to masculine ideals must come from not only comic books but also the realms of music, film, literature, education, and politics.

One of the most often cited alternative visions of black masculinity is put forth by Mitchell Duneier in *Slim's Table: Race, Respectability, and Masculinity* (1992), his acclaimed ethnography about the elderly black men who frequent Valois, a Chicago diner. The men of Valois have constructed for themselves what Duneier describes as a "community of caring." A world apart from the conventional understanding of black men caught up in masculine protests of violence, misogyny, and social alienation, these elderly men are unconcerned with—indeed, outrightly scornful of—displays of masculine posturing. Instead, the men profiled in *Slim's Table* spend their days offering support, respect, and love for each other in social and personal matters ranging from finances to sexual relationships. In relation to the issues I have been discussing in this essay, Bordo accurately sums up the vision of masculinity revealed in Duneier's work when she writes, "[T]he oppositions soft/hard, masculine/feminine have no purchase on their sense of manhood, which is tied to other qualities: sincerity, loyalty, honesty. Their world is not divided between the men and the wimps, but between those who live according to certain personal standards of decency and caring and those who try to 'perform' and impress others. They are scornful of and somewhat embarrassed by the 'cool pose' which has been adopted by many younger black men" (1993a, 730). But whereas Duneier, Bordo, and hooks see gentle, caring men of an older generation, like those who bid their time at Valois, as an ideal that might transform a younger, disillusioned generation, today's youth are likely to find little purchase in this ideal. Although these older men have certainly lived their lives in resistance to racism and other social pressures, young men today— young black men—live in an environment where the standards of hard versus soft and masculine versus feminine are an intricate and unavoidable fact that they must come to terms with. It is here that I think Milestone's reworked image of heroic black masculinity might prove uniquely helpful.

Unlike the communal response documented in *Slim's Table*, the Milestone books do not reject the properties of the cool pose and the dominant binary logic of our culture's key masculine-feminine gender distinction. Rather, it is a *reworking* that allows pervasive and popular conceptions of gender and race to be expanded by incorporating previously disassociated concepts of softness *with* hardness, of mind *with* body. Instead of merely championing the Clark Kent side of masculine duality as a legitimate role in and of itself, the Milestone books work to infuse gentler, more responsible, and more cerebral qualities within the codes of dominant masculinity. As the Milestone principals are well aware, images of cool black characters ("cool" as measured against existing definitions of what it means to be both black and a man in Western culture) and preadolescent fantasies of superhuman abilities are undeniably ingrained in anyone who might pick up a comic book and are powerful forms through which individuals must learn to negotiate their own lives. Rather than trying to ignore or eradicate the influential reality of existing norms of gender and race-informed patterns of behavior, the Milestone books seem to work most effectively for many of their readers by providing alternatives from within the dominant modes of discourse, by maintaining many of the fundamental conventions of comic book heroism at the same time that they expand the traditional definitions of the medium. "They're still great superhero stories," a young boy explained while his older brother waited for him at the cash register. "But they're different, ya know, and not just because of the color of their skin."

7

Drawing Conclusions

In the early 1970s the public service advertisement used by the Black-Owned
Communications Alliance asked, "What's wrong with this picture?" A young
black boy looked in the mirror and saw only the pale imaginative reflection of
a white superhero. Well, the child from that advertisement has grown up and
the world of superheroes has changed. In the 1990s Milestone Media, and
other black comic book publishers, have replied to that decades-old question
by creating a variety of new heroes, a variety of African American superheroes.
In fact, on the editorial page of the twentieth issue of the company's flagship
series *Icon* (December 1994), Milestone reprinted a photograph (fig. 7.1) of
Icon illustrator M. D. Bright standing next to a man dressed in an Icon costume
for a comics convention. This single image speaks volumes about the changes
in heroic ideals that are currently taking place in the world of comics. Young
boys, and grown men, can fantasize and read stories about superheroes of all
colors. Though the dominance of white-bread costumed heroes is far from
over, it is clearly on the decline. Likewise, young fans can now foresee a world
of possibilities as comic book writers and illustrators regardless of their cultural
background.

In juxtaposing the BOCA advertisement discussed in the introduction (fig.
1.1) with the photograph, reproduced here, of a grown man dressed as Icon, I
do not want to imply that new fantasies are now available to young black
comic book readers. To suggest this would, I think, be too literal-minded a way
of viewing the workings of fantasy. In fact, I think the BOCA advertisement
was too literal minded in its representation of imaginative play (though I do
understand the very real problems of misrepresentation, problems that they
were trying to counter at the time). If cultural studies' approach to audiences

7.1 Man dressed as Icon at convention. Courtesy of DC Comics and Milestone Media, Inc. Used with permission.

and fan groups has proven anything, it is that all people are uniquely adept at transcending boundaries in their fantasies. In the imagination there are no rules. Even Freud observed, in "A Child Is Being Beaten" (1919), that in fantasy people can occupy any number of possible subject positions, individually or simultaneously. I am quite sure that the little boy in the advertisement would have had no real problem imagining himself as a superhero, no problem seeing his own idealized reflection cast back at him from the bathroom mirror.

What the new heroes from Milestone do offer readers is a wider range of fictions, a larger scope of formalized subject positions. Fantasies are typically a fairly personal practice, internally exercised and usually too private a pleasure to share with others. Mass-produced fictions, on the other hand, are collaborative, shared, and very public versions of fantasy, especially for audience members who are active within the various subcultures of media fandom. As Ang has pointed out, "We are not the originators of the public fantasies offered to us in fiction [instead, they are] offered ready-made to audiences" (1996, 93). These public fantasies then are inextricably linked to the mass-produced texts from which they emanate. This is not to say that public fantasy is restricted by the textual fictions; quite the contrary, audiences negotiate the texts in such diverse ways as to construct an *almost* infinite range of personalized interpretations. But the mass-produced fictions do provide a focal point around which specific fantasies can emerge. More obviously than in any other medium, the fans and the creators of comic books interact in a collaborative sense in order to fine-tune the fictions and the public fantasies. Fans and creators have an open line of communication through personal contact at comicons as well as through letters, computer bulletin boards, chat lines, and a corporate system that allows fans to move into the ranks of the creators. The readers and the publishers often negotiate the comic book master narratives long before those narratives' conventions and internal mythology are deemed satisfying. So Milestone's creation of new heroes is not a birth of new fantasies out of whole cloth, but it is an important formalization of an imaginary subject position around which public fantasies can flourish. Milestone's comic book universe is a formalized fiction that arose out of both the publishers' imaginations and the fans' desires.

Although the readers' identification with the fictional characters has been a recurring theme of the research I have presented here, it was never my primary focus. My goal was to explore comic book fandom as a subculture according to the principles of interpretation that readers adopt in relation to the text. What I wanted to understand was how fans make sense of the comic book text. What I found out after talking with dozens of fans and retailers was that for many fans the act of reading a comic book is far from a passive activity. That does not necessarily mean that comic book fans are active resisters of hegemonic meanings, as several other audience ethnographers have found of the fan communities they studied. Rather, for the devoted comic book enthusiast interpretation is a complex process shaped by individual ways of *negotiating* genre conventions and intertextual information shared with, and about, the creators themselves.

The account I have offered here identifies six fundamentally interrelated principles and points of comparison that fans use to construct their understanding of the media texts, the superhero stories, and the African American characters published by Milestone Media.

The first principle of interpretation used by comic book fans is one that influences all of the other points of reception. Comic book fans relate to the texts according to very clearly defined subcultural modes of evaluation. The fans' interpretive practices are shaped by a particular set of critical strategies developed through participation in the world of comics fandom, strategies that shape the reception process in socially contingent ways. Although fan communities are often marginalized for their devotion to texts that the general popu-lace considers trivial and immature, in truth it is this very devotion that creates a system whereby fans learn to evaluate texts in much the same way that connoisseurs of high culture do. For example, where in high culture an institu-tionally sanctioned art critic is able to demonstrate his or her cultural capital by distinguishing between a Rembrandt and a Da Vinci, many comic book fans, like Jordan, the aspiring artist, can similarly verify their subcultural capital by discerning when a character is illustrated by Denys Cowan and when the same character is drawn by Humberto Ramos. Further, a fan like Jordan can also tell that the visual style of Ramos is heavily influenced by Japanese Manga and that his narrative style is influenced by such industry legends as Jack Kirby. Borrowing the framework and the language first used by Bourdieu, we see how the comic book fans' practices are similar to the cultural economy; in fact, they represent what Fiske (1992) has called a "shadow cultural economy," one that directly mimics the established system.

Comic book fans can actually gain the respect of their peers if they excel at evaluating the texts. Thomas, for example, became a highly respected fan due to his mastery of story lines and the ever-changing market value of resale comic books. He recalls with pride the times when younger fans would actively seek him out to ask his interpretations of a particular story or his advice on which comics would be worth collecting. Of prime importance to the fans are such defining characteristics as the popularity or skill of the artist and/or the writer, recognition of the actual or the potential market value of a book, and historical knowledge about the industry, the genre, the characters, and the creators. Moreover, this semiformalized system of evaluation is an example of how the fans and the publishers feed off each other. The publishers capitalized on early preferences within the fan community by promoting individual creators; in turn, creator recognition became essential for the fan's understanding of the books. And finally, the star system constructed by both the fans and the pub-lishers resulted in a market where popular creators, like those at Milestone, could leave the big companies and achieve success as independents. The most heralded incident of this kind was the departure of several extremely popular creators from Marvel, including Todd Mcfarlane, Rob Liefeld, and Jim Lee, who, between them, were responsible for the three best selling comic books of all time. Thanks to their large fan followings, these artists were able to suc-cessfully produce their own books under the aegis of Image Comics, which quickly became the third largest publishing concern behind longtime industry giants Marvel and DC Comics.

The cultural economy of comic book fandom provides the central frame of reference for interpreting individual works, particularly new comics like those produced by Milestone. In addition to forming understandings based on one's familiarity with the individual publishers, writers, and artists, the fan-based interpretations are also premised on how a text relates to other books that it can logically be associated with (e.g., a new female superhero title is measured against other female superhero books), how it is situated within specific genre traditions, and how it relates to dominant trends and market-leading books being published at the same time.

The second and more distinctive principle that fans utilize when interpreting the Milestone titles is based on their awareness of Milestone's corporate and creative identity. Many of the fans understand the texts as they understand the publisher. In other words, their reading is contingent upon their recognition of Milestone as a black–owned and controlled company. When Milestone first emerged on the comics scene in 1993 it was met with a great deal of media attention, attention that focused on the novelty of black writers and artists joining together to create black superheroes. This preoccupation with the ethnicity of Milestone and its characters influenced readers to the point where Milestone came to be regarded as *the* black comic book company. For some comic book fans, this perception of Milestone as the black comic book company is an incentive to follow the various titles they publish. Todd, for instance, very consciously became a Milestone fan because the characters are, for the most part, African American. Todd, who described himself as seeking out forms of entertainment that fit with his emerging sense of ethnic heritage, welcomed the Milestone project as chance to read about heroic black characters and to support a black-owned business. For fans like Todd, the Milestone line of comics are favored because they provide both personal pleasure and political progress.

On the other hand, with Milestone's designation by many fans as *the* black comic book company came the burden of racial representation on a political level. So despite Milestone's careful attempts to position itself as nonpolitical, as a new comics line that just happens to be black, many readers assumed that by virtue of the company's much lauded ethnicity the stories and the characters *must* be overwritten by an ideological agenda. Of course, Milestone never denied that their endeavors were inspired by an interest in racial politics and media representation of African Americans, but they did try to downplay these points in favor of promoting their new universe as good, old-fashioned superhero entertainment. Still, the perception of fans, and of many comic book readers who have never become Milestone fans, is that the Milestone line is inherently political and its interpretations are shaped by this belief. The retailer whom I cited earlier for declaring that he did not stock many Milestone comics "because it's a black thing" is not alone in his perception. In some cases this assumption of ideological intent is what attracts fans to the books, and in other cases it is what keeps some comic book fans away.

The third principle used by fans for negotiating their understanding of the Milestone titles is closely related to the first principle. Coupled with an awareness of Milestone's corporate and creative identity as a black publishing company is the reader's understanding of Milestone's position in relation to other African American comic book companies such as Ania. The consortium of independent African American comic book publishers known as Ania charged that the books produced by Milestone were not authentic black comics. The characters, they argued, were nothing more than superheroes in blackface. This brief debate, which flourished just as the Milestone line of comics was first being published, revolved around the companies' different beliefs on exactly what constitutes authenticity in black media representation. Expressing an essentialist view grounded in biological and cultural absolutes, Ania argued that because Milestone had entered into a printing and distribution partnership with mainstream publisher DC Comics its books could only be whitewashed versions of true African American work; Ania saw the Milestone characters as a type of "chocolate-dip Superman." Milestone, on the other hand, argued that its stories reflected a greater diversity of modern black life and catered to a multicultural group of readers, rather than considering the African American audience as a one-dimensional monolith. This debate between Ania and Milestone is grounded in the long disputed rhetoric of the Black Aesthetic and is representative of the overall ideological divide in black nationalism based on the oppositional strategies of trying to integrate with dominant culture and trying to separate from it.

Because this very public disagreement between Milestone and Ania often overshadows the interesting work being done by both of the companies, some readers consider the books in relation to each other. In particular many fans feel that the Milestone titles are much more desirable as comic book fantasy fare in comparison to the books published by Ania. The Ania titles are seen as being too political minded, as wearing their agenda on their sleeve, as falling too far outside of the acceptable norm of standard superhero stories. For many of the fans the perception of Milestone's books as quality superhero comics in the classical mold, and as relatively nonpolitical, is reinforced when the books are measured against the often heavy-handed messages of some of the more extreme underground African American publications.

The fourth, and perhaps the most obvious of the principles of interpretation and points of comparison, is how the texts relate to specific genre traditions and formulaic elements. This evaluative principle is one applied by fans to all superhero comic books, particularly books that are clearly identified as variations on the standard formula. Like all genres, the superhero comic is governed by a combination of conventions that have formalized over the years and the necessity of moderate variations that keep the genre fresh and appealing for new audience members. Fans understand the Milestone characters as one of these variations on the stock figure of the conventional costumed hero. For example, Will, who defines Milestone's "classic" formulaic superhero stories as an important element in their appeal for him, recognizes the characters' place within the overall lexicon of comic book characters. For Will, as for many other Milestone fans, the uniqueness of characters like Icon, Hardware, and Static is not simply that they are black but that they are black characters clearly aligned with the established conventions of the genre. Rather than radically diverging from the key elements of the time-honored formula, or simply repeating exactly what has come before, the Milestone characters are seen as mixing an appropriate amount of innovation with established conventions. As Eric, the rather vehement defender of Icon as a legitimate variation on the classic Superman typology argued, "Ike's not so different that you can't understand him. There ain't nothing wrong with having a black Superman. Hell, it's about time they got around to having one. Having him be like Superman is good; having him be black just makes the whole character fresher."

This recognition of the Milestone heroes' place in genre history is shared by both the creators and the fans. For those involved in the world of comic books, either as creators or as fans, there is a widespread and deeply ingrained familiarity with the basic tenets of the superhero genre. Fans expect certain generic elements from the stories they read, elements such as costumes and powers and a basic fight between good and evil. Likewise, the creators use these formalized conventions to construct an immediately recognizable story pattern or to expand on the basic reading of the formula, for example, by including subtle sexual references about characters who run around in skintight rubber costumes. Moreover, this level of familiarity has lead the comics medium to be incredibly self-referential. Both the fans and the creators revel in such genre homage as Milestone's month of tribute covers (see figs. 5.2 and 5.3 in chapter 5), where each series featured a cover illustration imitative of a famous scene from the Golden Age of comics. This precedent for self-referentiality in the comics medium facilitates the fans' understanding of individual works as they relate to the whole. Stories are constantly rewriting, reworking, reinventing, criticizing, glorifying, or paying homage to the historical traditions of the genre.

It is within this self-reflexive vein that the Milestone comic books are read. Specific characters are understood in relation to their closest precedent. For example, Icon is often compared to Superman, Hardware is compared to the likes of Batman and Iron-Man, and Static is compared to the early Spider-Man, not to mention the countless other fun-loving teenage superhero characters who have existed in the over sixty years of comic book history. Thus fans are apt to consider the influence of other comics in their interpretation of specific stories or situations, much in the way that Will altered his understanding of the awkward friendship between Icon and Hardware in the Milestone universe once he began to think of it as analogous to the legendary camaraderie of Superman and Batman in the DC universe. More generally, the entire line of Milestone comic books is read as self-reflexive variations on the classic super-hero world because the ethnicity of the characters (and of the creators) is in-cluded in the otherwise conventional mix. In other words, many readers interpret the Milestone books as a natural development of the genre, a devel-opment that brings into question the Aryan bias of the medium.

The fifth point of comparison used by comic book fans for interpreting the titles published by Milestone is based on how they compare to the typical blaxploitation comics from an earlier era. This is a comparison specific to the Milestone books and again is negotiated by both the creators' and the fans' awareness of genre history. For fans, like Todd, who are very familiar with the medium's prevailing representation of black characters, the new heroes published by Milestone are understood as a rectification of the one-dimen-sional blaxploitation comics of the 1970s. Through reprints, back issues, and the occasional guest appearances, such infamous landmark black characters as Luke Cage, the Black Panther, and Black Lightning have continued to over-shadow the representation of black comic book superheroes. The image of jive-talking, ghetto-based heroes stuck in the 1970s was the dominant comic book portrayal of black heroism until Milestone reworked those dated stereo-types in the early 1990s.

In a medium that revolves around creators and fans who are perhaps more self-consciously aware of the historical developments of the superhero genre than the participants in any other popular genre of entertainment, it was inevi-table that Milestone would explicitly address the blaxploitation period. The clearest example of this breaking with comics' blaxploitation past was worked out through the humorous portrayal of Buck Wild in the pages of *Icon*. Taking the bull by the horns, Milestone made it clear that while its characters owed a great deal to the industry's earlier attempts to create black superheroes, it was time to move beyond this narrow and dated character type. In testament to the interplay between the creators and the readers, it was at the fans' insis-tence that the blaxploitation era was addressed so literally within the pages of

Milestone comic books. It was the fans' repeated questions about the blaxploitation-Milestone relationship that prompted them to symbolically declare the official end of an era to the existing form of black representation in comic books. Yet, even this salve was not enough, and the fans demanded Buck's return until the creators at Milestone finally laid the character, and the stereotype, to rest—complete with a eulogy delivered by Icon. Even before Milestone expressly included reference to the blaxploitation era through such self-parodying characters as Buck Wild and Lysistra Jones, the fans understood the books as a conscious attempt to rework the dominant industry stereotypes. No matter how much the Milestone stories may avoid direct references to racial representation, the readers are nonetheless persistently conscious of the previous stereotypes against which they continually measure the Milestone universe. Moreover, these updated black superheroes are welcomed by fans as a much needed new ideal at the same time that they are appreciated for not ignoring the genre precedents that are so important to the fans' pleasure in the medium.

The final means of interpretation, and the most important strategy for the majority of contemporary comic book fans, is based on how the Milestone books compare to the highly visible line of Image comics. The Milestone stories are understood in contrast to the flashy, market-dominating comic books released by the various studios which fall under the publishing umbrella of Image Comics. Because Image is an artist-based publishing company, its comics are generally identifiable by their exaggeratedly stylized form of illustration. The Image comics have become a major force in the industry, a force known for their exaggerated vision of conventional gender types. Superhero comic books have always depicted for young readers a basic personification of masculinity as a fantasy of power based on the external trappings of what it means to be a man in Western culture. The conventional duality of the Superman–Clark Kent myth, which has always been an important element of the superhero story, illustrates a basic longing for such signs of masculinity as strength, muscles, respect, and confidence. But in many recent comics, primarily those published by Image, the dual nature of the fantasy has been all but erased. The he-man has done away with the common man from which he arises; the mask of muscles has obliterated the masquerader underneath. Moreover, following Image's lead, dozens of other publishers, both new companies and previously established ones, have begun to flood the market with similar comic books featuring exceedingly macho, and exceedingly muscular, costumed supermen.

It is in comparison to these dominant hypermasculine images produced by Image and the Image-like publishers that many fans have formed an understanding of the Milestone characters as an alternative masculine ideal. As "tough, but not *too* tough," one young fan told me. Or, as Ted, a young fan at a local Toronto comicon, explained the difference, "Static and Hardware and even Icon are a lot more realistic, not so cartoony. I mean . . . I know they're comic books but come on, look at those guys [in the Image books]; they're fucking *huge!* At least the characters at Milestone look like they could fit through a doorway." The Milestone model is an ideal that reverses the most prevalent contemporary superhero model of hypermasculinity by emphasizing brains *over* brawn. This reversal is especially powerful and progressive because it is written on the body of black men, who have historically been aligned with the unthinking, bestial side of Western culture's nature-versus-civilization dichotomy. Because the Milestone heroes have been cast in the mold of the most conventional superhero characters of times past, despite the obvious innovation of their recognizable ethnicity, they are regarded as new heroes tempered by the social responsibilities written into the most classic version of the superhero formula. For many fans the Milestone universe offers a novel (black) masculine ideal for comic books, one that stresses compassion and intelligence rather than physical force.

Milestone's fans are passionate and devoted. Unfortunately, they are not the largest segment of the comic book fans out there. The Milestone project has been a struggle since its inception; the company's attempt to carve out a significant niche of the market has been an uphill battle. It has been a struggle hampered by the criticism of other African American comics publishers and by the mainstream audience's perception that Milestone is a superhero universe featuring only black characters, black politics, black problems and is intended only for black readers. The Milestone project can also be considered a struggle in a more general sense as the creators and the fans negotiate the fictional characters as well as the intentions and the meanings of the narratives. For example, when Milestone first introduced their flagship character Icon, he immediately became a greatly contested figure. As a staunch Republican and an upper-middle-class black lawyer, Icon's personality became a point of some controversy. The writers defended the character in editorial pages and during interviews for fanzines. They also gave Icon a sidekick from the projects in order to temper his conservative ideological leanings. Still some readers questioned Icon's politics, his behavior, and his motivations. Fans of *Icon* wrote in with support and suggestions about how a conservative black superhero could and should act. In short, the debate helped both the creators and the fans to sharpen their perception of what Icon is all about; they forced each other to think about the nature of the character and the role of costumed heroism when it comes in a different skin color. Likewise, the overriding heritage of the blaxploitation type of comic book characters was a subject broached by both the creators and the fans. When Milestone introduced Buck Wild as a tongue-in-cheek commentary on those old norms, the fans latched onto the character as an important part of the Milestone equation. With Buck Wild the fans saw the publishers providing them with a link to the past and reference point for contextualizing why new heroes are needed. In fact, the character proved so popular, such an ideal access point for fans to understand the creators' viewpoint, that the readers literally demanded his return.

It is in this sense, as negotiators of meaning, that I would consider the Milestone audience to be active. Of course, many of them are active in more tangible and material ways, ways that are more akin to the media poachers that Jenkins (1992) describes, those who piece together their own videos from the television programs they adore, or the slash fiction writers that Bacon-Smith (1992) discusses, those who create their own homosexual love stories for *Star Trek*'s Kirk and Spock. Many Milestone fans do make their own drawings of the characters, some try writing their own stories, and others have even built their own action figures from the bits and pieces of old models. Some of these homemade, Milestone-inspired works are submitted to fanzines, and the best of them are occasionally reprinted in the magazines' pages. But these extreme forms of activity are not the normal pattern. What is much more common is the fans' use of associated knowledge and subcultural principles to negotiate an interpretation of the comics text. The Milestone fans, like most comic book fans, are active within the limited range of interpretive possibilities provided by the creators and within all of the influential dynamics that surround the text.

In the case of comic book fans, as I suspect it is with the fans of other media texts as well, the process of reception is much more collaborative (at least in a symbolic sense) than the bulk of previous audience studies have contended. The rift which has developed in cultural studies' view of media audiences has become polarized between seeing the text as a conveyor of meaning that hegemonically situates the reader within acceptable social norms and the opposing view which sees audiences as active resisters who can, and do, construct any sort of meaning they want from the text, especially counter-hegemonic interpretations. The ideological and political framework of the researchers would seem to have taken them into extremes that are most likely overstatements of the actual cases of media consumption. Well-intentioned desires to expose the dangers of cultural hegemony, or to bear witness to the ingenuity and resistance embodied in the common consumer, have lead to a skewed understanding of how audiences relate to media texts. Unlike these extremes, comic book fandom can best be understood as neither wholly complacent nor essentially resistant. Despite being one of the most active and well-organized fan communities to exist in modern times, comic book fandom should be considered an arena where the producers and the consumers of mass media meet to mutually construct meanings across a wide range of possible variables.

This study has been not only about a fan culture but also about boys' culture. I feel that it is important to point this out, although by this time it should be more than obvious, because it is an influential variable when it comes to the process of reception. The media subject has been comic books, and much more specifically it has been *Milestone* comic books, but the fan group has been young boys from a variety of ethnic backgrounds. In other words, although the African American identity of the Milestone publishers and characters situates them within the confines of a disadvantaged group in relation to media representations, the fans discussed here are generally mainstream, culturally mixed, and boys. As I pointed out earlier, a majority of the most widely recognized audience studies conducted within the last fifteen to twenty years have concentrated on fan communities composed primarily of women. The impetus for many of these studies was to demonstrate through ethnographic methods how real women use media texts to construct pleasures which are not evidence of their textual subordination but rather demonstrate their resistance to ideological impositions. Male fan cultures have typically been ignored on the premise that the popular media serve the existing patriarchy and thus men must simply be reading along with the text. For many of the Milestone fans this is simply not the case. The readings constructed by Milestone fans may not be active in the sense of their being "oppositional" (although I have doubts about how oppositional the writing of slash fiction really is even for women's groups), but in their negotiation of meaning the Milestone fans demonstrate that they do not just passively accept dominant messages. Even when it comes to self-serving notions of masculinity being based in physical power, many of the young readers who count the Milestone comics among their favorites actively sought out alternatives that countered the dominant hypermasculine rhetoric being fed to them by a majority of comic book publishers. This is not to say that all boys who read comic books, or even all boys who read Milestone comic books, seek out alternative models of masculinity. It *is* to say that some young men navigate gender roles in ways that are not always as readily apparent as are others. Dominant forms of masculinity do not always dominate.

Naturally, I would like to add a caveat at this point about the dangers of overgeneralization. An incredible number of comic book fans do in truth eagerly accept the excessively masculine model of gender behavior that is presented to them. But the fact that at least some young male comic book readers express a dissatisfaction with this current ideal suggests that a great deal more work needs to be done on how masculine fan groups *really* relate to media texts. It is an error to assume that male fans merely read along with media texts, even those media texts that have traditionally been identified as men's genres and would seem best able to satisfy traditionally misogynistic fantasies. Moreover it is an error that perpetuates an unequal consideration of the genders and may prove as limiting to our understanding of women as it does to our understanding of men.

The world of comics is a particularly unique medium. There are other fan groups that are every bit as devoted to their preferred media texts as comic book fans are, and many even have regional and national conventions as well as fanzines and computer networks, but very few have as large a network of specialty stores where participants can meet on a weekly or even a daily basis. Yet, perhaps most important is that no other mass entertainment industry has ties which are as closely knit between the producers and the consumers as the comic book industry does. The ties do exist between the fans and the producers in other media, but they are not as clear nor as well developed. In fact, the world of comics might not be so much unique as it is an exaggeration of the dynamics that either exist or are possible in other systems of mass-produced entertainment. It would be logical to assume that fans of other media forms might eventually be able to establish networks which could directly affect the construction of the text and its meaning in much the same way that comic book fans do. For example, television viewers may exercise a subtle control over the production of texts in ways that go beyond the statistical guidelines of Nielsen's ratings and textual poaching. Viewers may actually be influencing the producers, the writers, and even the actors through personal contact, written correspondence, and in other ways that have yet to be explored. It would seem that one of the ways for cultural studies to expand its consideration of media audiences beyond the purview of idiosyncratic enclaves, a limitation that the discipline has imposed on itself to satisfy ideological dictates, would be to consider how the audiences influence the texts to achieve a mutually satisfying content. Rather than blind compliance or active resistance, we can begin to understand the audience's relationship with mass-produced media texts and their creators as a type of continuum where meaning and content are negotiated within a given and mutually acceptable range of possibilities.

Appendix

Over the course of this study I conducted formal and semi-formal interviews with 128 male comic book fans. The majority of the research was conducted in the greater Toronto area with supplemental research in New York City and Chicago. The respondents ranged in age from five to thirty- three years of age, with a median age of thirteen years. Of the 128 fans 64 (50%) were White, 41 (32%) were Black, 18 (14%) were West Asian, and 5 (4%) were Hispanic or East Asian. The age and ethnicity range of the respondents used in this study closely parallels the general distribution found in comics fandom at large (see Parsons, 1991). Of the 128 fans that constituted the overall sample there were 25 young fans that were particularly helpful. This core group of twenty-five local fans introduced me to other enthusiasts, provided a wealth of technical information about the comics subculture, and provided useful feedback on my research. In this sub-group 14 (56%) were White, 8 (32%) were Black, and 3 (12%) were East Asian. All of these particularly helpful informants were between twelve and eighteen years old.

The bulk of people I spoke with over the course of this study counted themselves as serious comic books fans (purchasing at least two comic books per week). In fact, many of the fans considered the quantity of comics an individual buys each week to be as strong an indication of their commitment to the medium as was frequent participation in fandom activities such as attending comicons. Most regular comic book series are published on a monthly basis but publishers stagger their release so they can offer a variety of titles each week. An average comic book specialty store will stock twenty to forty new issues each week. Excluding special promotions, informants' estimates of their own purchasing practices ranged from six to thirty-five new comics a month. Due to fluctuations in the fans' disposable income, availability of comics and delays in printing the amount of comics purchased by an individual fan may vary considerably week to week. The consensus of the retailers in the Toronto area is that a serious fan will purchase between three and six comic books each week, on average.

Notes

2: A Milestone Development

1. A story arch is any adventure that requires more than two comic book issues to complete.

2. Ironically, since Milestone was so clearly distinguished as a *black* comic book publishing company, sales of their nonblack superhero titles soon faltered. Currently Milestone is down to three main series, *Icon, Hardware,* and *Static,* all of which feature African American heroes.

3: Comic Book Fandom

1. As the culture of collecting has grown since the mid-1980s, there has been a great deal of attention placed on books that sell well in the first month of their release. Since the demand for these books is initially greater than the supply, their resale value among collectors can increase dramatically. The sometimes fleeting "hotness" of a comic is regarded as a strong indication of audience trends or popularity shifts among fans.

2. In order to establish a dependable clientele, most comic book stores have instituted a "members" program. Membership is usually free and guarantees that a customer's favorite titles will be reserved for him and held in a safe place for up to a year. In addition to the monetary bonus of regular discounts, being a member also functions as a minor mark of status in the fan community.

3. DC Comic's *The Sandman,* written by Neil Gaiman, is generally considered the high-water mark of quality and sophistication for monthly comics. It has won numerous literary awards.

4. The most popular locations dedicated to the comic books of Milestone Media can be found at http://www.unm.edu/~djyoung/.milestone.html, http://www.wam. umd.edu/~recurve/Xombi.html, and http://www1.primenet.com/~kynn/dakota-l.

4: The Readers

1. Many Canadian comic book specialty stores offer the week's new releases at the suggested retail price for American retailers, often with a further 10 percent discount for members. For example, a normal Milestone issue is currently priced at Can$3.50 but is sold in specialty stores for Can$2.50, the current U.S. price. This is a considerable incen-

tive for fans who buy several comics each week to shop at specialty stores, particularly since some books can cost $7.00 or $8.00 an issue.

2. "Guide price" refers to the most recent value of a given comic book according to the *Official Overstreet Comic Book Price Guide*, or more recently, *Wizard: The Guide to Comics*. The prices listed in these books are considered a strong indication of a comic's market value but are rarely 100 percent accurate since a book's popularity changes on a weekly basis. A knowledgeable fan or retailer is aware of the "mood of the market" and knows when the value of a comic has risen or fallen in comparison to the price given in the guide.

3. An inker is responsible for going over the illustrator's original sketches in India ink to prepare them for coloring. More than a mere tracer, a talented inker can influence the look of the artwork to a great degree by how they emphasize the lines of an artist. Some fans claim that they can distinguish among an individual illustrator's art according to who the inker was that worked on it.

4. Manga is Japanese for comic book; Anime is Japanese for animation. Both Manga and Anime are characterized by a distinctive style of illustration, a style generally more *cartoony* than the styles traditionally associated with mainstream American comic books. Fans often joke about how hard it is to tell the characters apart in this style because they are all so simplified that differences in facial features and body types are minimal at best. In recent years Manga style has become increasingly influential for North American artists (see McCloud 1996; Horn 1996).

5. Each comic book page is made up of several different panels, often of varying size and shape, each containing a different scene. There are a variety of ways that the story can flow from one panel to the next (see McCloud 1993a), but if the transition between the panels is awkward the narrative thread can become confusing for even the most seasoned of readers.

6. Figure drawings are freestanding illustrations of characters. These are the most common type of illustrations for aspiring artists to work on because the characters can easily be posed in heroic stances. Most comic book professionals stress the need for young illustrators to develop their skill with the less glamorous aspects of comic illustration, such as backgrounds, page organization, or panel transitions.

7. *Vibe* is an American magazine devoted to black media and culture. The article Todd is referring to is "Toon Black, Toon Strong" (Tirella 1995).

8. A "pull list" is a comic book reservation list that members keep on file at their comic book specialty store. Each week, when the new books come in, the store will automatically pull whichever books the customer has reserved and store them in a safe location. This service is a mark of the fan's dedication to collecting, ensuring that he or she will never miss a desired book because it was sold out before they could make it to the store.

5: Reading Race and Genre

1. The owners of several comic book stores throughout the United States have been charged with selling offensive material to children. The charges are primarily related to "Adult Only" comics, which the retailers claim were never sold to minors. Given the long history of persecution that the comics industry has faced, the comic book community

(both creators and fans) have responded to this new wave of charges by establishing the Comic Book Legal Defense Fund to assist with legal fees.

2. These are extremely rare limited-edition books literally salvaged from trash cans by publishers in the 1940s. During this boom period of superhero expansion most of the highly competitive publishers were desperate to copyright as many potential superhero names and titles as possible. In order to do so the publishers would refurbish unsold comic books with fake covers and submit the bogus books as legitimate copies of undeveloped characters, thus securing all legal rights. For example, an old copy of Superman might have its cover replaced with a quickly sketched picture of "Miraculous Guy" so that they would have the rights to any character who might be developed in the future bearing that name.

3. From Kurt Busiek's acclaimed 1995 miniseries *Marvels*.

4. Buck Wild's exclamation of "Sweet Easter!" like all of his hokey, macho, 1970s ghetto-speak, is meant as a direct parody of Luke Cage, who was always shouting "Sweet Christmas!" presumably because stronger language was deemed inappropriate for a comic book.

5. Lysistra Jones is described on the back of her Milestone trading card: "She developed a unique but effective fighting style from viewing countless hours of cheesy martial-arts films. After a similar marathon session of viewing a series of 'blaxploitation' films, she decided to become the 'Black Queen of Crime (or 'Queen of Black Crime,' she's still deciding which). In addition to her criminal genius, she is also a talented choreographer."

Works Cited

The references for individual comic books are not included in the list of works cited. The issue number and the date accompanies all of the comic books mentioned in the body of this text. Those series or story lines which have been discussed as graphic novel reprints have been included in this list, as they are officially categorized by the Library of Congress as books and are available through the same distribution systems as are "real" books.

Abbott, Lawrence L. 1986. "Comic Art: Characteristics and Potentialities of a Narrative Medium." *Journal of Popular Culture* 19, no. 4: 155–76.

Allen, R. C., ed. 1987. *Channels of Discourse: Television and Contemporary Criticism.* Chapel Hill: University of North Carolina Press.

Allor, M. 1988. "Relocating the Site of the Audience." *Critical Studies in Mass Communication*, no. 5: 217–33.

Althusser, Louis. 1971. *Lenin and Philosophy and Other Essays.* London: Verso.

Andrae, Thomas. 1987. "From Menace to Messiah: The History and Historicity of Superman." *Discourse*, no. 2. 1980. Reprint. In *American Media and Mass Culture: Left Perspectives*, edited by Donald Lazere, 124–38. Los Angeles: University of California Press.

Ang, Ien. 1985. *Watching "Dallas": Soap Opera and the Melodramatic Imagination.* London: Metheun.

———. 1996. *Living Room Wars: Rethinking Media Audiences for a Postmodern World.* New York: Routledge.

Ang, Ien, and Joke Hermes. 1991. "Gender and/in Media Consumption." In *Mass Media and Society*, edited by J. Curran and M. Guvrevitch, 307–28. London: Edward Arnold.

Angus, Ian, and Suht Jhally, eds. 1989. *Cultural Politics in Contemporary America.* New York: Routledge.

Bacon-Smith, Camille. 1992. *Enterprising Women.* Philadelphia: University of Pennsylvania Press.

Barker, Martin. 1989. *Comics: Ideology, Power and the Critics.* Manchester, England: Manchester University Press.

———. 1993. "Seeing How Far You Can See: On Being a 'Fan' of 2000 AD." In *Reading Audiences: Young People and the Media*, edited by David Buckingham, 159–83. New York: Manchester University Press.

Barrier, Mike. 1973. "The Duck Man." In *The Comic-Book Book,* edited by Don Thompson and Dick Lupoff, 206–25. New York: Arlington.

Bass, Debra. 1995. "From Tha Unda Ground: Inside the "Black Age" of the Comic Book Industry." *The Source,* December, 18–20

Baugh, John. 1991. "The Politicization of Changing Terms of Self-Reference among American Slave Descendants." *American Speech* 66, no. 2: 133–46.

Bee, Jim. 1989. "First Citizen of the Semiotic Democracy?" *Cultural Studies* 3, no. 3: 353–59

Bennett, Lerone, Jr. 1971. "The Emancipation Orgasm: Sweetback in Wonderland." *Ebony* 26 (September): 106–16.

Bennett, Tony, and Janet Woollacott. 1987. *Bond and Beyond: The Political Career of a Popular Hero.* New York: Methuen.

Benton, Mike. 1991. *Superhero Comics of the Silver Age: The Illustrated History.* Dallas: Taylor Publishing.

———. 1993. *The Comic Book in America: An Illustrated History.* Dallas: Taylor Publishing.

Berger, Arthur Asa. 1978. "Taking Comics Seriously." *Wilson Quarterly* 2, no. 3 (summer): 95–101.

Berry, Michael. 1995. "Black Lightning Strikes Twice: Reviving His Hero of Yesteryear, Tony Isabella Explores Today's Problems." *Comics Scene,* no. 48 (January): 9–13.

Bevan, David. 1993. *Modern Myths.* Atlanta, Ga.: Rodopi.

Bierbaum, Tom. 1987. "As Typical Comics Reader Skews Older, More Adult Themes Raise Questions and Eyebrows of Kiddies."*Variety,* July 8, 27, 42.

Bingham, Dennis. 1994a. *Acting Male: Masculinities in the Films of James Stewart, Jack Nicholson, and Clint Eastwood.* New Brunswick, N.J.: Rutgers University Press.

———. 1994b. "Warren Beatty and the Elusive Male Body in Hollywood Cinema." *Michigan Quarterly Review* 33, no. 1: 149–76.

Bird, Elizabeth S. 1992. "Travels in Nowhere Land: Ethnography and the Impossible Audience." *Critical Studies in Mass Communication* 9, no. 1: 250–60.

Blackmore, Tim. 1993. "Blind Daring: Vision and Re-vision of Sophocle's Oedipus Tyrannus in Frank Miller's *Daredevil: Born Again.*" *Journal of Popular Culture* 27, no. 4: 135–62.

Bleich, David. 1986. "Gender Interests in Reading and Language." In *Gender and Reading: Essays on Readers, Texts, and Contexts,* edited by Elizabeth A. Flynn and Patrocinio P. Schweickart, 234–66. Baltimore: The Johns Hopkins University Press.

Bloom, Allan David. 1987. *The Closing of the American Mind.* New York: Simon and Schuster.

Bogle, David. 1973. *Toms, Coons, Mullatoes, Mammies, and Bucks: An Interpretive History of Blacks in American Films.* New York: Viking.

Bordo, Susan. 1993a. "Reading the Male Body." *The Michigan Quarterly Review* 32, no. 4: 696–737.

———. 1993b. *Unbearable Weight: Feminism, Western Culture, and the Body.* Los Angeles: University of California Press.

Bourdieu, Piere. 1980. "The Aristocracy of Culture." *Media, Culture, and Society,* no. 2: 246–61.

———. 1984. *Distinction: A Social Critique of the Judgement of Taste.* New York: Routledge.

Boyarin, Jonathan, ed. 1992. *The Ethnography of Reading.* Los Angeles: University of California Press.

Brannon, Robert. 1976. "The Male Sex Role: Our Culture's Blueprint of Manhood and What It's Done for Us Lately." In *The Forty-Nine Percent Majority: The Male Sex Role,* edited by Deborah S. David and Robert Brannon, 1–48. Reading, Mass.: Addison-Wesley.

Bratlinger, Patrick. 1990. *Crusoe's Footprints: Cultural Studies in Britain and America.* New York: Routledge.

Breines, Paul. 1990. *Tough Jews: Political Fantasy and the Moral Dilemma of American Jewry.* New York: Beacon Books.

Breznick, Alan. 1993. "Black Superheroes Ready to Fight Evil: Will Comic Line Expand Market?" *Crain's New York Business,* March 1–7, 1, 28.

Brown, Carolyn. 1994. "Marketing a New Universe of Heroes." *Black Enterprise* 25, no. 4 (November): 80–86.

Brown, Jeffrey A. 1995. " 'Putting on the Ritz': Masculinity and the Young Gary Cooper." *Screen* 36, no. 3: 193–213.

———. 1996. "Gender and the Action Heroine: Hardbodies and *The Point of No Return.*" *Cinema Journal* 35, no. 3: 52–71.

———. Forthcoming. "Comic Book Fandom and Cultural Capital." *Journal of Popular Culture.*

Brown, John Mason. 1948. "The Case against the Comics." *Saturday Review of Literature,* March 20, 31–32.

Browne, Ray, and Marshall Fishwick, eds. 1978. *Icons of America.* Bowling Green, Ohio: Popular Press.

Brunsdon, Charlotte. 1981. "Crossroads: Notes on Soap Opera." *Screen* 22, no.4: 32–37.

Brunsdon, Charlotte, and David Morley. 1978. *Eveyday Television: 'Nationwide.'* London: BFI.

Buckingham, David. 1993a. "Introduction: Young People and the Media." In *Reading Audiences: Young People and the Media,* edited by David Buckingham, 1–23. New York: Manchester University Press.

———. 1993b. *Reading Audiences: Young People and the Media.* New York: Manchester University Press.

Budd, Mike, Robert Entman, and Clay Stein. 1990. "The Affirmative Character of U.S. Cultural Studies." *Critical Studies in Mass Communication* 7, no. 2: 169–84.

Bukatman, Scott. 1994. "X-Bodies (the Torment of the Mutant Superhero)." In *Uncontrollable Bodies: Testimonies of Identity and Culture,* edited by Rodney Sappington and Tyler Stallings, 92–129. Seattle: Bay Press.

Burger, John R. 1995. *One-Handed Histories: The Eroto-politics of Gay Male Video Pornography.* New York: Haworth Press.

Burt, Ramsay. 1995. *The Male Dancer: Bodies, Spectacle, Sexualities.* New York: Routledge.

Busiek, Kurt, and Alex Ross. 1995. *Marvels.* New York: Marvel Comics. Graphic novel reprint.

Butler, Judith. 1990. *Gender Trouble: Feminism and the Subversion of Identity.* New York: Routledge.

Byrd, Veronica. 1992. "Making a Difference: The Men behind the Superheroes." *New York Times,* September 13, F-8.

Cadenhead, Roger. 1994. "Bad Girls: Who Says Female Characters Don't Sell? Don't Tell That to These Women . . . or Their Creators." *Wizard: The Guide to Comics*, no. 38 (October): 42–47.

Campbell, Joseph. 1949. *The Hero with a Thousand Faces*. New York: Pantheon Books.

Cawelti, John G. 1976. *Adventure Mystery and Romance: Formula Stories as Art and Popular Culture*. Chicago: University of Chicago Press.

Chambers, Iain. 1986. *Popular Culture: The Metropolitan Experience*. London: Metheun.

Chang, B. G. 1987. "Deconstructing the Audience: Who Are They and What Do We Know about Them?" In *Communication Yearbook* 10, edited by McLaughlin. Thousand Oaks, Calif.: Sage.

Christensen, William, and Mark Seifert. 1994. "Four-Color Culture: Minority Diversity in Comics." *Wizard: The Guide to Comics*, no. 20 (October): 40–43.

Christman, Eddy. 1984. "Direct Sales Rescues Comics." *Advertising Age*, June 25, 110.

Clark, Alan, and Laurel Clark. 1991. *Comics: An Illustrated History*. London: Greenwood Publishing.

Clifford, James. 1986. "Introduction: Partial Truths." In *Writing Culture: The Poetics and Politics of Ethnography*, edited by James Clifford and George Marcus. Berkeley: University of California Press.

Clifford, James, and George Marcus, eds. 1986. *Writing Culture: The Poetics and Politics of Ethnography*. Berkeley: University of California Press.

Clover, Carol. 1992. *Men, Women, and Chainsaws: Gender in the Modern Horror Film*. New York: Routledge.

Cohan, Steven. 1991. "Masquerading as the American Male in the Fifties: Picnic, William Holden, and the Spectacle of Masculinity in Hollywood Film." *Camera Obscura*, nos. 25–26: 43–74.

Cohan, Steven, and Ina Rae Hark. 1993. *Screening the Male: Exploring Masculinities in Hollywood Cinema*. New York: Routledge.

Coleman, Earle J. 1985. "The Funnies, the Movies, and Aesthetics." *Journal of Popular Culture* 18, no. 4: 89–100.

"Comic Books Regain Their Readership—and Outlets." 1985. *Publishers Weekly* 228, no. 23: 34–36.

Connell, R. W. 1995. *Masculinities*. Cambridge: Polity Press.

Cotta Vaz, Mark. 1989. *Tales of the Dark Knight: Batman's First Fifty Years, 1939–1989*. New York: Ballantine Books.

Cripps, T. 1977. *Slow Fade to Black: The Negro in American Film, 1900–1942*. New York: Oxford University Press.

Curran, J., and M. Gurevitch, eds. 1991. *Mass Media and Society*. New York: Edward Arnold.

D'Acci, Julie. 1994. *Defining Women: Television and the Case of Cagney and Lacey*. Chapel Hill: University of North Carolina Hill Press.

Daniels, Les. 1971. *Comix: A History of Comic Books in America*. New York: Bonanza Books.

———. 1991. *Marvel: Five Fabulous Decades of the World's Greatest Comics*. New York: Harry N. Abrams.

———. 1995. *DC Comics: Sixty Years of the World's Favorite Comic Book Heroes*. New York: Bullfinch Press.

Dates, J. L., and W. Barlow. 1990. *Split Image: African Americans in the Mass Media.* Washington, D.C.: Howard University Press.

Dauphin, Gary. 1994. "Superfly, the Comics Evolution: Black Superheroes Invade America." *Village Voice* 39, no. 20 (May 17): 31–38.

Davis, Kathy. 1991. "Remaking the She-Devil: A Critical Look at Feminist Approaches to Beauty." *Hypatia* 6, no. 2: 83–104.

De Certau, Michel. 1984. *The Practice of Everyday Life.* Berkeley: University of California Press.

Deming, C. J. 1985. "*Hill Street Blues* as Narrative." *Critical Studies in Mass Communication* 2: 1–22.

Denby, David. 1996. "Buried Alive: Our Children and the Avalanche of Crud." *New Yorker*, July 15, 48–58.

Dooley, Dennis, and Gary Engle. 1987. *Superman at Fifty: The Persistence of a Legend.* New York: Collier Books.

Dorfman, Ariel, and Armand Mattelart. 1976. *How to Read Donald Duck: Imperialist Ideology in the Disney Comic.* New York: International General.

Dorfman, Ariel. 1983. *The Empire's Old Clothes: What the Lone Ranger, Babar, and Other Innocent Heroes Do to Our Minds.* New York: Pantheon Books.

Duneier, Mitchell. 1992. *Slim's Table: Race, Respectability, and Masculinity.* Chicago: University of Chicago Press.

Dyer, Richard. 1982. "Don't Look Now." *Screen* 23, nos. 3–4 (September–October): 61–73.

Easthope, Antony. 1988. *British Post-Structualism.* New York: Routledge.

———. 1990. *What a Man's Gotta Do: The Masculine Myth in Popular Culture.* New York: Routledge.

Eco, Umberto. 1979. *The Role of the Reader: Explorations in the Semiotics of Texts.* Bloomington: Indiana University Press.

Eisner, Will. 1991. *Comics and Sequential Art.* Expanded ed. Tamarac, Fla.: Poorhouse Press.

Evans, W. 1990. "The Interpretive Turn in Media Research." *Critical Studies in Mass Communication* 7, no. 2: 145–68.

Fanon, Frantz. 1970. *Black Skin, White Masks.* London: Paladin.

Faust, Wolfgang M. 1971. "Comics and How to Read Them." *Journal of Popular Culture* 5, no. 1: 195–202.

Feder, Edward L. 1955. *Comic Book Regulation.* Berkely: Bureau of Public Administration.

Feiffer, Jules. 1965. *The Great Comic Book Heroes.* New York: Dial Press.

Feldman, David B. 1990. "Finding a Home for Fictional Characters: A Proposal for Change in Copyright Protection." *California Law Review* 78, no. 3: 687–720.

Fell, John L. 1975. *Film and the Narrative Tradition.* Norman: University of Oklahoma Press.

Fetterley, Judith. 1986. "Reading about Reading: 'A Jury of Her Peers,' 'The Murders in the Rue Morgue,' and 'The Yellow Wallpaper.' " In *Gender and Reading: Essays on Readers, Texts, and Contexts*, edited by Elizabeth A. Flynn and Patrocinio P. Schweickart, 147–64. Baltimore: The Johns Hopkins University Press.

Feuer, J., et al., eds. 1984. *MTM: Quality Television.* London: British Film Institute.

Fish, Stanley. 1980. *Is There a Text in This Class? The Authority of Interpretive Communities.* Cambridge: Harvard University Press.

Fiske, John. 1986. "Television: Polysemy and Popularity" *Critical Studies in Mass Com-munication* 3, no. 1: 391–408.

———. 1987a. "British Cultural Studies and Television." In *Channels of Discourse: Tele-vision and Contemporary Criticism*, edited by R. C. Allen, 254–90. Chapel Hill: Uni-versity of North Carolina Press.

———. 1987b. *Television Culture*. London: Metheun.

———. 1989a. *Reading the Popular*. Boston: Unwin Hyman.

———. 1989b. *Understanding Popular Culture*. Boston: Unwin Hyman.

———. 1992. "The Cultural Economy of Fandom." In *The Adoring Audience: Fan Cul-ture and the Popular Media*, edited by Lisa A. Lewis, 30–49. New York: Routledge.

Flynn, Elizabeth. 1986. "Gender and Reading." In *Gender and Reading: Essays on Read-ers, Texts, and Contexts*, edited by Elizabeth A. Flynn and Patrocinio P. Schweickart, 267–88. Baltimore: The Johns Hopkins University Press.

Flynn, Elizabeth A., and Patrocinio P. Schweickart, eds. 1986. *Gender and Reading: Es-says on Readers, Texts, and Contexts*. Baltimore: The Johns Hopkins University Press.

Focillon, Henri. 1942. *Life of Forms in Art*. New York: George Wittenborn.

Fost, Dan. 1991. "Comics Age with the Baby Boomer." *American Demographics* 13, no. 5: 16.

Frazer, Elizabeth. 1987. "Teenage Girls Reading Jackie." *Media, Culture, and Society* 9, no. 4: 407–25.

Freud, Sigmund. 1963. "'A Child Is Being Beaten': A Contribution to the Study of the Origin of Sexual Perversions." 1919. Reprint. In *Sexuality and the Psychology of Love*, edited by Phillip Reif, 107–32. New York: Colliers.

Fulce, John. 1990. *Comic Books Exposed: Seduction of the Innocent Revisited*. Baton Rouge, La.: Huntington House Publishers.

Fuller, Hoyt W. 1971. "Introduction: Towards a Black Aesthetic." In *The Black Aesthetic*, edited by Addison Gayle Jr. New York: Doubleday & Company.

Gabilliet, Jean-Paul. 1994. "Cultural and Mythical Aspects of a Superhero: The Silver Surfer, 1968–1970." *Journal of Popular Culture* 28, no. 3: 203–13.

Gayle, Addison, Jr. 1971. "Cultural Strangulation: Black Literature and the White Aes-thetic." In *The Black Aesthetic*, edited by Addison Gayle Jr., 38–45. New York: Dou-bleday & Company.

———, ed. 1971. *The Black Aesthetic*. New York: Doubleday & Company.

Geertz, Clifford. 1983. *Local Knowledge: Further Essays in Interpretative Anthropology*. New York: Basic Books.

Geppi, Steve. 1993. "Collector's Collectible Comics." *Wizard: The 100 Most Collectible Comics*, Special ed.: 6–7.

Gerald, Carolyn F. 1971. "The Black Writer and His Role." In *The Black Aesthetic*, edited by Addison Gayle Jr., 349–56. New York: Doubleday & Company.

Gilbert, James. 1986. *A Cycle of Outrage*. New York: Oxford University Press.

Gilmore, David. 1990. *Manhood in the Making*. New Haven: Yale University Press.

Gitlin, Todd. 1983. *Inside Prime Time*. New York: Pantheon Books.

Goar, Carol. 1995. "Issues of Race Will Confront Americans at Every Turn." *Toronto Star*, October 7, A-1, A-16.

Goulart, Ron. 1991. *Over Fifty Years of American Comic Books*. Lindlewood, Ill.: Publi-cation International.

Gramsci, Antonio. 1971. *The Prison Notebooks*. New York: International Publishers.

Grant, Barry Keith, ed. 1985. *Film Genre Reader*. Austin: University of Texas Press.

Gray, Ann, and Jim McGuigan, eds. 1993. *Studying Culture: An Introductory Reader*. New York: Edward Arnold Publishing.

Grossberg, Lawrence. 1988. "Putting the Pop Back into Postmodernism." In *Universal Abandon? The Politics of Postmodernism*, edited by Andrew Ross, 167–90. Minneapolis: University of Minnesota Press.

———. 1989. "MTV: Swinging on a (Postmodern) Star." In *Cultural Politics in Contemporary America*, edited by Ian Angus and Suht Jhally, 254–68. New York: Routledge.

Groth, Gary. 1993. "Nabile Hage: 'I Will Always Speak Out.'" *Comics Journal: The Magazine of Comics News and Criticism*, no. 160: 39–46.

Guerrero, Ed. 1994. *Framing Blackness: The African American Image in Film*. Philadelphia: Temple University Press.

Guzzo, Gary. 1996. "How Are Heroes Born? Where Does It All Begin?" Editorial in *Fatale #2*, April, New York: Broadway Comics.

Hall, Stuart. 1980. "Encoding and Decoding in the Television Discourse." In *Culture, Media, Language: Working Papers in Cultural Studies*, 1972–79, edited by S. Hall et al. London: Hutchinson Press.

Hall, Stuart, and Tony Jefferson. 1976. *Resistance through Rituals: Youth Subcultures in Post-war Britain*. London: Hutchinson Press.

Harney, Michael. 1993. "Mythogenesis of the Modern Super Hero." In *Modern Myths*, edited by David Bevan, 189–210. Atlanta, Ga.: Rodopi.

Harrington, C. Lee, and Denise D. Bielby. 1995. *Soap Fans: Pursuing Pleasure and Making Meaning in Everyday Life*. Philadelphia: Temple University Press.

Harris, Ian M. 1995. *Messages Men Hear: Constructing Masculinities*. London: Taylor & Francis.

Heath, Stephen. 1977. "Notes on Suture." *Screen* 18, no. 4: 48–76.

Hebdige, Dick. 1976. "The Meaning of Mod." In *Resistance through Rituals: Youth Subcultures in Post-war Britain*, edited by Stuart Hall and Tony Jefferson, 87–96. London: Hutchinson Press.

———. 1979. *Subculture: The Meaning of Style*. London: Metheun.

Helfand, Michael Todd. 1992. "When Mickey Mouse Is as Strong as Superman: The Convergence of Intellectual Property Laws to Protect Fictional Literary and Pictorial Characters." *Stanford Law Review* 44: 623–74.

Herman, Edward S., and Noam Chomsky. 1988. *Manufacturing Consent: The Political Economy of the Mass Media*. New York: Pantheon Books.

Hersey, George L. 1996. *The Evolution of Allure: Sexual Selection from the Medici Venus to the Incredible Hulk*. New York: MIT Press.

Hirsch, Eric Donald. 1987. *Cultural Literacy: What Every American Needs to Know*. Boston: Houghton Mifflin.

Hitly, Joan. 1994. "Peppermint Patty and Her Sisters: Sometimes Others Called Them Sir." In *Dagger: On Butch Women*, edited by Lily Burana and Roxxie Linnea Due, 42–52. Pittsburgh: Cleis Press.

Hobson, Dorothy. 1982. "*Crossroads*": *The Drama of a Soap Opera*. London: Metheun.

hooks, bell. 1992. *Black Looks: Race and Representation*. Toronto: Between the Lines Press.

———. 1994. "Feminism Inside: Toward a Black Body Politic." In *Black Male: Representations of Masculinity in Contemporary American Art*, edited by Thelma Golden, 83–101. New York: Whitney Museum of American Art.

Horn, Carl Gustav. 1996. "American Manga." *Wizard: The Guide to Comics*, no. 56 (April): 52–57.

Horn, Maurice. 1985. *Sex in the Comics*. New York: Chelsea House Publishers.

Hunter, Andrea G., and James Earl Davis. 1994. "Hidden Voices of Black Men: The Meaning, Structure, and Complexity of Manhood." *Journal of Black Studies* 25, no. 1: 20–40.

Inge, Thomas. 1984. "Collecting Comic Books." *American Book Collector* 5, no. 2 (March/April): 1–13.

Jenkins, Henry. 1988. "Star Trek Rerun, Reread, Rewritten: Fan Writing as Textual Poaching." *Critical Studies in Mass Communication* 5, no. 2: 85–107.

———. 1992. *Textual Poachers: Television Fans and Participatory Culture*. New York: Routledge.

Jensen, Jeff. 1994. "Comics' High Tech Weapons." *Advertising Age* 65 (September 12): 20.

Jenson, Joli. 1992. "Fandom as Pathology: The Consequences of Characterization." In *The Adoring Audience: Fan Culture and the Popular Media*, edited by Lisa A. Lewis, 9–29. New York: Routledge.

Jewett, Robert, and John Shelton Lawrence. 1977. *The American Monomyth*. New York: Anchor Press/Doubleday.

Kalmar, Ivan. 1993. *The Trotskys, Freuds, and Woody Allens: Portrait of a Culture*. Toronto: Penguin.

Kimmel, Michael, ed. 1989. *Men Confront Pornography*. New York: Crown Publications.

Klein, Alan M. 1993. *Little Big Men: Bodybuilding Subculture and Gender Construction*. Albany: SUNY Press.

Kupperberg, Paul. 1993. "Two Major Milestones . . . *Hardware* and *Blood Syndicate!*" *DC Direct Currents* #61.

Kurtz, Leslie A. 1986. "The Independent Legal Lives of Fictional Characters." *Wisconsin Law Review* 1: 429–525.

Lacan, Jacques. 1977. *Ecrits: A Selection*. London: Tavistock.

Lacassin, Francis. 1972. "The Comic Strip and Film Language." *Film Quarterly* 26, no. 1: 11–23.

Lacher, Irene. 1993. "Heroes of a Different Color." *Los Angeles Times*, November 14, View section, E-1.

Lang, Jeffrey. 1994. "Worlds Collide When DC and Milestone Cross Over." *CBG Price Guide* (June): 24–25, 41.

Lang, Robert. 1990. "Batman and Robin: A Family Romance." *American Imago* 47, nos. 3–4 (fall–winter): 293–319.

Lazere, Donald, ed. 1987. *American Media and Mass Culture: Left Perspectives*. Los Angeles: University of California Press.

Leverenz, David. 1994. "The Last Real Man in America: From Natty Bumppo to Batman." In *Fictions of Masculinity: Crossing Cultures, Crossing Sexualities*, edited by Peter F. Murphy, 21–53. New York: N.Y.U. Press.

Lewis, Lisa A. 1990. *Gender Politics and MTV: Voicing the Difference*. Philadelphia: Temple University Press.

———. 1992a. "Something More Than Love: Fan Stories on Film." In *The Adoring Audience: Fan Culture and Popular Media*, edited by Lisa A. Lewis, 135–62. New York: Routledge.

————, ed. 1992b. *The Adoring Audience: Fan Culture and Popular Media.* New York: Routledge.

Lindlof, T. R., and D. Grodin. 1990. "When Media Use Can't Be Observed: Some Problems and Tactics of Collaborative Audience Research." *Journal of Communication* 40, no.4: 8–28.

Linstead, Stephen. 1993. "From Postmodern Anthropology to Deconstructive Ethnography." *Human Relations* 46, no. 1: 97–120.

Loach, Loretta. 1993. "Bad Girls: Women Who Use Pornography." In *Sex Exposed: Sexuality and the Pornography Debate*, edited by Lynne Segal and Mary McIntosh, 266–74. New Brunswick, N.J.: Rutgers University Press.

Long, Elizabeth. 1985. *The American Dream and the Popular Novel.* Boston: Routledge and Keegan Paul.

————. 1986. "Women, Reading, and Cultural Authority: Some Implications of the Audience Perspective in Cultural Studies." *American Quarterly* 38, no. 4: 591–612.

———— 1987. "Reading Groups and the Postmodern Crisis of Authority." *Cultural Studies* 1, no. 3: 42–67.

————. 1992. "Textual Interpretation as Collective Action." In *The Ethnography of Reading*, edited by Jonathan Boyarin, 180–211. Los Angeles: University of California Press.

Lott, Tommy L. 1995. "A No-Theory Theory of Contemporary Black Cinema." *African American Review* 25, no.2. 1991. Reprint. In *Cinemas of the Black Diaspora*, edited by Michael T. Martin, 40–55. Detroit: Wayne State University Press.

Lotterman, Andrew. 1981. "Superman as a Male Latency Stage Myth." *Bulletin of the Menninger Clinic* 45, no. 6: 491–98.

Lowery, Sharon. 1983. *Milestones in Mass Communication Research: Media Effects.* New York: Longman.

Lull, J. 1988. "The Audience as Nuisance." *Critical Studies in Mass Communication* 5, no. 3: 239–42.

Lyle, Jack, and Heidi Hoffman. 1971. "Children's Use of Television and Other Media." *Television and Social Behavior* 4: 3–17.

Lyness, Paul. 1952. "The Place of Mass Media in the Lives of Boys and Girls." *Journalism Quarterly* 29, no. 1: 43–55.

McAllister, Matthew Paul. 1990. "Cultural Argument and Organizational Constraint in the Comic Book Industry." *Journal of Communication* 40, no. 1 (winter): 55–71.

MacCabe, Collin. 1974. "Realism and the Cinema: Notes on Some Brechtian Theses." *Screen* 15, no. 2: 7–27.

McCloud, Scott. 1993a. "Comics and the Visual Revolution." *Publishers Weekly*, October 11: 47–53.

————. 1993b. *Understanding Comics: The Invisible Art.* Northampton, Mass.: Kitchen Sink Press.

————. 1996. "Understanding Manga." *Wizard: The Guide to Comics*, no. 56 (April): 44–48.

McRobbie, Angela. 1980. "Settling Accounts with Subcultures: A Feminist Critique." *Screen Education*, no. 34: 37–49.

————. 1981. "Just Like a Jackie Story." In *Feminism for Girls: An Adventure Story*, edited by Angela McRobbie and Trisha McCabe, 23–42. London: Routledge and Keegan Paul.

———. 1982a. "Jackie: An Ideology of Adolescent Femininity." In *Popular Culture: Past and Present*, edited by B. Waites, T. Bennett, and G. Martin, 262–83. Open London: University Press.

———. 1982b. "The Politics of Feminist Research: Between Talk, Text, and Action." *Feminist Review*, no. 12: 46–57.

———. 1991. *Feminism and Youth Culture: From "Jackie" to "Just Seventeen."* London: MacMillan.

McRobbie, Angela, and Jenny Garber. 1976. "Girls and Subcultures." In *Resistance through Rituals: Youth Subcultures in Post-war Britain*, edited by Stuart Hall and Tony Jefferson, 209–22. London: Hutchinson Press.

McRobbie, Angela, and Trisha McCabe, eds. 1981. *Feminism for Girls: An Adventure Story*. London: Routledge and Keegan Paul.

McRobbie, Angela, and Mica Nava, eds. 1984. *Gender and Generation*. London: MacMillan.

Majors, Richard G. 1986. "Cool Pose: The Proud Signature of Black Survival." *Changing Men: Issues in Gender, Sex, and Politics* 17: 5–6.

———. 1990. "Cool Pose: Black Masculinity and Sport." In *Critical Perspectives on Sport, Men, and Masculinity*, edited by M. A. Messner and D. Sabo, 120–42. Champaign, Ill.: Human Kinetics Press.

Majors, Richard G., and J. Billson. 1992. *Cool Pose: The Dilemmas of Black Manhood in America*. New York: Lexington Books.

Majors, Richard, et al. 1994. "Cool Pose: A Symbolic Mechanism for Masculine Role Enactment and Coping by Black Males." In *The American Black Male: His Present Status and His Future*, edited by Richard G. Majors and Jacob U. Gordon, 245–59. Chicago: Nelson-Hall Publishers.

Marcus, G. E., and M. J. Fischer. 1986. *Anthropology as Cultural Critque*. Chicago: University of Chicago Press.

Martin, Michael T., ed. 1995. *Cinema of the Black Diaspora: Diversity, Dependence, and Oppositionality*. Detroit: Wayne State University Press.

Mayfield, Julian. 1971. "You Touch My Black Aesthetic and I'll Touch Yours." In *The Black Aesthetic*, edited by Addison Gayle Jr., 23–30. New York: Doubleday & Company.

Mayne, Judith. 1988. "*L.A. Law* and Prime Time Feminism." *Discourse* 10: 129–41.

———. 1993. *Cinema and Spectatorship*. New York: Routledge.

Medhurst, Andy. 1991. "Batman, Deviance and Camp." In *The Many Lives of the Batman: Critical Approaches to A Superhero and His Media*, edited by Roberta E. Pearson and William Uricchio, 149–63. New York: Routledge.

Mercer, Kobena. 1994. *Welcome to the Jungle: New Positions in Black Cultural Studies*. New York: Routledge.

Messner, Michael, and Donald Sabo, eds. 1990. *Sport, Men, and the Gender Order*. Champaign, Ill.: Human Kinetics Press.

Meyer, T. P. 1976. "The Impact of *All in the Family* on Children." *Journal of Broadcasting* 20, no. 1 (winter): 17–28.

Middleton, Peter. 1992. *The Inward Gaze: Masculinity and Subjectivity in Modern Culture*. New York: Routledge.

Miller, Adam David. 1971. "Some Observations on a Black Aesthetic." In *The Black Aesthetic*, edited by Addison Gayle Jr., 374–80. New York: Doubleday & Company.

Miller, Frank. 1986. *Batman: The Dark Knight Returns*. New York: DC Comics. Graphic novel reprint.

Modleski, Tania. 1984. *Loving with a Vengeance*. London: Metheun.

———. 1989. "Some Functions of Feminist Criticism, or The Scandal of the Mute Body." *October*, no. 49: 3–24.

Moore, Alan. 1986. "The Mark of Batman: An Introduction." In *Batman: The Dark Knight Returns*, by Frank Miller, 1–4. New York: DC Comics. Graphic novel reprint.

Moore, Alan, and Dave Gibbons. 1986. *Watchmen*. New York: DC Comics. Graphic novel reprint.

Moores, Shaun. 1993. *Interpreting Audiences: The Ethnography of Media Consumption*. London: Sage Publications.

Morley, David. 1980. *The Nationwide Audience: Structure and Decoding*. London: BFI.

———. 1981. "The 'Nationwide' Audience: A Critical Postscript." *Screen Education*, no.39: 3–14.

———. 1986. *Family Television: Cultural Power and Domestic Leisure*. London: Comedia.

———. 1992. *Television, Audiences, and Cultural Studies*. New York: Routledge.

———. 1993. "Active Audience Theory: Pendulums and Pitfalls." *Journal of Communication* 43, no. 4: 13–19.

Morris, Meaghan. 1988. "The Banality of Cultural Studies." *Discourse* 10, no.2: 14–43.

Morrow, Raymond A. 1991. "Introduction: The Challenge of Cultural Studies to Canadian Sociology and Anthropology." *Canadian Review of Sociology and Anthropology* 28, no. 2: 153–72. Special issue on cultural studies in Canada.

Moss, Gemma. 1993. "Girls Tell the Teen Romance: Four Reading Histories." In *Reading Audiences: Young People and the Media*, edited by David Buckingham, 116–34. New York: Manchester University Press.

Muhlen, Norbert. 1949. "Comic Books and Other Horrors." *Commentary* 7: 80–87.

Mukerji, Chandra, and Michael Schudson. 1991. *Rethinking Popular Culture: Contemporary Perspectives in Cultural Studies*. Los Angeles: University of California Press.

Mulvey, Laura. 1992. "Visual Pleasure and the Narrative Cinema." *Visual Pleasure and the Narrative Cinema* 16, no. 3, 1975. Reprint. In *The Sexual Subject: A Screen Reader in Sexuality*. New York: Routledge.

Murphy, Peter F., ed. 1994. *Fictions of Masculinity: Crossing Cultures, Crossing Sexualities*. New York: N.Y.U. Press.

Nakayama, Thomas K. 1994. "Show/Down Time: 'Race,' Gender, Sexuality, and Popular Culture." *Critical Studies in Mass Communication* 11: 162–79.

Nash, Jesse W. 1992. "Gotham's Dark Knight: The Postmodern Transformation of the Arthurian Mythos." In *Popular Arthurian Traditions*, edited by Sally K. Slocum, 36–45. Bowling Green, Ohio: B.G.S.U. Popular Press.

Nazzaro, Joe. 1993. "Welcome to Dakota: Milestone Media Unwraps a New Universe of Urban Realities." *Comics Scene*, no. 36 (August): 46–51, 64.

Neal, Larry. 1971. "The Black Arts Movement." In *The Black Aesthetic*, edited by Addison Gayle Jr., 257–74. New York: Doubleday & Company.

"New Superheroes Free the Comics from the Old Boys' Network." 1993. *New York Times*, August 6, Living Arts section, B-1, B-6.

Newswatch. 1993. "Some Milestone Comics Drop Comics Code." *Comics Journal*, no. 160 (July): 12. Special issue on black comics artists.

Newton, Huey P. 1971. "He Won't Bleed Me: A Revolutionary Analysis of Sweet Sweet-back's Baadassss Song." *Black Panther*, no. 6 (January 19): A–L.

Nightingale, Virginia. 1989. "What's Ethnographic about Ethnographic Audience Re-search?" *Australian Journal of Communication*, no. 16: 50–63.

Norman, Tony. 1993. "Milestone." *Comics Journal*, no. 160 (July): 67–77.

Nyberg, Amy Kiste. 1994. "Seal of Approval: The Origins and History of the Comics Code." Doctoral thesis, University of Wisconsin-Madison.

O'Neil, Patrick Daniel. 1993. "Marking Milestones." *Wizard: The Guide to Comics*, no. 20 (April): 44–49.

Orr, Philip. 1994. "The Anoedipal Mythos of Batman and Catwoman." *Journal of Popular Culture* 27, no. 4: 169–82.

Ortner, Sherry. 1984. "Theory in Anthropology since the Sixties." *Comparative Studies in Society and History* 26, no. 1: 126–66.

Overstreet, Robert M. 1989. *The Official Overstreet Comic Book Price Guide*, No. 19. New York: House of Collectibles.

Parsons, Patrick. 1991. "Batman and His Audience: The Dialectic of Culture." In *The Many Lives of the Batman: Critical Approaches to a Superhero and His Media*, edited by Roberta E. Pearson and William Uricchio, 66–89. New York: Routledge.

Pearson, Geoffrey, and John Twohig. 1977. "Sociological Imperialism, Blind Spots, and Ecstasies." In *Resistance through Rituals: Youth Subcultures in Post-war Britain*, edited by Stuart Hall and Tony Jefferson, 112–31. London: Hutchinson Press.

Pearson, Roberta E., and Williams Uricchio. 1991a. "'I'm Not Fooled by That Cheap Disguise.'" In *The Many Lives of the Batman: Critical Approaches to a Superhero and His Media*, edited by Roberta E. Pearson and William Uricchio, 182–213. New York: Routledge.

———, eds. 1991b. *The Many Lives of the Batman: Critical Approaches to a Superhero and His Media*. New York: Routledge.

Pecora, Norma. 1992. "Superman/Superboys/Supermen: The Comic Book Hero as So-cializing Agent." In *Men, Masculinity, and the Media*, edited by Steve Craig, 61–77. London: Sage Publications.

Penley, Constance. 1991. "Brownian Motion: Women, Tactics, and Technology." In *Technoculture*, edited by Constance Penley and Andrew Ross, 135–62. Minneapolis: University of Minnesota Press.

Postman, Neil. 1985. *Amusing Ourselves to Death: Public Discourse in the Age of Show Business*. New York: Viking Penguin.

Pumphrey, Martin. 1992. "Why Do Cowboys Wear Hats in the Bath? Style Politics and the Older Man." *Critical Quarterly* 31, no.3: 78–100.

Rackham, Neil. 1968. "Comics versus Education." *New Education* 4: 4–8.

Radner, H. 1989. "'This Time's for Me': Making Up and Feminine Practise." *Cultural Studies* 3, no.3: 301–22.

Radway, Janice. 1984. *Reading the Romance: Women, Patriarchy, and Popular Litera-ture*. Chapel Hill and London: University of North Carolina Press.

———. 1987. "Reading *Reading the Romance*." Introduction in *Reading the Romance: Women, Patriarchy, and Popular Literature*. Chapel Hill and London: University of North Carolina Press, 1984. Reprinted in *Studying Culture: An Introductory Reader*, edited by Gray and McGuigan, 62–79. London: Edward Arnold Press.

———. 1988. "Reception Study: Ethnography and the Problems of Dispersed Audiences and Nomadic Subjects." *Cultural Studies* 2, no. 3: 359–76.

Raglan, Lord. 1936. *The Hero*. London: Metheun.

Rank, Otto 1909. *The Myth of the Birth of the Hero*. Translated in 1914 by F. Robbins and Smith Ely Jelliffe. Nervous and Mental Disease Monograph Series, no. 18. New York: Journal of Nervous and Mental Disease Publishing.

Rappaport, Roy A. 1993. "Distinguished Lecture in General Anthropology: The Anthropology of Trouble." *American Anthropologist* 95, no. 2: 293–303.

Reed, Cory A. 1995. "*Batman Returns*: From the Comic(s) to the Grotesque." *Post Script* 14, no. 3: 37–50.

Reid, Calvin. 1990. "Picture This: Batman, Popular Syndicated Cartoons, and Sophisticated Graphic Novels Have Paved the Way for the Comics' Success in All Markets." *Publishers Weekly* 237, no. 4 (October 12): 17–23.

Reid, Mark A. 1988. "The Black Action Film: The End of the Patiently Enduring Black Hero." *Film History* 2, no. 1: 23–36.

Reif, Phillip, ed. 1963. *Sexuality and the Psychology of Love*. New York: Colliers.

Reitberger, Reinhold, and Wolfgang Fuchs. 1972. *Comics: The Anatomy of a Mass Medium*. Boston: Little, Brown.

Reynolds, Richard. 1992. *Super Heroes: A Modern Mythology*. London: B. T. Batsford.

Rimmels, Beth Hannan. 1995. "You've Come a Long Way, Baby? The Evolution of the Female Comic Book Character Has Been Long and Tough . . . and Many Believe It's Not Over Yet." *Wizard: The Guide to Comics*, no. 32 (August): 36–42.

Riviere, Joan. 1986. "Womanliness as a Masquerade." 1929. Reprint. In *Formations of Fantasy*, edited by Victor Burgin, James Donald, and Cora Kaplan, 35–44. London: Routledge.

Robbins, Trina. 1996. *The Great Super-Heroines*. New York: Gold Book.

Robinson, Doug. 1994. *No Less a Man: Masculinist Art in a Feminist Age*. Bowling Green, Ohio: Popular Press.

Robinson, James, Paul Smith, and Richard Ory. 1995. *The Golden Age: A Different Look at a Different Era*. New York: DC Comics. Graphic novel reprint.

Rodi, Robert. 1995. *What They Did to Princess Paragon*. New York: Plume.

Rollin, Roger B. 1970. "Beowulf to Batman: The Epic Hero and Pop Culture." *College English* 31, no. 5: 431–49.

Ross, Andrew. 1988. *Universal Abandon? The Politics of Postmodernism*. Minneapolis: University of Minnesota Press.

———. 1989. *No Respect: Intellectuals and Popular Culture*. New York: Routledge.

Rovin, Jeff. 1985. *The Encyclopedia of Superheroes*. New York: Facts on File Publications.

Sabin, Roger. 1993. *Adult Comics: An Introduction*. London: Routledge.

Salamon, Jeff. 1992. "Up, Up, and Oy Vay: The Further Adventures of Supermensch." *Village Voice* 37, no. 31 (August 4): 86–88.

Sanders, Joe, ed. 1991. *Science Fiction Fandom*. Westport, Conn.: Greenwood Press.

Sanjek, David. 1990. "Fans' Notes: The Horror Film Fanzine." *Literature/Film Quarterly* 18, no. 3: 150–59.

Sassienie, Paul. 1994. *The Comic Book: The One Essential Guide for Comic Book Fans Everywhere*. Toronto: Smithbooks.

Savage, William. 1990. *Comic Books and America, 1945–1954*. Norman: University of Oklahoma Press.

Schatz, Thomas. 1981. *Hollywood Genres: Formulas, Filmmaking, and the Studio System*. New York: Random House.

Schecter, Harold. 1978. "Comicons." In *Icons of America*, edited by Ray Browne and Marshall Fishwick, 263–70. Bowling Green, Ohio: Popular Press.

———. 1980. *The New Gods: Psyche and Symbol in Popular Art*. Bowling Green, Ohio: B.G.S.U. Popular Press.

Schibanoff, Susan. 1986. "Taking the Gold Out of Egypt: The Art of Reading as a Woman." In *Gender and Reading: Essays on Readers, Texts, and Contexts*, edited by Elizabeth A. Flynn and Patrocinio P. Schweickart, 83–106. Baltimore: The Johns Hopkins University Press.

Schmitt, Ronald. 1992. "Deconstructive Comics." *Journal of Popular Culture* 25, no. 4: 153–61.

Schulze, Laurie. 1990. "On the Muscle." In *Fabrications: Costume and the Female Body*, edited by Jane Gaines and Charlotte Herzog, 59–78. New York: Routledge.

Schweizer, Reinhard. 1992. *Ideologie und Propaganda in den Marvel-Superheldencomics*. Frankfurt am Main: Peter Lang.

Screen. 1992. *The Sexual Subject: A Screen Reader in Sexuality*. New York: Routledge.

Seaman, William R. 1992. "Active Audience Theory: Pointless Populism." *Media, Culture, and Society* 14: 301–11.

Segal, Lynne, and Mary McIntosh. 1993. *Sex Exposed: Sexuality and the Pornography Debate*. New Brunswick, N.J.: Rutgers University Press.

Segel, Elizabeth. 1986. " 'As the Twig Is Bent . . .': Gender and Childhood Reading." In *Gender and Reading: Essays on Readers, Texts, and Contexts*, edited by Elizabeth A. Flynn and Patrocinio P. Schweickart, 165–86. Baltimore: The Johns Hopkins University Press.

Shetterly, Will. 1991. "Graphic Comics Stir Controversy: Is Censoring Violence, Sex, and "Immorality" in Comic Books the Answer?" *Utne Reader* (May–June): 32–33.

Shutt, Craig. 1994. "If It Ain't Broke . . . Fix It!" *Wizard: The Guide to Comics*, no. 38 (October): 80–86.

Silk, C., and J. Silk. 1990. *Racism and Anti-racism in American Popular Culture*. Manchester, U.K.: Manchester University Press.

Silverman, Edward. 1993. "DC Charged: Black Writers, Artists Join with Major Publisher to Launch a New Hero." *Newsday*, January 18, City Business section, 31.

Singletary, Michelle. 1992. "Zap! Pow! Superheroes of Distinction: Milestone Media Gets DC Comics to Distribute Its Multicultural Message." *Washington Post*, September 8, E-1, E-4.

Slocum, Sally K., ed. 1992. *Popular Arthurian Traditions*. Bowling Green, Ohio: B.G.S.U. Popular Press.

Spotnitz, Frank. 1993. "A New Shade of Superhero: Black Comics Are Ultrahip—But They're Battling Each Other." *Entertainment Weekly*, May 28, 12.

Starker, Steven. 1989. *Evil Influences: Crusades against the Mass Media*. New Brunswick, N.J.: Transaction Publisher.

Steele, Valerie. 1996. *Fetish: Fashion, Sex, and Power*. New York: Oxford University Press.

Stock, Brian. 1983. *The Implications of Literacy: Written Language and Models of Interpretation in the Eleventh and Twelfth Centuries*. Princeton: Princeton University Press.

Suleiman, Susan. R. 1986. "Malraux's Women: A Re-vision." In *Gender and Reading: Essays on Readers, Texts, and Contexts*, edited by Elizabeth A. Flynn and Patrocinio P. Schweickart, 124–46. Baltimore: The Johns Hopkins University Press.

Tan, Alexis, and Kermit Scuggs. 1980. "Does Exposure to Comic Book Violence Lead to Aggression in Children?" *Journalism Quarterly* 57, no. 4: 579–83.

Tannen, Deborah. 1994. *Gender and Discourse*. New York: Oxford University Press.

Tasker, Yvonne. 1993. *Spectacular Bodies: Gender, Genre, and the Action Cinema*. New York: Routledge.

Terrill, Robert E. 1993. "Put on a Happy Face: Batman as Schizophrenic Savior." *Quarterly Journal of Speech*, no. 79: 319–35.

Theweleit, Klaus. 1977. *Male Fantasies*. Vol. 1, 2. Translated by Stephen Conway. Minneapolis: University of Minnesota Press.

Thompson, Don, and Dick Lupoff, eds. 1973. *The Comic-Book Book*. New York: Don Arlington.

Thrasher, Frederic M. 1949. "The Comics and Delinquency: Cause or Scapegoat?" *Journal of Educational Sociology* 23 (December): 195–205.

Tirella, Joseph V. 1995. "Toon Black, Toon Strong." *Vibe* 3, no. 8 (October): 102–05.

Tomlinson, John. 1991. *Cultural Imperialism: A Critical Introduction*. London: Pinter Publishers.

Tompkins, Jane, ed. 1980. *Reader-Response Criticism: From Formalism to Post-Structuralism*. Baltimore: The Johns Hopkins University Press.

Tulloch, John, and Henry Jenkins. 1995. *The Science Fiction Audience: Dr. Who, Star Trek, and Their Fans*. New York: Routledge.

Turner, Graeme. 1990. *British Cultural Studies: An Introduction*. New York: Routledge.

U.S. Congress. 1954. *Comic Books and Juvenile Delinquency: Hearings before the Subcommittee to Investigate Juvenile Delinquency*. 84th Cong., April 21, 22, and June 4. Rept. 62.

van Zoonen, L. 1991. "Feminist Perspectives on the Media." In *Mass Media and Society*, edited by J. Curran and M. Gurevitch, 33–54. New York: Edward Arnold.

Vidmar, N., and M. Rokeach. 1974. "Archie Bunker's Bigotry: A Study in Selective Perception and Exposure." *Journal of Communication* 24, no. 1: 36–47.

Wagner, Dave. 1973. "Donald Duck: An Interview." *Radical America* 7, no. 1: 12–16.

Waites, B., T. Bennett, and G. Martin, eds. 1982. *Popular Culture: Past and Present*. London: Open University Press.

Walkerdine, Valerie. 1984. "Some Day My Prince Will Come: Young Girls and the Preparation for Adolescent Sexuality." In *Gender and Generation*, edited by Angela McRobbie and Mica Nava, 162–84. London: MacMillan.

———— 1990. *Schoolgirl Fictions*. London: Verso.

Waters, Harry F. 1993. "Another Kind of Superhero: The Clash of the Black Comic Book Titans." *Newsweek*, August 16, 58–59.

Waugh, Coulton. 1947. *The Comics*. London: University Press of Mississippi.

Wertham, Frederic. 1948. "The Comics . . . Very Funny." *Saturday Review*, May 29, 6–7, 27–29.

————. 1954. *Seduction of the Innocent*. New York: Holt, Rinehart and Winston.

Whitlark, James. 1981. "Superheroes as Dream Doubles." In *Aspects of Fantasy: Selected Essays from the Second International Conference on the Fantastic in Literature and Film*, edited by William Coyle, 107–12. London: Greenwood Press.

Wiater, Stanley, and Stephen R. Bissette. 1993. *Comic Book Rebels: Conversations with the Creators of the New Comics*. New York: Donald I. Fine.

Wilhoit, G. C., and H. de Bock. 1976. "*All in the Family* in Holland." *Journal of Communication* 26, no. 3: 75–86.

Williams, J. P. 1988. "When You Care Enough to Watch the Very Best: The Mystique of *Moonlighting.*" *Journal of Popular Film and Television* 16, no. 3: 90–100.

Willinsky, J., and R. M. Hunniford. 1986. "Reading the Romance Younger: The Mirrors and Fears of Preparatory Literature." In *Reading-Canada-Lecture* 4, no. 1: 12–31.

Willis, Paul. 1977. *Learning to Labour: How Working Class Kids Get Working Class Jobs.* London: Saxon House.

———. 1978. *Profane Culture.* London: Routledge.

———. 1990. *Common Culture: Symbolic Work at Play in the Everyday Cultures of the Young.* Boulder, Colo.: Westview Press.

Witek, Joseph. 1989. *Comic Books as History: The Narrative Art of Jack Johnson, Art Spiegleman, and Harvey Pekar.* Jackson: University Press of Mississippi.

Wynter, Leon E. 1993. "Business and Race: To Diversify Products, Big Firms Tap Outsiders." *Wall Street Journal,* March 30, B-6.

Young, Thomas. 1991. "Are Comic Book Super-Heroes Sexist?" *Sociology and Social Research* 75, no. 4: 218.

Index